山东省职业教育优质教材

高等职业教育财经商贸类专业基础课系列教材

国际商务礼仪
（双语版）

封海燕　范文艳　主　编
彭　琰　马　婷　副主编

清华大学出版社
北京

内 容 简 介

本书为职业教育商务英语专业国家教学资源库商务英语课程配套教材,山东省职业教育优质教材,山东省职业教育在线精品课商务礼仪配套教材。全书包括初识商务礼仪、职场形象礼仪、商务交往礼仪、位次空间礼仪、商务活动礼仪、商务宴请礼仪、跨文化商务礼仪七个模块,以满足外贸新业态发展下国际商务人士对相关知识与技能的需求。本书为新形态一体化教材,配有动画、微课、视频、教学课件、思维导图、企业案例、同步测试、实训项目等丰富的数字化教学资源,本书精选其中优质资源做成二维码在书中进行了关联标注。

本书是由高等职业院校教师和行业企业专家共同打造的"双元"教材,既可作为商务英语、国际经济与贸易、国际商务、跨境电子商务等涉外经贸类专业的学生教材,也可供从事国际商务相关工作人士参考使用。

图书在版编目(CIP)数据

国际商务礼仪:中文、英文 / 封海燕,范文艳主编 . — 北京:清华大学出版社,2023.10(2025.2重印)
高等职业教育财经商贸类专业基础课系列教材
ISBN 978-7-302-64275-6

Ⅰ.①国… Ⅱ.①封… ②范… Ⅲ.①国际商务-礼仪-双语教学-高等学校-教材-汉、英 Ⅳ.① F718

中国国家版本馆 CIP 数据核字(2023)第 139109 号

责任编辑:左卫霞
封面设计:傅瑞学
责任校对:刘 静
责任印制:宋 林

出版发行:清华大学出版社
  网 址:https://www.tup.com.cn,https://www.wqxuetang.com
  地 址:北京清华大学学研大厦A座 邮 编:100084
  社 总 机:010-83470000 邮 购:010-62786544
  投稿与读者服务:010-62776969,c-service@tup.tsinghua.edu.cn
  质量反馈:010-62772015,zhiliang@tup.tsinghua.edu.cn
  课件下载:https://www.tup.com.con,010-83470410
印 装 者:大厂回族自治县彩虹印刷有限公司
经 销:全国新华书店
开 本:185mm×260mm 印 张:19.25 字 数:467千字
版 次:2023年10月第1版 印 次:2025年2月第3次印刷
定 价:59.00元

产品编号:100566-01

前言
Preface

随着经济全球化的发展，国际商务合作日益频繁。恰当得体的国际商务礼仪是确保国际商务活动顺利进行的重要环节。遵守国际商务礼仪不仅能够为应对全球化背景下日益频繁的国际商务交流活动奠定基础，而且能够展示中国国民的素质，提升中国国际形象。

本书以国际商务活动为主线，以企业真实案例为依据，以适度、够用为标准，既涵盖国际商务礼仪的理论知识，又强调实践能力的培养，采用"项目引导、任务驱动"的编写思路进行教学内容组织。本书具有以下特点。

1. 落实立德树人，融入课程思政

党的二十大报告指出"用社会主义核心价值观铸魂育人"，本书全面贯彻党的二十大精神，落实立德树人根本任务，以社会主义核心价值观为引领，以培养熟练掌握国际商务礼仪基本知识和操作方法，具有较高实践操作技能，具有良好职业道德的新时代高素养商务人员为使命，设计素养目标、知识目标和能力目标"三位一体"的学习目标。在学习目标下，设计"价值链""知识链""能力链"，将书中的知识点和能力点串联成线，形成知识链和能力链，将其背后蕴含的价值要素串联成价值链，三条链合成一体，由此构成了"一个引领、三位一体、三链合一"的教材思政体系。本书设置"思政课堂"和"中华礼仪"专栏，深化爱国主义教育，坚守中华文化立场，着力培养"讲好中国故事、传播好中国声音，展现可信、可爱、可敬的中国形象"的新时代商务人士，加强国际传播能力建设，全面提升国际传播效能，推动中华文化更好地走向世界。

2. 校企"双元"合作开发，突出"教、学、做"一体化

本书由学校教师和行业企业专家共同开发，按照"分析岗位需求→确定育人目标（素养、知识、能力目标）→项目任务设计→形成项目模块"的思路，设有情境导入、知识储备、拓展阅读、同步测试、案例分析、实训项目、思政课堂和中华礼仪等栏目，突出"教、学、做"一体化，让学生在学中做、做中学。一体化实训项目覆盖所有教学内容，是校企"双元"合作开发，产教融合的集体成果，以任务工作单、任务实施单、任务检查单、任务评价单的形式呈现，体现了《国家职业教育改革实施方案》倡导的工作手册式教材形式。

3. 配套数字化教学资源，更新及时

本书依托职业教育商务英语专业国家教学资源库商务礼仪课程和山东省职业教育在线精品课程商务礼仪的数字化资源：微课、动画、图片、视频、测试等，帮助学生理解教材中的重点及难点，这些资源将结合实际不断更新，本书精选其中优质资源做成二维码在书中进行了关联标注，扫描本页下方二维码即可在线学习该课程。

本书由山东外贸职业学院与青岛贝来科技文化有限公司联合开发。具体分工如下：山东外贸职业学院封海燕为第一主编，拟定编写大纲及体例，对全书进行校对及统稿工作，并编写模块 1、模块 4、模块 5 任务 1 及模块 7 任务 1；山东外贸职业学院范文艳为第二主编，主要负责模块 3 任务 1、2，模块 5 任务 2，模块 7 任务 4、6 的编写；山东外贸职业学院彭琰为第一副主编，主要负责模块 3 任务 3、模块 6 及模块 7 任务 5 的编写；山东外贸职业学院马婷为第二副主编，主要负责模块 2 及模块 7 任务 2、3 的编写；山东外贸职业学院国晓立参与本书数字化资源录制；山东商务职业学院李刚、淄博职业学院张银成、山东经贸职业学院刘奎芬参与"思政课堂"栏目编写；青岛贝来科技文化有限公司总经理王士忠负责本书企业案例素材收集与审核。王士忠与中国海洋大学张德玉教授共同担任本书主审。

本书在编写过程中，编者参考并借鉴了大量资料，在此向这些资料作者表示衷心的感谢。由于编者水平有限，书中难免有不足之处，敬请同行、专家和广大读者指正。

编　者
2023 年 4 月

职业教育商务英语专业国家教学资源库
商务礼仪在线开放课程

目 录
Contents

Module 6　Banquet Etiquette

模块 6　商务宴请礼仪

Module 7　Intercultural Business Etiquette

模块 7　跨文化商务礼仪

Module 1
Fundamentals of Business Etiquette

 ### Profile of the Module

Business etiquette is a set of social and professional rules that govern the way people interact with one another in business settings. Business or corporate etiquette is instrumental in helping advance your career. It helps you show others the kind of values and belief systems you follow. Business opportunities always favour individuals who can present themselves in an appropriate manner because some may represent the organization externally. Whether you interact with clients or convince customers, your corporate etiquette can help you create a powerful impression. In addition to showing courtesy and respect to others, you demonstrate self-control and better emotional management.

Task 1

The Importance of Business Etiquette

◎ Learning Objectives

■ Moral Objectives
- To cultivate students' values of civilization, harmony, patriotism, friendship.
- To establish cultural confidence.

■ Knowledge Objectives
- To get familiar with the concept and importance of international business etiquette.
- To grasp the international practices to be followed in international business activities.

■ Ability Objectives

• To be able to correctly abide by international practices in business activities.
• To focus on individual business image and corporate image.

 Lead-in: Case Study

Situation: Sean is an overseas teacher in a Chinese training program. After class, he is chatting with Alice, one of his students.

Sean: Alice, your English is really good.

Alice: (Looking down) Oh, no, my English is not very good.

Sean: Why are you saying that? You are doing a good job in class.

Alice: (Waving her hand and looking shy) No, I am not a good student. Michael is doing a much better job than me.

Sean: Michael is also a good student. But you should be proud of your English, Alice.

Alice: No, it's not true. My English is so bad.

Sean is surprised by Alice's response and wonders why she doubts his compliment. He feels embarrassed and wonders if he should pay her a compliment.

Discussion: What made Sean so embarrassed?

 Basic Knowledge

1.1.1 The Definition of Etiquette and Business Etiquette

Etiquette refers to guidelines which control the way a responsible individual should behave in the society. It is a set of practices and forms which are followed in a wide variety of situations. Each society has its own distinct etiquette, and various cultures within a society also have their own rules and social norms. Learning these codes of behavior can be very challenging for people who are new to a particular culture, and even old hands sometimes have a rough time.

Business etiquette is a set of ordinarily agreed-upon rules for behaving in the business environment. Within a place of business, it involves treating coworkers and employers with respect and courtesy in a way that creates a pleasant work environment for everyone. Business etiquette is not just knowing what to discuss during a business dinner or how to address colleagues; it is a way of presenting yourself in such a way that you will be taken seriously.

知识链接：中华礼仪与西方礼仪渊源

1.1.2 The Importance of Business Etiquette

1. Building strong relationship

Professional behavior helps build strong relationship among management, staff and clients

微课：商务
礼仪的意义

because proper business etiquette entails honest and fair dealings with everyone. People appreciate honesty in their business dealings. Loyalty to a business is generated through the solid relationships developed by consistent professionalism and integrity shown by all company employees.

2. Promoting positive atmosphere

A good working environment is fostered by good business etiquette. When management and workers treat one another with the respect and sensitivity dictated by good business manners, it creates a positive working atmosphere.

3. Helping earn respect

Good etiquette helps you earn respect. Rude and offensive behaviors do not go down well with anyone. And as the saying goes, "Respect a man, and he will do the more." Hence, if you treat others with respect and acknowledgement, you are most likely to be respected, trusted and cared for.

4. Preventing misunderstanding

Knowing the proper business etiquette can help you avoid misunderstandings and save you a great deal of time, resources and money. Good business etiquette is cost-effective. They increase the quality of life in the workplace, contribute to optimum employee morale, embellish the company image, and hence play a major role in generating profit. On the other hand, negative behavior, whether it is based on selfness or ignorance, can cost a person a promotion, even a job.

Extended Reading

拓展阅读：商务
礼仪的重要性

Scan the QR code, read the passage about "The Importance of Business Etiquette" and finish the following tasks.

After-reading tasks

When you finish reading the text above, finish the following tasks.

Task 1　Read the statements and decide whether they are true or not. Mark "T" for true and "F" for false.

（1）Etiquette is only confined to courtesy. （　　）

（2）It is important to treat others without any arrogance. （　　）

（3）Being punctual is vital to win others' respect. （　　）

（4）It is OK to interrupt your coworkers. （　　）

（5）Being overdressed is preferable to being underdressed when you are not sure about the dressing code. （　　）

Task 2　Critical thinking

Share your experience of building relationship by good etiquette or business etiquette or your experience of being offended by others' bad manners.

Basic Knowledge Test

Read the statements and decide whether they are true or not. Mark "T" for true and "F" for false.

同步测试：汉语版－M1T1 判断正误

（1）Good business etiquette not only means showing courtesy and respect to others, but also means your self control and better emotional management. （　　）

（2）Comporting yourself professionally means not only presenting oneself with confidence but also taking the feelings and attitudes of others into consideration. （　　）

（3）Managers and coworkers who scream at and berate others when under pressure create a good working environment. （　　）

（4）Keeping a cool head when you face business challenges and try to meet tough deadlines or deal with difficult customers lead to success. （　　）

（5）A good business etiquette requires that you put some extra thought into your work outfit – that way, you'll be showing your employees and colleagues that you respect your position and care about the company's image. （　　）

Case Study

• Case 1

Joe Girard is the greatest car salesman in the world. One day, a middle-aged woman went from the opposite Ford car showroom into Joe Girard's car showroom. She wanted to buy a white Ford. "Welcome, madam." Joe Girard said with a smile. "Today is my 55th birthday and I want to buy a white Ford as a birthday present for myself," the woman told him excitedly. "Happy birthday, madam." Joe Girard congratulated her warmly. Then, he whispered a few words

微课：玫瑰花与雪佛兰的故事

to his assistant. Joe Girard led the lady as she walked around and enthusiastically introduced the Chevy in the showroom. After a while, the assistant came in and gave Joe Girard a bunch of roses. Joe Girard sent the beautiful roses to the lady and wished her a happy birthday one more time. The lady was moved to tears and immediately bought a white Chevy from Joe Girard.

Discussion: Joe Girard succeeded in selling a Chevy to the lady who was going to buy a Ford. What business etiquettes did Joe Girard adopt?

• Case 2

A French client arrived in Beijing on a 7:00 p.m. flight and was picked up by a driver sent by the Chinese firm. The driver took the Frenchman to his hotel at 8:00 p.m.. Chinese executives assumed their guest would want to relax after a long flight and planned to meet him the next morning. The French client felt offended.

微课：派谁去机场接客呢

Discussion: What annoyed the French client?

 Skills Training Tasks

The Importance of Honesty

微课：我该承认
错误吗

Harvey, a HR officer, mistakenly approved full pay to an employee on sick leave. After he discovered the mistake, he told the employee and explained that he had to correct the mistake by subtracting the overpaid amount from the next paycheck. The employee said that this would cause him serious financial problems, so he asked for the overpaid salary to be deducted in installments. But Harvey had to get approval from his superiors. "I know it's going to upset the boss," Harvey said, "As I thought about how to deal with the situation in a better way, I realized that all was my fault and I had to admit it to boss." So Harvey went to the boss, told the details and admitted his mistake. After listening to this, the boss lost his temper. He first criticized the personnel department and accounting department for their negligence, and then blamed the other two colleagues in the office. However, Harvey repeatedly explained that it was all his fault and it had nothing to do with other colleagues. Finally, the boss looked at him and said, "Well, it's your fault. Now let's solve this problem." The correction of this mistake did not cause any trouble to anyone. Since then, the boss has trusted Harvey more.

Scan the following QR codes to complete the tasks.

1.1 任务工作单　　　1.1 任务实施单　　　1.1 任务检查单　　　1.1 任务评价单

Curriculum Ideology and Politics

An Olympic of Civility and Etiquette

The 29th Summer Olympic Games in 2008 was held in Beijing, the capital of China. To this end, the country put forward the slogan of "to welcome the Olympic Games, to stress civilization, to cultivate new trends, to participate, to contribute, to be happy". To respond to this call, Chinese people must do their little bit and consciously observe etiquette rules, so as to make this Olympic Games a truly "Olympic of Civility and Etiquette". The essence of the humanistic Olympics is to enhance the spirit of a nation.

Deng Yaping played an edge ball in the final with the Korean player, so the Korean player scored a point. However, the referee did not find it and gave Deng Yaping a score. Deng Yaping immediately said to the referee, "This is an edge ball; I should not score." After that, the coach praised the Chinese player for doing the right thing, reflecting the demeanor of a great country athlete.

Deng Yaping's civilized etiquette shows the demeanor of a great country athlete and shows the world the demeanor and image of a great country with Chinese civilization and etiquette.

Discussion: How did Deng Yaping promote Chinese image as a great power? What does Ms Deng's behavior convey to the world?

 Chinese Etiquette

Etiquette, "Li", comes from the fear and the respect of the nature. We find all the forms of "Li" from heaven, earth and nature. "Li" represents the authority of emperors who was given by heaven. "Li" also represents hierarchy. In social life, it means that people get along with each other harmoniously and respect the elderly. "Li" comes from the heart of people, showing respect to heaven, the earth and people who are important.

（Source: Hello, China）

Task 2

The Rules of Business Etiquette

🎯 Learning Objectives

■ Moral Objectives

- To cultivate students' personal appreciation and aesthetic quality, and to pay attention to ecological civilization.
- To have a sense of etiquette, dedication and social responsibility.
- To behave appropriately and show good professional ethics and professionalism.
- To cultivate cultural confidence among students.

■ Knowledge Objectives

- To get familiar with the customs of different countries and cultural differences between China and foreign countries.
- To grasp the basic knowledge, rules and skills related to international business etiquette.

■ Ability Objectives

- To be able to communicate with customers in accordance with business practices.
- To be able to use business etiquette knowledge to deal with problems and special situations.

Lead-in: Case Study

Situation: Shirly is from China. She was transferred to London, the transnational corporation's headquarters, last month. Now she is talking with her colleague Michael, a British native.

Shirly: I am going to Northern Ireland this weekend.

Michael: I wish I were going with you. How long are you going to be there?

Shirly: Four days. This is my first time to be there, and I have been eager for the ancient city for a long time. (I am new here and I hope he will offer me a ride to the airport.)

Michael: (If she wants a ride, she'll ask me.) Have a great time.

Shirly: (If he had wanted to give me a ride, he would have offered it. I had better ask somebody else.) Thank you. I'll see you when I get back.

Discussion: Why can't Michael get Shirly's point?

Basic Knowledge

International business etiquette refers to the code of conduct that guides people to show respect and friendliness to others in international business activities. International business etiquette, a kind of Esperanto, is the "traffic rules" that people should abide by in international exchanges. International exchanges emphasize "seeking common ground while reserving differences" and "abiding by conventions". With the deep development of world economic integration, the development of international economic trade will, to a certain extent, affect the economic prospects of a country or a region. As international business activities become more and more frequent, it is increasingly important to learn international business etiquette. There are three basic business etiquette rules.

1.2.1　The Rule of Respect & Courtesy

The core of etiquette is respect. In international business communication, people are equal. Despite one's rank, nation and race, there is no distinction between nobleness and lowliness. In business activities, we should not only be self-respected, but also be respectful. In international business activities, it is an essential basic quality for international businessmen to master standard speech and good behavior. Use normative behavior and politeness to express

微课：商务
礼仪的原则

respect for each other and sincerity in communication. We display courtesy or respect by communicating and behaving properly. This includes, but is not limited to, saying "please" "thank you" "excuse me" "being on time", etc. that portray basic politeness.

1.2.2　The Rule of "Do as the Romans do"

In international business exchanges, as a visitor, you must abide by the local customs, etiquette practices and do as the Romans do. Only when we fully understand the unique local etiquette customs and business practices can we fully respect the local etiquette customs and conduct business activities according to the host's etiquette customs.

When you are the host and you want to give the guests a sincere welcome, you can also use the guests' etiquette and customs to express your enthusiasm and respect for the guests, reflecting "Hosts come first." For example, when you are at a Chinese banquet, you can place chopsticks, knives and forks on the banquet table at the same time to show respect for Western guests.

There are two basic principles of interpersonal communication, that is, golden rule and platinum rule. Golden rule whose essence is "Treat others as you would like to be treated", applies to the situation when we communicate with people sharing the same cultural and religious values. Platinum rule whose essence is "Treat others as they would like to be treated", applies to cross-cultural communication.

1.2.3　The Rule of Moderation

When we apply the rules of international business etiquette, it is necessary to grasp the scale of communication and pay attention to the moderation of speech and behavior. We should not only abide by all kinds of etiquette norms, make our behavior conform to business norms, international practices and industry rules, but also avoid being servile, frivolous and flattering. In international business activities, we should not only be polite, warm and generous, but also maintain the image of the enterprise and the nation.

 Extended Reading

Scan the QR code, read the passage about "10 Easy-To-Follow Business Etiquette Rules" and finish the following tasks.

拓展阅读：十项
商务礼仪原则

After-reading tasks

When you finish reading the text above, finish the following tasks.

Task 1　Read the statements and decide whether they are true or not. Mark "T" for true and "F" for false.

（1）Office gossip between coworkers brings people closer. （　　）

（2）Remembering others' names can help you gain others' respect. （　　）

（3）Maintaining eye contact is vital in the conversation, so we should stare at others all the time. （　　）

（4）Responses like nodding your head, smiling, or giving gestures are helpful in showing that you are listening. （　　）

（5）Without specific purposes, interrupting others when they are talking or working is improper. （　　）

Task 2　Critical thinking

Can you list other good business etiquette rules besides those mentioned in the text? Share with others your experience concerning good manners or bad manners.

 Basic Knowledge Test

Read the statements and decide whether they are true or not. Mark "T" for true and "F" for false.

（1）Treating others with courtesy and kindness is the essential business etiquette rule. （　　）

（2）The rule of "Do as the Romans do" will help you assimilate into foreign cultures. （　　）

（3）When we are courteous or respectful to others, we should be as humble as possible. （　　）

（4）Platinum rule whose essence is "Treat others as they would like to be treated" applies to cross-cultural communication. （　　）

（5）In international communication, we should avoid being servile, frivolous and flattering. （　　）

同步测试：汉语版 –M1T2 判断正误

 Case Study

Some Italian clients are coming to visit Xijie Logistics International for business in China. Xijie Logistics International sends an e-mail to Italian clients saying that they will arrange the meeting on September 13, Friday. One day later, Xijie Logistics International receives an e-mail saying that the Italian clients insist on another date of meeting. Xijie Logistics International rearranges the meeting on September 11, Wednesday, and prepares special gifts for them. The meeting goes well, and the two sides are about to sign an agreement next day. Xijie Logistics International sends the Italian clients special gifts—handkerchiefs with chrysanthemum patterns. When Italian clients open the gift, they seem very annoyed with the gift and leave unhappily.

微课：白金原则

Discussion: Why are Italian clients annoyed with the initial meeting date—September 13, Friday and annoyed with the gift?

 Skills Training Tasks

Basic Rules of Business Etiquette

Wenwen and Zhenzhen, employees from Tongte Space Design in China went on business in England and were invited to their British business partner Michael's home for afternoon tea.

Wenwen and Zhenzhen dressed formally and arrived at Michael's home 10 minutes earlier. When Michael opened the door, he seemed surprised and a little embarrassed. Michael's wife Lucy was preparing the snacks in the kitchen.

微课：英国商务拜访案例

Wenwen and Zhenzhen said hello to Lucy and gave her the gifts: a bunch of white lilies wrapped with dark green, a fine china cup with the company's logo on it and a clock in the shape of an owl. When Lucy took the flowers, she squirmed a bit. When she opened the box and found the gifts, she seemed embarrassed. Wenwen and Zhenzhen were puzzled and wondered what was going on.

When they had tea, Wenwen and Zhenzhen kept talking about Brexit. Michael and Lucy didn't talk much about it, just nodding when listening.

Scan the following QR codes to complete the tasks.

1.2 任务工作单   1.2 任务实施单   1.2 任务检查单   1.2 任务评价单

 ## Curriculum Ideology and Politics

Treating People with Kindness

"Civilization is founded on poetry, established on etiquette and accomplished on music", This saying proves the significance of etiquette and music to civilization. Chinese etiquette is profound, which is embodied in every word and move of characters. Chinese etiquette is the world's most time-honored etiquette. Looking back on the past and towards the future, China as a great country has been encouraging the virtue of treating people with courtesy in the 21st century. This is also reflected in our foreign policy in the international political arena. Treating people with courtesy is a symbol of our cultural confidence. Treating people with kindness is an embodiment of our moral principles as a great country. We respect the different voices of all countries, and we also hope to gain the respect of other countries. China's foreign policy is always to maintain world peace and promote common development. Only by treating each other with courtesy and kindness can we achieve Great Harmony.

（Source: Hey, The World）

Discussion: What is the essence of China's treating others with courtesy? Can you illustrate how China has been playing its role in achieving Great Harmony as a great country?

 ## Chinese Etiquette

Born in 551 BC, Confucius, kong zi, has made the greatest contribution to Chinese culture in history. He developed his thoughts into a system of philosophy known as Confucianism. Confucianism emphasized self-cultivation, harmonious relationships with each other and respect for the elderly. Friends should be honest to each other. Rulers should make an effort to provide a happy life for people.

（Source: Hello, China）

模块 1
初识商务礼仪

 模块导读

　　商务礼仪是一套社会和职业准则，能够规范人们在商务环境中相互交流的方式。商务礼仪不仅有助于个人的职业发展，还能向他人展示自身所遵循的价值观和信仰体系。企业对于能够以合宜的方式展示自身修养的人青睐有加，因为他们可以代表公司形象。无论是与客户互动还是说服客户，个人所代表的企业形象都会给对方留下深刻印象。遵循商务礼仪原则，不仅需要在与他人的交往中表现出对他人的礼貌和尊重，也需要在交往中能够控制并更好地管理情绪。

任务 1

商务礼仪的意义

◎ **学习目标**

■ **素养目标**
- 弘扬文明、和谐、爱国、友善等价值观。
- 树立文化自信。

■ **知识目标**
- 了解国际商务礼仪的概念及重要性。
- 掌握国际商务活动中应遵循的国际惯例。

■ **能力目标**
- 能够在商务活动中正确遵守国际惯例。
- 能够注重个人商务形象与企业形象。

情境导入

> **情境：** 肖恩是一位汉语培训机构的英语教师，一天下课后，他和学生爱丽丝聊天。
>
> **肖恩：** 爱丽丝，你的英语真的很好。
>
> **爱丽丝，**（低头）啊 不，我的英语不是很好。
>
> **肖恩：** 你为什么这么说？你在课堂上做得很好。
>
> **爱丽丝：**（摆摆手，看起来很害羞）不，我不是一个好学生。迈克尔做得比我好得多。
>
> **肖恩：** 迈克尔也是个好学生。但你应该为你的英语感到骄傲，爱丽丝。
>
> **爱丽斯：** 不，这不是真的。我的英语太差了。
>
> 肖恩对爱丽丝的回答感到惊讶，他不明白爱丽丝为什么不认同他的赞美。他感到很尴尬，不知道是否该接着夸赞她。
>
> 讨论： 为什么肖恩会感到很尴尬？

 知识储备

1.1.1 礼仪和商务礼仪的内涵

礼仪是指控制一个人在社会中的行为方式的准则。它是在各种各样的情况下应遵循的一套做法和准则。每个社会都有自己独特的礼仪，一个社会中的各种文化也有自己的规则和社会规范。

商务礼仪是商业环境中约定俗成的一套行为规则。在一个商业场所，它涉及尊重和礼貌地对待同事和雇主，为每个人创造一个愉快的工作环境。商务礼仪不仅是知道在商务晚宴上讨论什么或如何与同事交谈，还要能够以某种方式展现自己，从而让自己被他人认真对待。

1.1.2 商务礼仪的重要性

1. 增强关系

职业行为有助于在管理层、员工和客户之间建立牢固的关系，因为恰当的商业礼仪要求与每个人都诚实、公平地打交道。人们在商业交易中欣赏诚实。公司员工一贯秉承的专业精神及诚信使员工与公司之间关系稳固，而这种稳固的关系又会促成员工对企业的忠诚。

2. 创造良好的工作氛围

良好的工作环境是由良好的商务礼仪培养出来的。当管理层和员工以良好的商业礼仪尊重、体贴地对待对方时，就会创造一种积极的工作氛围。

3. 赢得尊重

良好的礼仪有助于你赢得尊重。任何人都无法接受粗鲁无礼的行为。俗话说："尊重一个人，他会做得更多。"因此，如果你尊重他人，认可他人，你最有可能得到尊重、信任和关心。

4. 避免误会

了解正确的商务礼仪可以帮助你避免误解，节省大量的时间、资源和金钱。良好的商务礼仪是有成效的，因为会提高工作场所的生活质量，有助于提振员工士气，树立公司形象，因此在创造利润方面发挥着重要作用。另外，消极的行为，无论是基于自私还是无知，都会让一个人失去晋升机会，甚至是工作职位。

 **同步测试**

扫码做题。

同步测试：汉语版－M1T1 判断正误

 **案例分析**

● **案例 1**

乔·吉拉德是世界上最优秀的汽车推销员。一天，一位中年妇女从对面的福特汽车展销室走进了乔·吉拉德的汽车展销室。她原本想买一辆白色的福特轿车。"夫人，欢迎您来看我的车。"乔·吉拉德微笑着说。妇女兴奋地告诉他："今天是我55岁的生日，我想买一辆白色的福特轿车作为送给自己的生日礼物。""夫人，祝您生日快乐！"乔·吉拉德热情地祝贺。随后，他轻声地向身边的助手交代了几句。乔·吉拉德领着这位夫人边看边热情地介绍展销室里的雪佛兰轿车。一会儿，刚才的那位助手走了进来，把一束玫瑰花交给了乔·吉拉德。乔·吉拉德把这束漂亮的玫瑰花送给了这位夫人，再次向她表示祝贺。那位夫人感动得热泪盈眶，当即在乔·吉拉德这里买了一辆白色的雪佛兰轿车。

讨论：乔·吉拉德成功地将雪佛兰车卖给了准备买一辆福特轿车的女士。他用了哪些商业礼仪规则？

● **案例 2**

一位法国客户乘坐晚上7点的航班抵达北京，中国公司仅派了一名司机去机场迎接。司机于晚上8点将这位法国人带到酒店，中国公司的代表认为客人在长途飞行后需要休息，因此并没有当晚就拜访客户，计划第二天早上与他见面。这位法国客户对中国公司的接待行为大为不满。

讨论：是什么使这位法国客户不悦？

 **实训项目**

分析商务礼仪的重要性

1. 实训目的

通过训练，掌握商务礼仪的意义。

2．实训内容

（1）背景资料：公司某员工请了病假，财务处哈维在核算工资时却没有扣除病假工资，给这位员工付了全薪；之后哈维向这位员工解释工资核算错误，需要更正，但是这位员工希望分期扣除以避免由此给自己带来的财务问题；哈维向上级坦白了自己的错误，并承担了所有的责任。公司老板虽然不满哈维带来的工作上的麻烦，但还是很欣赏哈维的坦诚。

（2）以小组为单位，分析此案例中商务礼仪的重要性；分享身边案例，讨论基本礼仪的重要性。

3．实训要求

（1）采取"组内异质，组间同质"的原则，将学生分为若干小组，每组4～6人。

（2）每组提交一份商务礼仪重要性实训报告，内容包括本案例商务礼仪的意义以及生活中基本礼仪的意义。

（3）每组讲解和展示本组的工作成果。

4．实训考核

（1）评价方式：采取小组自评、小组互评、教师评价、企业导师评价四维评价方式，总评成绩＝小组自评×20%＋小组互评×20%＋教师评价×30%＋企业导师评价×30%。

（2）评价指标：从素质目标、知识目标、能力目标3方面进行评价。

　1.1 任务工作单　　　　1.1 任务实施单　　　　1.1 任务检查单　　　　1.1 任务评价单

 思政课堂

文明奥运　礼仪奥运

2008年第29届夏季奥林匹克运动会在首都北京召开。为此，国家提出了"迎奥运、讲文明、树新风、我参与、我奉献、我快乐"的口号。要响应这一号召，国人就必须切实从自己做起，有意识地用礼仪规范来约束自己的言行，才能将这一届奥运会办成名副其实的"礼仪奥运""文明奥运"。人文奥运的核心就是提升民族精神。

邓亚萍与韩国选手决赛时，打了一个擦边球，应该韩国选手得分。但是裁判没有发现这是个擦边球，判邓亚萍得分。邓亚萍立即对裁判说："这是一个擦边球，我不应该得分。"事后，教练夸赞中国队员做得对，体现了一个大国运动员的风范。

邓亚萍的文明礼仪展现了一个大国运动员的风范，向世界展示了中华文明礼仪之邦的大国风范和形象。

（资料来源：https://cn.chinadaily.com.cn/a/202107/15/WS60f00176a3101e7ce9759e3b.html）

讨论：党的二十大报告指出"传播好中国声音，展现可信、可爱、可敬的中国形象"。本案例中邓亚萍的行为体现了什么？向世界传达了什么？

中华礼仪

我国对于礼的认知首先来自对大自然的敬畏。天、地、自然万物,我们从中发现了秩序,也找到了礼的格式。礼,在官方体现了皇权天授的威严。礼,也体现了等级。礼在民间指的是人们和谐交流,长幼有序。发自内心的礼,在规矩之上。礼是中国人对天、地、人的敬重。

任务 2

商务礼仪的原则

学习目标

■ **素养目标**

• 展现个人鉴赏力和审美素质,关注生态文明。
• 拥有礼仪意识、敬业精神及社会责任感。
• 展现出良好的职业道德和职业素养。
• 树立文化自信。

■ **知识目标**

• 了解不同国家的风俗和中外文化差异。
• 掌握与国际商务礼仪相关的基本知识、规则和技巧。

■ **能力目标**

• 能够遵循商务交往的惯例与客户沟通。
• 能够运用商务礼仪知识处理问题、应对特殊情境。

 情境导入

情境:雪莉来自中国,上个月被调到跨国公司的总部伦敦。她现在正和同事英国人迈克尔交谈。

雪莉:这个周末我要去北爱尔兰。

迈克尔:我真希望和你一起去。你打算在那里待多久?

雪莉:四天。这是我第一次去那里,我渴望这座古城很久了。(我是新来的,我希望他能送我去机场。)

> 迈克尔：（如果她想搭便车，她会问我的。）祝你玩得愉快。
>
> 雪莉：（如果他想载我一程，他会主动提出的。我最好问问别人。）谢谢。我回来后见。
>
> 讨论：为什么迈克尔无法理解雪莉的弦外之音？

 知识储备

国际商务礼仪是指人们在国际商务活动中，对交往对象表示尊重与友好的行为规范。国际商务礼仪是人们在国际交往中应该遵守的"交通规则"，它是一种世界语。国际交往强调"求同存异"与"遵守惯例"。随着世界经济一体化的深度发展，开展国际经济贸易在一定程度上影响一个国家和地区的经济前景。随着国际商务活动越来越频繁，学习国际商务礼仪也变得越来越重要。商务礼仪有3个基本原则。

1.2.1 尊重与礼貌原则

礼仪的核心是尊重。在国际商务交往中，人与人之间是平等的。无论职务高低、民族大小、种族强弱，都没有贵贱之分，强调要以尊重为本。在商务活动中，不仅要自尊，更要尊重他人。在国际商务活动中，掌握规范的言语、行为举止是商务人士必备的基本素质。人们通过适当的沟通和行为来表达礼貌或尊重，这包括但不限于表示基本礼貌的"请""谢谢""对不起""准时"等。

1.2.2 入乡随俗原则

在国际商务交往中，作为访问者一定要遵守当地的风俗习惯和礼仪惯例，做到入乡随俗。在充分了解当地特有的礼仪习俗、商业惯例等前提下，才能对当地的礼仪习俗予以充分尊重，并按照主方的礼仪习惯完成商务活动。

当自己身为东道主时，为了表达对客人的诚挚欢迎之心，也可以沿用客方的礼仪习俗表达对客人的热情和尊重，体现"主随客意"。例如，在中式宴请时，可以在宴会桌上同时摆放筷子和刀叉，以示尊重和方便西方客人。

人际交往有两个基本原则：黄金法则和白金法则。黄金法则的精髓是"以自己想被对待的方式那样来对待别人"，适用于与具有相同文化和宗教价值观的人交流的情况。白金法则的精髓是"以他人希望被对待的方式来对待他人"，适用于跨文化交际。

1.2.3 适度原则

在运用国际商务礼仪原则时，需要把握交流沟通的尺度，注意谈吐和举止的适度。既要遵守各种礼仪规范，使自己的行为符合商务规范、国际惯例和行业规则，又要避免行为举止卑躬屈膝、轻浮诙媚。在国际商务活动中，既要彬彬有礼、热情大方，又要维护好企业和国家的形象。

 同步测试

同步测试：汉语版 –M1T2 判断正误

扫码做题。

 案例分析

意大利客户来希杰物流国际公司考察中国业务。希杰物流国际公司向意大利客户发送了一封电子邮件，称他们将在 9 月 13 日（星期五）安排会议。一天之后，希杰物流国际公司收到一封电子邮件，称意大利客户坚持另约一个会议日期。希杰物流国际重新安排了 9 月 11 日（星期三）的会议，并为意大利客户准备了特别的礼物。会议进展顺利，双方第二天即将签署协议。希杰物流国际为意大利客户送上带有菊花图案的特制手帕作为礼品。当意大利客户打开礼物时，他们似乎对礼物非常恼火，气愤地离开了。

讨论：为什么意大利客户对最初的见面日期 9 月 13 日（星期五）感到恼火，并对收到的礼物很不满意？

 实训项目

分析商务礼仪的原则

1. 实训目的

通过训练，掌握商务礼仪的基本原则。

2. 实训内容

（1）背景资料：来自中国通特空间设计公司的员工文文和珍珍在英国出差，他们应邀到英国商业伙伴迈克尔家中喝下午茶。

文文和珍珍穿着正式，提前 10 分钟到达迈克尔家。当迈克尔打开门时，他似乎很惊讶，有点儿尴尬，迈克尔的妻子露西正在厨房准备点心。

文文和珍珍向露西问好，并送给她礼物：一束用深绿色包装纸包裹的白色百合花，一个印有公司商标的精美瓷杯和一个猫头鹰形状的钟。露西接过花时，她似乎有点局促不安。当她打开盒子看到礼物时，表情似乎很尴尬。文文和珍珍很困惑，不知道发生了什么。

喝茶的时候，文文和珍珍一直在谈论英国脱欧。迈克尔和露西没怎么谈，只是边听边点头。

（2）以小组为单位，分析此案例中文文和珍珍有哪些不妥之处，违背了哪些商务礼仪的基本原则；讨论生活中的案例，总结礼仪的基本原则。

3. 实训要求

（1）采取"组内异质，组间同质"的原则，将学生分为若干小组，每组 4～6 人。

（2）每组提交一份商务礼仪的基本原则实训报告，内容包括商务礼仪的原则及案例。

（3）每组讲解和展示本组的工作成果。

4. 实训考核

（1）评价方式：采取小组自评、小组互评、教师评价、企业导师评价四维评价方式，

总评成绩＝小组自评×20%＋小组互评×20%＋教师评价×30%＋企业导师评价×30%。

（2）评价指标：从素质目标、知识目标、能力目标 3 方面进行评价。

1.2 任务工作单　　　1.2 任务实施单　　　1.2 任务检查单　　　1.2 任务评价单

以 礼 待 人

"兴于诗，立于礼，成于乐，"这是礼乐文明。中华礼仪博大精深，博大精深藏在我们的一言一行、一举一动当中。中华礼仪是世界上最古老的礼仪。传承传统，面向未来，这种流在骨血里的大国风范和以礼待人的风貌一直延续到 21 世纪，更体现在国际政治舞台上。待人以礼是我们的文化自信，与人为善是我们的大国风范。我们尊重各种不同的声音，同时也希望获得各个不同国家的尊重。中国的外交政策始终是维护世界和平，促进共同发展。当我们人人有礼的时候，才能够实现真正的天下大同。

讨论：党的二十大报告指出"推进文化自信自强，铸就社会主义文化新辉煌"。中国以礼相待的本质是什么？举例说明中国作为一个伟大的国家在实现大同方面是如何发挥作用的。

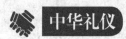

孔子于公元前 551 年出生，是历史上对中华文化影响最大的人。后来，他创立了儒家思想。儒家思想注重人的自我修养，强调与人建立和谐的关系，对待长辈要尊敬有礼；与朋友交往要诚实守信；统治者应该致力于让人民生活幸福。

Module 2
Professional Image in Business Etiquette

Profile of the Module

A professional image is a way of presenting yourself in a professional manner. Establishing a strong professional image helps individuals maintain positive workplace relationships and present themselves appropriately. When people see your image, they instantly associate it with competency and credibility. Cultivating this image is essential if you want to be successful. It builds trust between your business and the consumer. Being mindful of your grooming, dressing and behaving around others is important when fulfilling your daily duties or when trying to advance into a new role. Learning more about what a professional image is and understanding the etiquettes in business activities can help you present yourself consistently at work.

Task 1

Business Grooming Etiquette

◎ Learning Objectives

- Moral Objectives
  - To cultivate students' professional qualities of focusing on business grooming.
  - To develop students' self-esteem and self-confidence.

- Knowledge Objectives
  - To get familiar with the importance of grooming etiquette in business activities.

• To master the basic principles and taboos of grooming etiquette.

■ Ability Objectives

• To be able to choose makeup suitable for business occasions according to the principles of grooming etiquette.

 Lead-in: Case Study

Situation: A company wanted to recruit a foreign secretary personnel. Many graduates were attracted to the interview by the favorable salary and benefits, including Wang Li, an English major graduate. The contents of her resume were excellent: she came out on top in all subjects in college, translated many novels, did translation work for many foreign affairs activities, and once served as the host of school celebrations. She was very eloquent. However, she showed up for the interview in a miniskirt, bright red lipstick and dyed blonde hair, revealing a sparkly manicure and a jingling bracelet as she handed her resume to the interviewer. Then she sat down, smiling and waiting for the question. Unexpectedly, the interviewer said: "Wang Li, please go back and wait for the notice!" Wang Li thought the interviewer was pleased with her and said happily, "Yes!" She picked up her little leather bag and ran out.

Discussion: Do you think the interviewer was satisfied with Wang Li and wanted to hire her? Why?

 Basic Knowledge

The Basic Code of Business Grooming Etiquette

Professional grooming is not only limited to certain situations but it is considered at all times initiating from the job interviews to client meetings, and every day on the job. The grooming of the person is reflecting his capabilities. Make-up, hair care, nails, teeth, odors, cloths, shoes and accessories are few of the vital components that should be considered with significance in having a professional grooming.

微课：仪容礼仪
的基本要求

1. Professional makeup to support confidence

Here are nine simple steps for businesswomen's perfect work makeup look without having to hire a makeup artist.

2. Make your hair tidy, clean and fresh

Even though the length of the hair is not given much importance, but to have it in good shape and trimmed is more important. Hair also includes

知识储备：商务
美妆程序与禁忌

知识链接：商务
化妆工具

eyebrows that should be neat and tidy.

3. Have your nails well manicured

Individuals should clip and clean their nails in a well manicured shape. It is better to cut nails short to the extent that it does not give the impression of being chewed.

4. Focus on your odors

Dousing cologne, aftershave, deodorants, and perfumes should not be the case. A light fragrance from the individual makes them look and smell fresh, and at the same time it does not create the impression of being offensive.

5. Keep your teeth clean and shiny

Teeth are another area that needs to be clean and food won't be stuck in teeth. We particularly need to have a look at our teeth after lunch and tea breaks, as food is likely to get stuck after the intake of food.

6. Proper choice of clothes, shoes and accessories

Individuals should wear shoes that are matching their outfits and are in good condition. In additions, indiriduals also need to polish their shoes properly so that it can give a clean look.

For women, the jewelry should not be too loud, as it would create a nonprofessional look, and for men belts should completely match to their outfit and should not be worn or very old, as it would lead to ruining the overall appearance. Furthermore, the individuals should also keep their watches simple and elegant.

7. Tattoos and piercings as few as possible

In order to appear oneself in a more professional look, they should properly cover their body art so that it is not visible. Additionally, the individuals should also limit the number of visible piercings in order to give a more professional impression.

📖 Extended Reading

Scan the QR code, read the passage about "The Importance of Appearance in the Workplace" and finish the following tasks.

拓展阅读：职场
仪容的重要性

After-reading tasks

When you finish reading the text above, finish the following tasks.

Task 1   Read the statements and decide whether they are true or not. Mark "T" for true and "F" for false.

（1）Your workplace appearance does not matter so long as you have the capability and knowledge at your work. (   )

（2）It is difficult for us to forget our first impression of someone once it is formed. (   )

（3）Personal appearance also plays a vital role in your job hunting. （　　）

（4）Professional appearance has nothing to do with your job promotion or your salary. （　　）

（5）Both verbal and nonverbal languages matter in improving your workplace appearance. （　　）

Task 2　Critical thinking

Suppose you are going to a company for internship during the summer vacation, what should you pay attention to regarding your appearance?

Basic Knowledge Test

Read the statements and decide whether they are true or not. Mark "T" for true and "F" for false.

（1）It is easy for individuals to change their first impressions about someone they have met. （　　）

（2）Compared with the shape and style of individual's hair, the length of hair is less important. （　　）

（3）If there is unclean area or stuck food in teeth of an individual, others may be distracted when they are communicating. （　　）

（4）Individuals should wear shoes that are suitable for their attire and make sure they are polished. （　　）

（5）Too many visible piercings will make one look unprofessional. （　　）

同步测试：汉语版 –M2T1 判断正误

Case Study

When a foreign trade company receives foreign clients, it sends a newcomer to do the business reception. This new employee did a great job, but her face looks pale and listless when she met the clients. The client was in a low mood when he saw her, and then he found that the employee had no makeup and looked even morbid under the lights of the business reception room. The customer is deeply hesitant to hand over his order to such a foreign trade saleswoman: The intensity of foreign trade work is so great. Can she handle it well?

Discussion: Why was the client worried and reluctant to do business with the company?

Skills Training Tasks

Who has the Most Professional Makeup?

One day, Lucy, a professional dresser was invited by an international trade company to teach their employees knowledge about business etiquette and instruct them how to wear makeup. She found that everyone had some problems in their makeup. Shirley who's in her 40s barely wore any makeup, only with a very red lip. Peggy, who's in her 30s, had a very beautiful makeup.

However, there was a distinct border between her face and neck, as if she was wearing a white mask. Another employee, Anne had drawn rather thick black eyeliners which looked like two big brackets around her eyes. The last lady, Jenny, chose an orange lipstick color while she was wearing a blue dress.

微课：谁的妆容最职业

Tasks:

（1）List the problems of each employees' makeup.

（2）What suggestions would the dresser give to each employee's makeup?

Scan the following QR codes to complete the tasks.

2.1 任务工作单　　　　2.1 任务实施单　　　　2.1 任务检查单　　　　2.1 任务评价单

 Curriculum Ideology and Politics

Recently, the Palace Museum has released its new series of product — Limited Edition of a Lipstick Collection in Six Colors on T-mall, provoking excitement among netizens and fashion lovers.

According to reports, this lipstick collection was released by the Palace Museum's Cultural, Creative Center and the national beauty brand Runbaiyan. The six lipstick colors are Lang Yao glaze red, rose-purple, bean paste red, tourmaline purple, maple red and mermaid pink, as shown in Figure 2-1. The lipstick paste color is derived from the red national treasures in the Palace Museum's collection, and the lipstick tube design is inspired by colors and patterns of clothes belonging to empresses and imperial concubines of the Qing Dynasty, one exterior design corresponding to a paste color. The color of the lipstick paste, and the outer tube tone are very harmonious and coordinated.

It is worth mentioning that the Place Museum lipstick also uses 3D printing technology to print traditional patterns on lipstick tubes to present the texture of embroidery. In addition, the lipstick balm is soft and moisturizing, which can effectively help relieve wrinkles on lips, even in dry autumn and winter.

故宫限量版六色口红系列彩图

Figure 2-1　Limited Edition of a Lipstick Collection in Six Colors

（Source：China Daily）

Discussion: What other inspirations for modern makeup can we borrow from traditional Chinese culture?

The Makeup of Ancient China

The live-action *Mulan* is quite a hit around the world. While screaming with excitement for the stirring fight scenes, some netizens also showed great interest in Mulan's make-up. It is said that Buddhism flourished at Northern Wei Dynasty when Mulan lived, and they were inspired by shiny Buddha statues covered with gold, so they painted their foreheads into yellow, which is called "Buddha makeup". This yellow color is called "ehuang"（额黄）in Chinese, which means the yellow color of forehead. And the red flower that you can see in the middle of her forehead is called "huadian"（花钿）, which means flower. Southern and Northern Dynasty is a golden age for men to go after trends of beauty. Not only women did make-ups but also men did it, so you may have heard of many male characters in the history who were famous for their looks like Panan, King Lanling and Caozhi.

Task 2

Business Dressing Etiquette

 Learning Objectives

- Moral Objectives
  - To cultivate students' professional qualities in business dressing.
  - To develop self-esteem and self-confidence.

- Knowledge Objectives
  - To get familiar with the importance of business dressing etiquette in business activities.
  - To get familiar with the types of business attires and accessories.
  - To master the dress code of business attires and accessories in different business activities.

- Ability Objectives
  - To be able to choose business attires and accessories for different business activities.

Lead-in: Case Study

Situation: Conventional wisdom has it that those blessed with a pretty face are more likely to be a shoo-in for top jobs. Previous research has claimed that attractive people get hired more quickly and are rewarded with promotion sooner. But now a new study suggests the secret to a successful job interview is probably more down to locks and socks than looks and appeal. Chicago and California Universities followed the career paths of 14,600 men and women over 13 years, starting when they were still at school. The study states: "We find that attractive individuals earn roughly 20 percent more than people of average attractiveness, but this gap is reduced when controlling for dressing, suggesting that the beauty premium can be actively cultivated." Dressing appropriately for occasions is key. If you are going for a work-related meeting, then make the effort to follow the dress code for your industry.

Discussion:

（1）Why does an individual's dress play a significant role in the career development?

（2）Can you list any dress codes in business situation?

Basic Knowledge

2.2.1   Types of Business Attires

You might decide how to dress depending on the scenario, such as an interview or for a meeting or the type of industry you work in. Based on the setting, you can decide which kind of business attire is appropriate.

知识储备：不同类型商务服装举例说明

1. Casual

Casual business attire is informal clothing worn not only in most business settings but also in many settings outside of work, as shown in Figure 2-2. You should avoid wearing casual dress with clients and in interviews, even if the office is casual overall.

2. Smart casual

Smart casual is another form of casual business attire with a stylish twist, as shown in Figure 2-3. You might also choose to wear smart casual in an interview for a more informal office.

3. Business casual

Business casual is a common form of dress worn in many offices, as shown in Figure 2-4. Business casual is appropriate for many interviews, client meetings and office settings.

4. Business professional

Business professional is a traditional form of attire used in more conservative settings or companies with strict dress codes, as shown in Figure 2-5. Business professional clothes should be well-fitted and may be tailored to fit you specifically.

5. Business formal

Business formal is reserved for the most formal settings such as award ceremonies, special dinners, benefits or other important evening events, as shown in Figure 2-6. Business formal is similar to "black tie," but should be reserved to maintain professionalism.

Figure 2-2　Casual

Figure 2-3　Smart casual

Figure 2-4　Business casual

Figure 2-5　Business professional

Figure 2-6　Business formal

🔗 Knowledge Related

Black Tie

"Black tie" is sometimes called the "tux" or "tuxedo" dress code, as shown in Figure 2-7. They were first called "dinner jackets," as they were perfect for informal evening events. These days, tuxedos and other black-tie attire are reserved for very formal events like weddings, dinners, balls, galas and fundraisers, as dress codes overall have shifted toward the casual.

Figure 2-7　Black Tie

Black-tie events are sometimes labeled "black tie required" to distinguish them from the less formal "black tie optional". Other invitations may indicate "black tie preferred" or "black tie requested".

2.2.2   Principles and Dress Codes of Business Attires

Business dressing has three basic principles. The first principle is harmony. Business personnel's dress must be in harmony with their own age, gender, skin color, figure, profession and other conditions. They need to develop strengths and avoid weaknesses, after fully considering their own conditions. The second principle is TPO which stands for time, place and object. This principle requires business personnel to strive to make their

微课：仪表礼仪
的基本原则

clothes appropriate to the time, the place and the object of the occasion, after fully considering these three factors. The third principle is "no more than three colors". It means the colors of all clothing and accessories should be limited to three kinds. Besides, the color of one's shoes, belt and briefcase should be the same, usually black.

1. Dress code for businessmen

There are three "three principles" in business suit dress code. The first one is "three colors principle" which means the colors of all the clothes should be no more than three. The second one is "three in one", indicating that the shoes, belt and briefcase should be of the same color. What's more, there are three taboos. Don't keep the label on the suit. Don't choose shoes that don't match the suit. Don't wear the suit without a tie.

微课：男士
仪表礼仪

Different types of suits have different numbers of buttons. For a three-button suit, you can just keep the upper two or the middle one buttoned up. For a two-buttons suit, just keep the first one buttoned up. If your suit has just one button, you can button it up or just unbutton it.

2. Dress code for businesswomen

In business occasion, women usually wear a suit dress. The best fabrics for a suit dress are wool and linen. Never wear leather skirts, because in western countries, black leather skirts are the standard dress for street girls. And the best color is black, gray, brown, beige, etc. In formal business occasions, no matter what season it is, the suit dress must be long-sleeved. And the skirt should be long enough to cover the knee. The suit dress should

微课：女士
仪表礼仪

match the shirt, the shoes and the stockings. The best fabrics of shirt are cotton and silk. The style should be brief and without lace and wrinkles. Shoes should be high-heeled step-ins made of leather. Boots or sandals are not appropriate. Long stockings are a must to a suit dress. They should by no means be replaced by knee-deep socks.

3. Dress code for accessories

Accessories can add a polished finish to your professional attire. Here are the dress codes to consider when choosing your business casual accessories.

1）Belts

It's generally considered good practice to match your belt to your shoes. For example, if you are wearing a black pair of loafers, you may wish to select a closely matching black belt.

2）Watches

Watches are an accessory that can provide both function and style. If you choose to wear a watch, your options include both analog and digital choices, as well as even smartphone-connected wearables.

3）Cufflinks

This accessory connects the open cuffs of a dress shirt. Cufflinks are a slightly more formal accessory and come in a variety of materials and designs.

4）Tie bars

A tie bar or tie clip attaches a necktie to the placket of a dress shirt. Like cufflinks, tie bars and clips come in a variety of materials and designs. Some people also choose to use a tie tack, which performs a similar function but actually pierces the material of the tie and shirt.

5）Bags

Consider the materials and colors you most often wear and try choosing a bag that coordinates. If your workplace is more casual, you may even opt for a tasteful business backpack in a material like suede or leather.

知识链接：如何挑选职场服装颜色

Extended Reading

Scan the QR code, read the passage about "Business Attire: What This Dress Code Means" and finish the following tasks.

拓展阅读：正确理解商务着装规范

After-reading tasks

When you finish reading the text above, finish the following tasks.

Task 1 Read the statements and decide whether they are true or not. Mark "T" for true and "F" for false.

（1）The unwritten rules of dress code may be less valid as the written ones. （   ）

（2）The dress code is seen as a way to demonstrate the cultures and values of an organization or company, and even helps it achieve its goal. （   ）

（3）Different climates in different countries can lead to different dress codes. （   ）

（4）Employees engaged in IT industry tend to wear very casually at work since their clients don't care so much about their dressing. （   ）

（5）Diamond earrings are more suitable for businesswomen because the diamond will give them a more business-like and professional look. （   ）

Task 2 Critical thinking

Suppose that you are going to have a job interview with the HR from an international trade company. Please choose a set of proper business attire.

Basic Knowledge Test

Read the statements and decide whether they are true or not. Mark "T" for true and "F" for false.

（1）You should always choose the same business attire for different settings or occasions.（　　）

（2）Casual business attire is only appropriate for settings outside work.（　　）

（3）Business professional clothes should be well-fitted and tailored to fit you specifically.（　　）

（4）It is inappropriate to dress yourself in a similar way to the people who hold the position you would like to reach.（　　）

（5）Business formal is only suitable for the most formal settings such as award ceremonies, special dinners, benefits or other important evening events.（　　）

同步测试：汉语
版 –M2T2 判断
正误

 Case Study

Once a foreign customer came to a garment processing factory, and a middle-aged woman in the factory received him. The customer found that the lady's clothes was very simple, similar to the style of the 1980s. Her attire was not professional at all. At that time, the foreign customer wanted to know about the production of the current popular clothing, so he was invited to the workshop where he found that the workers are not wearing uniforms. Instead, they are wearing casual clothes and some of them looks rather sloppy. After he had seen this lady and other workers, he frowned and the order was not successfully made.

微课：服装厂的
一次参观

Discussion:

（1）What led to the failure of this business visit?

（2）Why is individual's dressing important for business activity?

 Skills Training Tasks

Business Attire on Friday

Susie is a secretary for the president of an international trade company. She enjoys her job, but some colleagues have noticed her little habits.

Last Friday, causal Friday, Susie arrived to work wearing sweatpants, a tank top and flip flops. Usually on Fridays there are no major appointments however this was no usual Friday. On this Friday, a representative from another company had a meeting with the president. This meeting entailed major decisions towards both companies' futures. Susie's company has been trying to purchase the other one, which would make them the number one sales in the country.

In the meeting the representative noticed and frowned on Susie's attire. The representative was hesitant about this business decision due to the first impression of Susie and finally didn't agree to do the acquisition.

After the meeting, the president was very mad about Susie's attire and needed to speak with her about her future with the company.

Tasks:

（1）List what Susie did wrong in the case.

（2）Give Susie some suggestions about her business attire.

Scan the following QR codes to complete the tasks.

2.2 任务工作单   2.2 任务实施单   2.2 任务检查单   2.2 任务评价单

 Curriculum Ideology and Politics

Behind the Uniform Design for Chinese Athletes at Tokyo Olympics

It took two years to complete the design work for the Chinese Olympic delegation's entry uniform. After several rounds of selections and evaluations, final uniform designs with the theme of "making a good start" were officially confirmed in March 2020 for the Chinese Olympic delegation participating in the Tokyo Olympics, as shown in Figure 2-8.

After designing uniforms for the 2008 Beijing Olympics and Paralympics, the Beijing Institute of Fashion Technology has since taken on the task of costume design for a number of major international sporting events, creating uniforms for athletes that confidently express the national identity and image of China.

Since the appearance of the athletes is a focus of the opening ceremony, an eye-catching color like red is a top choice, especially since it is the primary shade in China's national flag and also symbolizes energy, passion and joy in traditional Chinese culture.

White — which represents brightness, purity and divinity — plays a buffering role in the costume design. The combination of red and white at the occasion of the opening ceremony of the Olympics makes an auspicious statement echoing the theme of the design: "making a good start".

Color along with graphics can convey the visual characteristics of a country and express a more accurate national image. The hem of the white dress for female athletes features China's national flower, the peony, and the source for the pattern was drawn from a Ming Dynasty (1368－1644) peony bowl, which is representative of traditional Chinese aesthetics.

The design of the men's shirts is inspired by the five-star graphic pattern of China's national flag. It reflects the spirit of the Chinese Olympic team to fight together for national honor.

Professor He Yang, one of the designers behind the uniform, said that one of the considerations during the design process was that the uniform should display the traditional Chinese cultural character in an intelligible and identifiable way. "We need to strike a balance between cultural representation, etiquette and the spirit of modern Chinese sportsmen." said he.

中国奥运代表团礼
服"开门红"彩图

Figure 2-8 "Making a Good Start" — the Uniform of Chinese Olympic Delegation

（Source: China Daily）

Discussion: What significant roles do the Chinese athletes' uniforms play in the Olympics and Paralympics?

 Chinese Etiquette

A Tang Suit (Tangzhuang) is not a suit of the Tang Dynasty (618－907) but a suit with Chinese style. Tangzhuang are tailored according to specific procedures. Brocade is the first choice of materials for Tangzhuang. Stand-up collars and symmetrical lapels are typical styles. Exquisite embroidery is another feature of Tangzhuang. Even the little buttons are made with great details. These unique buttons are the finishing touches of Tangzhuang. Nowadays people put on Tangzhuang for the Spring Festival or weddings. People regard Tangzhuang as special clothing for important ceremonies. Absorbing some elements from Western designs, Tangzhuang now has a more fashionable, beautiful look.

Task 3

Business Body Language Etiquette

 Learning Objectives

- **Moral Objectives**
  - To cultivate students' professional qualities in business body language.
  - To develop students' self-esteem and self-confidence.

- **Knowledge Objectives**
  - To get familiar with the principles of business body language etiquette in business activities.
  - To master the requirements of the etiquette for hand gesture, posture and facial expressions, etc. in business activities.

- **Ability Objectives**
  - To be able to demonstrate appropriate body language according to the principles of business body language etiquette.

Lead-in: Case Study

Situation: One day, Jack is paying a visit to a customer's company and meets two employees at the reception desk. The two employees give off totally different impressions. One of the employee looks like bored or tired. By slouching over, he appears fearful or lethargic. He props his head up on the desk with a dull expression, because his attention is occupied by the desk toy. As for the other employee, he's standing tall with his back straight and shoulders pulled back while facing people with a smile. Thanks to this good posture, he looks alert, friendly, and ready to give his full attention. Jack instinctively draws near to the second employee and avoids communication with the first one. Not surprisingly, the second employee receives him warmly and leads him to see the boss of the company.

Discussion:
（1）What impressions do the two employees make on the visitor respectively?
（2）What is the importance of body language in business situation?

Basic Knowledge

2.3.1　The Importance of Business Body Language Etiquette

According to research made by Japanese researchers, as for the impressions people make on others, 55% of them come from body language, 38% come from speech content, and only 7% come from the content of the conversation. Therefore, your body language plays a vital role in business. People would like to do business with people who make them feel comfortable. Making some small adjustments to your body language can boost your confidence and as a result improve your professional relationships and job performance.

知识链接：体语学——我们的肢体语言

2.3.2　Posture Etiquette

1. Standing

As shown in Figure 2-9, a balanced standing posture required you to stand up straight and tall. Then you should keep your shoulders back, pull your stomach in, keep your head level and let your arms hang down naturally at your sides. When standing, make sure you put your weight mostly on the balls of your feet while maintaining your feet about shoulder-width apart.

微课：仪态礼仪的基本要求

2. Sitting

When seated, don't cross your legs. Relax your shoulders, and they should not be rounded or pulled backwards. As shown in Figure 2-10, make sure that your back is fully supported. Make sure that your thighs and hips are supported. You should have a well-padded seat, and your thighs and hips should be parallel to the floor.

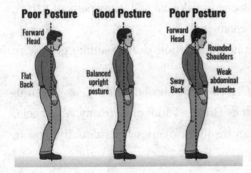

Figure 2-9　Standing

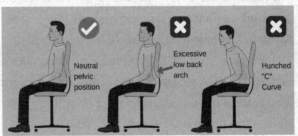

Figure 2-10　Sitting

3. Walking

As shown in Figure 2-11, when walking, keep your eyes forward to avoid looking down. Let your shoulders be back and relaxed. Suck in your stomach and tuck in your behind. You shouldn't have your butt sticking out while you're walking.

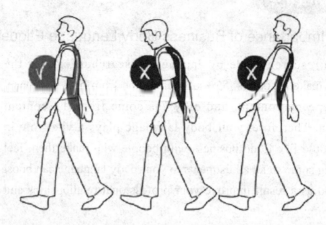

Figure 2-11 Walking

2.3.3 Hand Gesture Etiquette

Hand gestures are a great way of reinforcing what you're saying. But be cautious: they can mean different things in different cultures.

The age-old "V sign" comes in two formats: one with the palm faced outwards, and one with the palm inwards, as shown in Figure 2-12. In the United States, the two hand signals mean the same thing. However, if the outside of your hand is facing your target, you're giving somebody a long-established insult in Great Britain and many English-speaking countries such as Australia, Ireland and New Zealand.

Opening your palm to your target and stretching out your fingers seems harmless enough to most Westerners. Most of us would think you're waving, as shown in Figure 2-13. In Greece, however, the gesture is one of their most traditional manual insults. With fingers slightly apart, you thrust your hand into your target's face, usually coupling the gesture with a brash "na!" meaning "here you go!" The gesture is also an insulting one in Pakistan and many parts of Africa. The Japanese use a very similar sign to insult their old enemies.

Curling your index finger towards you in a summoning motion is an insulting gesture in Australia and Indonesia, as shown in Figure 2-14。

Essentially the "OK" sign meaning comes out as "great", or "absolutely fine", as shown in Figure 2-15. Not so, however, in a few countries such as Brazil, Türkiye, Germany, Venezuela, where the numerical interpretation gives the signal an insulting overtone. Essentially, you're telling them that you think they're a "zero".

In the United States, crossing one's fingers is a positive sign, as shown in Figure 2-16. It means that you're wishing luck upon yourself or another. However, in Vietnam, it's best avoided because it gives an insulting signal.

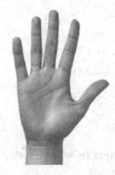

| Figure 2-12   "V Sign" with the Palm Inwards | Figure 2-13   "Waving" Sign | Figure 2-14   "Dog-Summoning" Sign |

| Figure 2-15   "OK" Sign | Figure 2-16   "Fingers Crossed" Sign |

2.3.4   Facial Expressions Etiquette

Smiling is also a great way to provide feedback. When you don't know what to say about a comment that was made to you, a smile can provide assurance and direct acknowledgement.

2.3.5   Eye Contact Etiquette

Imagine a line below your business associate's eyes. This will serve as the base of a triangle and the peak will be at their mid-forehead. To maintain a professional contact, keep your eyes in the middle of that triangle when speaking to others.

If you know the other person on a personal level, invert the triangle so that its peak is now at their mouth. Still, keep your eyes focused in the middle of the triangle, which is now at the bridge of their nose. Also, always be aware that spending too much time looking at the lower half of someone's face may give off inappropriate nonverbal messages.

When thinking about eye contact, you should also be aware of the cultures involved. Direct and prolonged eye contact is seen as a sign of trustworthiness and is more appreciated in Western cultures. On the other hand, it may be seen as a sign of disrespect to look directly at a superior in Eastern cultures.

Extended Reading

Scan the QR code, read the passage about "Ten Tips for Improving Your Nonverbal Communication" and finish the following tasks.

拓展阅读：提升非语言交际的十十技巧

After-reading tasks

When you finish reading the text above, finish the following tasks.

Task 1   Read the statements and decide whether they are true or not. Mark "T" for true and "F" for false.

（1）Nonverbal communication is less important in our daily interpersonal communication compared to verbal language. （   ）

（2）When people refused to look others' eyes directly, there is possibility that they are unconfident or trying to hide something. （   ）

（3）You are encouraged to ask questions if you don't understand another person's body language. （   ）

（4）It is always true that if a person's handshake is very weak, he can be seen as lacking in strength. （   ）

（5）Nonverbal communication is a skill that anyone can improve by practicing. （   ）

Task 2   Critical thinking

Supposing that you are going to have a business negotiation with your clients, list the non-verbal languages you need to pay attention to during the negotiation.

Basic Knowledge Test

Read the statements and decide whether they are true or not. Mark "T" for true and "F" for false.

（1）The body language you are having when communicating with others will influence others' response to you. （   ）

（2）Since your posture is the result of habits formed over a long period of time, it can be hardly changed. （   ）

同步测试：汉语版 –M2T3 判断正误

（3）When you are having dinner with your clients and find something on the ground, you can pick it up using your hand. （   ）

（4）When you don't understand what others' words mean, you can just smile as a response. （   ）

（5）When you are talking about something important with your client, blinking eyes will undermine the credibility of your message. （   ）

 Case Study

Lulu is an employee of Qingdao Brandland International Co., Ltd. In the icebreaker phase of a recent teleconference with her clients abroad, she shared an unforgettable experience of her own.

"I thought I was in my practice Zoom window, using the screen as a mirror, checking my make-up, hair, teeth. But alas, I wasn't there! I had clicked on the 'view in video' phase on my scheduled meeting. Yes, others were watching me primp. It is now a long-standing joke with this particular group. And of course, I always smile and let myself enjoy the teasing, as I do want to leave a good impression of myself."

Discussion:

（1）What is acceptable about Lulu's behaviors? And what is unacceptable?

（2）Share your ideas with your partner about how we should present ourselves in a teleconference.

 Skills Training Tasks

The Importance of Business Body Language

Situation: The salesman of a garment factory came to Qingdao Brandland International Co., Ltd. to promote the latest garment samples. The general manager of the company received him.

Salesman: Hello, this is our latest garment sample. Please have a look. (His back leaning on a chair and his legs crossed, the salesman handed the sample to the general manager with just one hand.)

General Manager: OK, these new clothes are very beautiful. What is the material of this dress?

Salesman: It's silk. (Scratching his head involuntarily as he speaks).

General Manager: I hope you can give me a discount on your price.

Salesman: Sorry, the cost is too high this time. We can't supply at the previous discount. (He looks the general manager in the eye impatiently and fidgets with his collar.)

In the end, the general manager did not accept this order, and made a phone call to the head of the garment factory, hoping to send other salesmen to negotiate in the future.

Tasks:

（1）Please list the mistakes the salesman had made during the negotiation and then correct them.

（2）Do a role play of the negotiation with your partner and make sure your body language is appropriate.

Scan the following QR codes to complete the tasks.

2.3 任务工作单　　　　2.3 任务实施单　　　　2.3 任务检查单　　　　2.3 任务评价单

Curriculum Ideology and Politics

Tian'anmen Square Duty Fulfilled by Elite Unit of PLA

Generations of soldiers have vowed to guard the national flag with their lives, and they have overcome demanding physical challenges to make sure the ritual is flawless every morning.

All soldiers selected in the national flag guard unit have to be between 180 cm and 190 cm tall and meet other physical requirements, including neck length, shoulder width and leg shape. They then have to undergo months of rigorous training that involves standing, marching and holding a gun. While the skills sound basic, the program is intense.

One major training drill is learning to march with legs extended in a goose step. To make sure the formation is in perfect unison, each step has to be 75 cm long and 30 cm above the ground. The steps are measured by instructors to ensure they are precise, and the exercise is repeated daily until muscle memory is formed.

Another training drill is to hold a rifle with a bayonet attached while standing in a fixed position. They need to fix the hand in position, hold the gun, and press the wrist against it with the hand solidly pinned. The rifle is about 3.5 kg to 4 kg and they have to hold it still for three to four hours.

They also need to practice hoisting the rifle over their shoulders vigorously. After each training session their hands and shoulders will be bruised and swollen.

One soldier said: "It felt completely different when you stood among the audience. That kind of atmosphere and enthusiasm are something you can never feel while being in the formation. It represents the dignity and the image of a country. Every day people come here to watch the ceremony. The moment we step on the avenue in perfect unison and the moment I unfurl the flag, the perfect display is to let people see and feel from the bottom of their hearts that our army is strong. And only when the army is strong, can the country be strong and peaceful."

（Source: China Daily）

Discussion: Why is the training program of the national flag guard soldiers extremely rigid?

Chinese Etiquette

There is walking etiquette since people need to pay attention to interpersonal relationships during walking. In ancient China, there is "bowing etiquette", that is, when walking in front of people of high status, people of low status need to bow down and take small steps to show respect to the venerable. In addition, there is also the protocol of "No walking in the middle of the road; no standing halfway in and out". You can't walk in the middle of the road but walk by the roadside. And you can't stand halfway in and out but by the door. This not only shows respect to the venerable, but also gives way to pedestrians.

模块 2
职场形象礼仪

模块导读

　　职业形象是一种以专业的行为举止展示自身形象的方式。打造良好的职业形象有助于职场人士构建积极的职场人际关系，并恰如其分地展示自我。人们往往会把一个人的职业形象与其能力和信誉联系起来。积极的职业形象能使企业与客户之间建立信任关系，因此塑造良好的职业形象是成功的必要因素。无论是履行日常职责还是尝试新职场角色，打理好自身仪容、仪表和仪态对商务人士至关重要。了解职业形象的要点及商务活动中的职业形象礼仪可以帮助商务人士在工作中始终如一地展示自己。

任务 1
商务仪容礼仪

◎ 学习目标

■ **素养目标**
- 注重商务仪容的职业素养。
- 培养自尊心及自信心。

■ **知识目标**
- 了解仪容礼仪在商务活动中的重要性。
- 掌握仪容礼仪的基本原则和禁忌。

■ **能力目标**
- 能够根据仪容礼仪原则选择适合商务场合的妆容。

情境导入

情境： 某公司招聘外事文秘人员，由于待遇优厚，应者如云。英语专业毕业的王丽前往面试。她的简历内容非常优秀：大学期间各门成绩名列前茅，翻译过多本小说，为许多外事活动做过翻译工作，也曾经担任过学校庆典活动的主持人，口才很好。然而，她画眼叫穿着 件述你裙，涂着鲜红的辰膏，染着金黄色的头发，将简历递给面试官时，露出了亮闪闪的美甲和叮当作响的手链。之后她坐了下来，笑眯眯地等着问话。不料，面试官说："王丽小姐，请回去等通知吧！"王丽以为面试官对自己很满意，高兴地说："好！"拎起自己的小皮包飞奔了出去。

讨论： 面试官是否对王丽感到满意并愿意录用她？为什么？

知识储备

商务仪容礼仪的基本规范

专业仪容涉及多种情况，工作面试、客户会议以及日常工作等场合都包含在内。仪容是自身能力的体现。在打理职业仪容时，妆容、发饰、指甲、牙齿、体味、服装、鞋子和配饰等这些关键方面都应该着重考虑。

1. 专业妆容，提升自信

这里有 9 个简单的步骤，让职场女性无须聘请化妆师就能拥有完美的职场妆容。扫描二维码了解具体程序与禁忌。

2. 确保头发整洁清新

头发的长度并不重要，保持良好的造型和修剪更重要。梳理头发时还应把眉毛修整干净、利落。

3. 认真修剪指甲

职场人士应时常修剪、清理自己的指甲。指甲要剪得短一些，但不要短得看起来像是咬过的那样。

4. 注意自己的体味

不要使用古龙水、须后水、除臭剂和香水。身上散发出淡淡的香味才能使人看起来、闻起来清爽，同时也不会令人反感。

5. 牙齿要干净闪亮

牙齿是另一个需要清洁的区域，不要使牙齿间塞满食物，尤其应该在午餐和喝下午茶后检查自己的牙齿，很可能在吃完东西后牙齿上有残留食物。

6. 巧搭衣着、鞋子与配饰

鞋子与衣着要匹配，并应该干净。可以适当地打光鞋子，给人清爽的感觉。

女士的珠宝不要叮当作响，否则会给自己的职业形象减分。男士的腰带应与衣着完美匹配，不能佩戴陈旧磨损的腰带，那样会破坏整体形象。此外，手表的佩戴也要力求简洁、美观。

7. 避免文身与穿刺

为了让自己看起来更专业，应该适当地掩盖自己的文身与穿刺，不被别人看到。此外，职场人士应尽量少在身上穿刺，让自己显得更职业化。

 同步测试

扫码做题。

同步测试：汉语版 –M2T1 判断正误

案例分析

某外贸公司接待国外客户时，派出一名外贸新人。这位外贸新人的接待工作做得非常到位，但是她面无血色，显得无精打采。客户看到她就心情欠佳，仔细观察才发现这位接待员没化妆，在商务接待室的灯光照射下显得病态十足。客户对将自己的单子交给这样一位业务人员十分犹豫：外贸工作强度那么大，她能承受得了吗？

讨论： 为何客户感到担忧？

 **实训项目**

分析商务妆容的得体性

1. 实训目的

通过训练，掌握商务场合妆容的禁忌与规范。

2. 实训内容

（1）背景资料：职业化妆师露西从专业角度指导某公司女员工的商务妆容。很显然，女职员们的美妆存在各种各样的问题，甚至违反了商务妆容禁忌，例如化妆不足、底妆不自然、过于浓妆艳抹、妆面与服饰不协调等。这些问题都需要专业化妆师指出并提出改进意见。

（2）以小组为单位，分析此案例中女员工违反了哪些商务美妆禁忌；给出可供选择的改进方案。

3. 实训要求

（1）采取"组内异质，组间同质"的原则，将学生分为若干小组，每组 4～6 人。

（2）每组提交一份实训报告，内容包括本案例中存在的问题及相应的改进方案。

（3）每组讲解和展示本组的工作成果。

4. 实训考核

（1）评价方式：采取小组自评、小组互评、教师评价、企业导师评价四维评价方式，总评成绩 = 小组自评 ×20% + 小组互评 ×20% + 教师评价 ×30% + 企业导师评价 ×30%。

（2）评价指标：从素质目标、知识目标、能力目标 3 方面进行评价。

2.1 任务工作单

2.1 任务实施单

2.1 任务检查单

2.1 任务评价单

 思政课堂

近日，故宫在天猫上发布新产品——限量版六色口红系列，令网友和时尚爱好者激动不已。

据报道，这个口红系列由故宫博物院文化创意馆联合国产美妆品牌润百颜发布。六款口红颜色分别为郎窑红、玫紫色、豆沙红、碧玺色、枫叶红和变色人鱼姬，如图2-1所示。这些口红膏体颜色均来自故宫博物院所藏的红色国宝器物，口红管外观设计则从清宫后妃服饰的颜色和图案上汲取灵感，一个外观设计对应一款膏体色。口红膏体颜色和外观色调十分协调、搭调。

值得一提的是，故宫口红还采用了3D打印科技，将传统图案打印在口红管上，呈现出刺绣的质感。此外，口红膏体柔软滋润，能有效帮助改善唇纹，即使是在干燥的秋冬季节，也可高效保湿、丰润滋养。

故宫限量版六色口红系列彩图

图 2-1 故宫限量版六色口红系列

讨论： 党的二十大报告指出"坚持和发展马克思主义，必须同中华优秀传统文化相结合"。现代美妆还可以借鉴中华传统文化的哪些内容？

 **中华礼仪**

中国古代美妆

真人版《花木兰》在全世界大受欢迎。在为激动人心的打斗场面兴奋尖叫的同时，也有网友对花木兰的妆容表现出极大的兴趣。据说佛教在木兰生活时的北魏时期兴盛起来，人们受到金光佛像的启发，将额头涂成黄色，称为"佛妆"。这种黄色妆容称为"额黄"，意思是额头的黄色。额头中间可以看到红色的花朵，称为"花钿"，意思是花饰。南北朝是男人追求美的黄金时代。不仅女人化妆，男人也化妆，所以你可能听说过历史上很多以貌美闻名的男性，例如潘安、兰陵王、曹植。

任务 2

商务仪表礼仪

 学习目标

- **素养目标**
  - 注重商务仪表的职业素养。
  - 培养自尊心及自信心。

- **知识目标**
  - 了解仪表礼仪在商务活动中的重要性。
  - 了解商务着装及配饰的基本类型。
  - 掌握不同商务活动中着装及配饰的穿戴规范。

- **能力目标**
  - 能够根据不同的职业场合搭配合适的商务着装和配饰。

 情境导入

情境： 传统观点认为，那些长得漂亮的人更容易赢得热门职位。并且以往研究表明，有外貌优势的人能更快获得职位，也能更快得到晋升。但是现在一项新的研究表明，成功通过工作面试的秘诀不再是吸引人的外表，而是穿戴。芝加哥和加利福尼亚大学跟踪调查了 14600 人的职业道路，从他们还在学校的时候就开始，持续了 13 年。研究这样陈述："我们发现有外貌优势的个体比外貌一般的个体薪水大约高 20%，但是当着装开始起作用时，这种差距就会缩小。也就是说，美貌优势是可以培养的。"穿着与场合相符的服饰是关键。如果你打算去参加一场与工作相关的会议，那么应尽量遵循你所属行业的着装规范。"

讨论：

（1）为何一个人的着装对其事业的发展起重要作用？

（2）你能说出一些商务场合中的着装要求吗？

知识储备

2.2.1 商务着装的基本类型

职场人士根据不同的职业场景选择着装，例如面试、会议或所在的行业类型，需要根据特定的场合选择合适的着装。

1. 商务便装

商务便装是一种非正式的服装，可在大多数商业环境中穿着，也可在工作之余穿着，如图 2-2 所示。即使公司整体着装是休闲风格，也要避免在客户面前或面试中穿着休闲装。

2. 商务时尚休闲装

时尚休闲装是另一种具有时尚感的商务休闲装，如图 2-3 所示。对于应聘办公氛围更宽松的公司，你也可以选择在面试中穿时尚休闲装。

3. 商务休闲装

商务休闲装是许多办公人士穿的一种常见服装，如图 2-4 所示。商务休闲装适合多种面试、客户会议和办公室环境。

4. 商务职业装

商务职业装是一种传统的着装形式，用于较为保守的场合或着装要求严格的公司，如图 2-5 所示。商务职业装应该是量身定做的。

5. 商务正式装

商务正式装只适用于最正式的场合，如颁奖典礼、特殊晚宴、慈善活动或其他重要的晚间活动，如图 2-6 所示。商务正式装类似于"佩戴黑领结的男子晚礼服"，但应保持职业性。

图 2-2　商务便装

图 2-3　商务时尚休闲装

图 2-4　商务休闲装

图 2-5　商务职业装

图 2-6　商务正式装

黑领结晚礼服

"黑领结晚礼服"通常是指"燕尾服"或"无尾礼服"，如图 2-7 所示。最初被叫作"晚礼服"，因为这种礼服非常适合非正式的晚间活动。如今，晚礼服和其他黑领结服装被保留在非常正式的场合，如婚礼、晚宴、舞会、庆典和筹款等活动。

图 2-7　黑领结晚礼服

黑领结活动有时会被贴上"必须穿着黑领结礼服"的标签，以区别于不太正式的"可选择黑领结礼服"的场合。其他的邀请可能会注明"首选黑领结礼服"或"要求穿黑领结礼服"。

2.2.2　商务着装的基本原则和规范

商务仪表礼仪包含三个基本原则。一是和谐原则。商务人士的着装需与自己的年龄、性别、肤色、身材、职业等条件相协调，在充分考虑自身特点的基础上扬长避短。二是TPO 原则，分别是指时间、地点和对象（time、placet 和 object），商务人士要充分考虑商务活动的时间、地点和交流对象，选择合适的着装。三是"最多三色"。是指全身的衣服及配件的颜色加在一起不应超过三种，并且鞋子、腰带和公文包的颜色最好是同一种，首选黑色。

1. 商务男士着装规范

商务男士套装着装规范中有三个"三原则"。一是"三色原则"，指所有衣服的颜色不应超过三种。二是"三合一"，指鞋子、腰带和公文包的颜色应相一致。三是"三个禁忌"，即不要把标签挂在衣服上、忌鞋衣不配、忌不打领带。

不同类型的西装有不同的纽扣。对于带三个纽扣的西装，应把上两个或中间的一个扣起来。穿两个纽扣的西装时，把第一个纽扣扣好即可。如果西装只有一个纽扣，扣起来或者不扣都可以。

2. 商务女士着装规范

在商务场合，女士通常也要穿商务套装。做套装最好的面料是羊毛和亚麻。不可穿皮裙，因为在西方国家，皮裙是站街女的标准着装。最合适的颜色是黑色、灰色、棕色、米色等。无论什么季节，女士的西装都必须是长袖的。裙子应该足够长，遮住膝盖。西装裙应与衬衫、鞋子和长筒袜相配。衬衫最好的面料是棉和丝绸，款式要简洁，没有花边和褶皱。鞋子应该是皮革做的高跟鞋。靴子或凉鞋不合适。长筒袜是商务套装的必备品。不可穿齐膝长的袜子。

3. 配饰的佩戴规范

配饰可以为商务着装锦上添花。下面是几条可供参考的配饰穿戴规范。

1）腰带

一般来说，腰带最好能与鞋子相匹配。例如，如果穿着一双黑色的乐福鞋，不妨选择一条与之搭配的黑色腰带。

2）手表

手表是一种既有功能性又有装饰性的配饰。如果想戴手表，可以选机械表或电子表，或是可连接手机的智能手表。

3）袖扣

袖扣可以用来扣紧衬衫袖口。适用于正式场合，可以由多种材质制作，样式繁多。

4）领带夹

领带夹用来将领带固定在衬衫的门襟上。和袖扣一样，领带夹也有各种各样的材质和设计。有些人使用领带钉，它也有类似的功能，但会刺穿领带和衬衫。

5）包

想想自己最常穿的衣服的材料和颜色是什么，试着选择一个与之搭配的包。如果工作场所比较随意，可以选择一个有品位的商务背包，材质可以是绒面革或皮革。

 **同步测试**

扫码做题。

同步测试：汉语版 –M2T2 判断正误

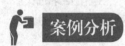 **案例分析**

有一次，一个外国客户来到一家服装加工厂，工厂里的一位中年妇女接待了他。那位妇女的衣服很简单，跟 20 世纪 80 年代的款式差不多，并且一点也不专业。当时外国客户想知道时下流行的服装的打样方法，于是他被邀请到车间。在车间他发现工人们都没有穿制服，大多数人衣着随意，有些人甚至看起来十分邋遢。他看到这些，皱起眉头，没有下订单。

讨论：

（1）这次商务接待失败的原因是什么？

（2）为什么个人着装对商务活动至关重要？

 实训项目

分析工作场合中的商务着装

1. 实训目的

通过训练，掌握职场商务着装的规范。

2. 实训内容

（1）背景资料：周五原本是公司的休闲便装日，然而本周五却不同寻常，案例中苏茜所在公司的总裁要与另一家外贸公司的业务代表会面，会议涉及对两家公司未来的重大决定。在会议上，苏茜穿着运动裤、背心和人字拖，给对方谈判代表留下了不好的第一印象，从而间接导致谈判失败。会后，总裁对苏茜的着装非常生气，要求与她谈谈她在公司的未来发展。

（2）以小组为单位，分析此案例中苏茜应该穿着的职场商务服装类型和依据；分享身边案例，讨论商务着装的原则和规范。

3.实训要求

（1）采取"组内异质，组间同质"的原则，将学生分为若干小组，每组 4～6 人。

（2）每组提交一份职场商务着装实训报告，内容包括本案例中职场商务着装的类型和依据，以及不同工作场景中的商务着装类型、原则及规范。

（3）每组讲解和展示本组的工作成果。

4.实训考核

（1）评价方式：采取小组自评、小组互评、教师评价、企业导师评价四维评价方式，总评成绩 = 小组自评×20% + 小组互评×20% + 教师评价×30% + 企业导师评价×30%。

（2）评价指标：从素质目标、知识目标、能力目标 3 方面进行评价。

2.2 任务工作单　　　2.2 任务实施单　　　2.2 任务检查单　　　2.2 任务评价单

 思政课堂

东京奥运会开幕式上中国代表团的礼服暗藏"玄机"

中国奥运代表团入场的礼服设计工作历时两年完成。经过多轮选拔和评审，2020 年 3 月，东京奥运会中国奥运代表团的礼服正式确定为以"开门红"为主题的最终设计，如图 2-8 所示。

在为 2008 年北京奥运会和残奥会设计礼服之后，北京服装学院此后承担了多个重大国际体育赛事的服装设计任务，为运动员打造了自信展现民族身份和形象的礼服。

由于运动员的出场是开幕式的一个重头戏，像红色这样引人注目的颜色是首选，尤其红色还是中国国旗的主要色调，也是中国传统文化中能量、激情和欢乐的象征。

图 2-8　中国奥运代表团礼服"开门红"

白色代表光明、纯洁和神圣，它在服装设计中起着缓冲作用。在奥运会开幕式上，红白两色的组合构成了一种吉祥的寓意，与设计主题"开好头"相呼应。

色彩和图形可以传达一个国家的视觉特征，更准确地表达国家形象。女运动员白裙的下摆以中国国花牡丹为装饰，图案来源于代表中国传统美学的明代（1368—1644 年）牡丹碗。

男式衬衫的设计灵感来自中国国旗的五星图案。它体现了中国奥运代表团为国家荣誉而奋斗的精神。

此次礼服设计团队成员贺阳教授说，"设计过程中需要考虑一个因素，制服应该以一种易于理解和识别的方式展示中国传统文化特征。我们需要在文化表述、礼仪和现代中国运动员精神之间取得平衡"。

讨论： 党的二十大报告指出，到 2035 年，我国发展的总体目标之一是要建成教育强国、科技强国、人才强国、文化强国、体育强国、健康中国，国家文化软实力显著增强。中国运动员的服装在奥运会和残奥会中发挥了什么重要作用？

中华礼仪

唐装并不是唐朝（618—907 年）人穿的服装，而是把具有中国式风格的服装统称为唐装。唐装做工讲究，织锦缎面料是首选。立起的领子、对称的衣襟是唐装的标准样式，精美的刺绣也是唐装的一大特点，就连小小的扣子也大有讲究，盘扣造型别致、工艺精美，是唐装的点睛之笔。现在人们多在结婚或过年的时候穿唐装，在大型的庆典场合，人们会把唐装当作一种礼服穿在身上。如今唐装又融入了一些西方的设计理念，显得更加时尚和美观。

任务 3

商务仪态礼仪

◎ 学习目标

■ **素养目标**
- 培养注重商务仪态的职业素养。
- 培养自尊心及自信心。

■ **知识目标**
- 了解仪态礼仪在商务活动中的重要性。

●掌握商务场合中的手势、姿势、表情等礼仪的要求。

■ 能力目标
●能够根据仪态礼仪的原则展示出恰当的仪态。

情境导入

情境：一天，杰克去拜访一个客户的公司，在前台遇到两位该公司的员工。这两位员工给人留下的印象完全不同。其中一位员工看起来百无聊赖、无精打采。他耷拉着身子，显得有些胆怯并且没精神。他用手支撑着头，表情呆滞，注意力都被桌上的摆件吸引了。而另一位员工，站得笔直，背挺阔，肩膀向后拉，面带微笑。这种良好的姿势使他看起来机敏、友好，时刻都做好回应对方的准备。杰克本能地靠近第二位员工，避免与第一位员工交流。不出所料，第二位员工热情地接待了他，并带他去见了公司老板。

讨论：
（1）这两位员工分别给来访者留下了怎样的印象？
（2）肢体语言在商务场合中有怎样的重要性？

知识储备

2.3.1　商务仪态礼仪的重要性

日本学者曾研究表明，人们在给交往对象留下的印象中，55% 来源于肢体语言，38% 来源于言语内容，而谈话内容只占 7%。可见，肢体语言在商业中起着至关重要的作用。人们愿意和那些让他们感到舒服的人做生意。通过细微调整肢体语言，可增强自信，改善职业关系和工作表现。

2.3.2　姿势礼仪

1. 站姿

如图 2-9 所示，左右两边为不良站姿。左边站姿：头部前倾，平背；右边站姿：头部前倾，背部下凹，圆肩挺肚。要想拥有平稳、良好的站姿，首先要站得笔直、挺拔。然后要挺胸、收腹，保持头部水平，手臂自然下垂在身体两侧。站立时，确保重心主要放在脚掌上，同时保持双脚与肩同宽。

2. 坐姿

坐着的时候，不要跷二郎腿。肩膀要放松，不要圆肩或后拉。如图 2-10 所示，让背部得到充分的支撑。让大腿和臀部有支撑，因此椅子表面要垫起来，从而使大腿和臀部与地面平行。图 2-10 后面两个坐姿，过度弓背或驼背 "C" 曲线都是不良坐姿。

3. 走姿

如图 2-11 所示，走路时眼睛向前看，避免向下看。让肩膀向后放松。收腹并收起臀部。走路的时候不要撅着屁股。

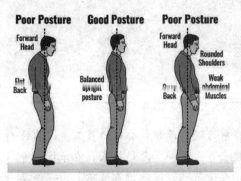

图 2-9　站姿

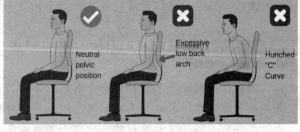

图 2-10　坐姿

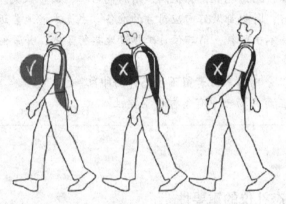

图 2-11　走姿

2.3.3　手势礼仪

手势是强化说话内容的好方法。但请注意，在不同的文化中，它们的含义可能不同。

古老的"V"字手势有两种形式：一种是掌心朝外；另一种是掌心朝内，如图 2-12 所示。在美国，这两个手势的意思是一样的。然而，在英国、澳大利亚、爱尔兰、新西兰等国，如果你的手背正对着说话对象，则有侮辱人之意，这一用法由来已久。

在大多数西方人看来，向说话对象张开手掌并伸出手指这一手势并无不当含义，一般可认为是在向人挥手，如图 2-13 所示。然而，在希腊，这个手势是他们最传统的肢体侮辱之一。手指微微分开，把你的手伸到对方的脸上，通常伴随着一个无礼的语气"呐！"，意思是"给你！"。在巴基斯坦和非洲许多国家或地区，这一举动也是一种侮辱。日本人就用一个非常相似的标志来侮辱他们的宿敌。

在澳大利亚和印度尼西亚，将食指指向自己的方向是一种侮辱性的召唤动作，如图 2-14 所示。

从本质上说，图 2-15 所示手势的意思是"很棒"或"非常好"。然而，在一些国家，如巴西、土耳其、德国、委内瑞拉并非如此，在这些国家，如果把手势从数字角度解读会有侮辱意味。实际上，做这个手势的人是在告诉对方，你认为他们是"零"，即一无是处。

在美国，图 2-16 中手指交叉是一个积极的信号。这意味着你祝愿自己或他人好运。然而，在越南最好避免这样做，因为这是一种侮辱的信号。

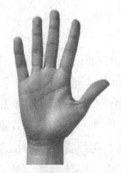

图 2-12　反 "V" 字手势　　　图 2-13　"挥手" 手势　　　图 2-14　"唤狗" 手势

图 2-15　"OK" 手势　　　　图 2-16　手指交叉

2.3.4　面部表情礼仪

微笑也是给人以反馈的好方法。当别人评价了你，而你又不知道说什么，那么微笑吧，微笑能表明你的确信和直接的认可。

2.3.5　目光交流礼仪

想象你的商业伙伴的眼睛下面有一条线。这将作为一个三角形的底部，尖部将在他们的前额中部。当你和别人说话时，把你的眼睛保持在那个三角形的中间，以保持眼神交流的专业性。

如果你和对方私交甚密，把三角形倒转一下，这样三角形的顶点就在对方的嘴巴处。不过，把你的眼睛集中在三角形的中间，也就是他们鼻梁的位置。此外，要时刻注意，花太多时间看别人的下半张脸可能会传递出不恰当的非语言信息。

眼神交流时，要意识到其中的文化因素。在西方文化中，直接、长久的眼神接触被视为值得信任的标志，更受赞赏。然而，在东方文化中，直视上级可能被视为一种不尊重。

 同步测试

扫码做题。

同步测试：汉语版 –M2T3 判断正误

 案例分析

露露是青岛贝来国际贸易有限公司的员工。在最近一次与海外客户的电话会议的开场阶段，她分享了一段经历，给人留下深刻的印象：

"我以为自己还在练习 Zoom 的预览窗口，于是把屏幕当镜子，对着计算机检查自己的化妆、头发和牙齿是否整洁。但是，这并不是预览！在找锁定的会议中，我头队上已经点击了'观看视频'阶段。是的，其他人在观看我打扮。于是这件事成为同事和客户中的笑料，我被笑话了好久。当然，我对此总是保持微笑，让自己享受嘲笑，因为我真的想让自己给别人留下好印象。"

讨论：
（1）露露的行为有哪些合适和不合适的地方？
（2）电话会议中应如何关注个人外表，请互相讨论。

实训项目

分析商务仪态礼仪

1. 实训目的

通过训练，掌握商务仪态礼仪的要点，理解其重要性。

2. 实训内容

（1）背景资料：某服装厂的业务员来到青岛贝来国际贸易有限公司，推广其工厂最新的服装样品，公司总经理接待了他。然而该服装厂业务员缺乏基本的商务礼仪素养，在仪态方面做出了不少出格的举动。例如，他在谈判中倚靠着坐在椅子上，跷起二郎腿，并一只手将样品交到对方手里；说话时手乱动，不由自主地用手挠头皮，用手摆弄自己的衣领；谈到价格时情绪很急躁，眼睛直盯着对方等。这一系列不礼貌的肢体行为给公司总经理留下了不好的印象，从而导致谈判的失败。

（2）以小组为单位，分析此案例中的业务员有哪些不恰当的肢体行为；分享身边案例，讨论商务仪态礼仪的重要性。

3. 实训要求

（1）采取"组内异质，组间同质"的原则，将学生分为若干小组，每组 4~6 人。

（2）每组提交一份关于商务仪态礼仪的实训报告，内容包含现实商务场合中商务仪态礼仪的要点（坐姿、手势、眼神等）及重要性，并提出改进方案。

（3）每组讲解和展示本组的工作成果。

4. 实训考核

（1）评价方式：采取小组自评、小组互评、教师评价、企业导师评价四维评价方式，总评成绩 = 小组自评 × 20% + 小组互评 × 20% + 教师评价 × 30% + 企业导师评价 × 30%。

（2）评价指标：从素质目标、知识目标、能力目标 3 方面进行评价。

2.3 任务工作单　　2.3 任务实施单　　2.3 任务检查单　　2.3 任务评价单

思政课堂

国旗护卫队在天安门广场执行任务的背后

一代又一代的士兵发誓用生命保卫国旗，他们克服了严苛的体力挑战，以确保每天早上的升旗仪式是完美的。

所有入选国旗护卫队的士兵身高必须在 180～190cm，并满足颈长、肩宽和腿型等方面的要求。然后，他们必须接受几个月的严格训练，包括站立、行进和持枪。虽然这些技能听起来很基础，但训练是高强度的。

其中一项主要训练是双腿伸直走正步。为了确保队形完美一致，每一步伐需长 75cm，离地 30cm。教练会测量每一步，以确保准确性。每天重复练习，直到形成肌肉记忆。

另一种训练是手持带有刺刀的步枪，站在固定的位置。他们需要拿着枪，把手腕压在枪上，手要牢牢地固定住。这种步枪重 3.5～4kg，一拿就是 3～4 小时。

士兵们还需要练习用力将步枪举过肩膀。每次训练结束后，他们的手和肩膀都会青肿。

一名士兵说："当你站在观众中间时，感觉完全不同。那种氛围和热情是你在队列中永远感受不到的。它代表着一个国家的尊严和形象。每天人们都来这里观看仪式。我们齐步走在林荫道上的那一刻，我完美地展开国旗的那一刻，就是让人们从心底看到和感受到我们的军队是强大的。只有军队强大，国家才能强大和平。"

讨论：党的二十大报告指出要"不断提升国家文化软实力和中华文化影响力"。为什么国旗护卫队士兵的训练如此严苛？升国旗仪式对于提升国家文化软实力有何意义？

中华礼仪

人们在行走过程中要注意人际关系的处理，因此有行走的礼节。古代中国人常行"趋礼"，即地位低的人在地位高的人面前走过时，一定要低头弯腰，以小步快走的方式表示对尊者的礼敬。另外，还有"行不中道，立不中门"的原则，即走路不可走在路中间，应该靠边行走，站立不可站在门中间。这样既表示对尊者的礼敬，又可避让行人。

Module 3
Business Communication Etiquette

 Profile of the Module

Business communication is a bridge and link for people to exchange emotions, establish friendship and carry out various activities in foreign business activities. Whether the greeting and introduction are appropriate, handshaking and business card are performed properly, and various communication tools are used effectively directly affect the success of business activities to a large extent. Good business communication etiquette can not only demonstrate personal charm and image, but also help businessmen gain respect and trust from others in business activities. Understanding the significance and basic etiquette of business communication etiquette and mastering various rules and skills are the necessary abilities and qualities for businessmen.

Task 1

Business Addressing, Greetings and Introduction Etiquette

◎ **Learning Objectives**

■ Moral Objectives
- To cultivate students' values of civility and courtesy.
- To establish good social image, respect others and build self-confidence and esteem.
- To be culturally confident to introduce China to the world.

■ Knowledge Objectives
- To get familiar with the importance of business addressing, greetings and introduction etiquette.

- To grasp the basic rules of business addressing, greetings and introduction in international business activities.

■ Ability Objectives
- To be able to correctly address, greet and introduce others in different business occasions and situations.

Lead-in: Case Study

Situation: American teacher Elizabeth Dahl is an associate professor who came to China to teach international relations theory. She is young, unmarried and beautiful. One day she met her student Lily for the first time.

Lily: Hello. Nice to meet you. I'm Lily Wang, a student of the international relations theory. May I ask your name?

Elizabeth: Hello. My name is Elizabeth Dahl. Nice to meet you.

Lily: Sorry, but how can I address you, Miss Dahl or Elizabeth? I was told that American children can call their parents and grandparents by their first names, bringing them closer to each other.

Elizabeth: (A smile on her face) That's true. But I'd rather you call me professor.

Discussion: What can we learn from the dialogue?

Basic Knowledge

3.1.1 Business Addressing Etiquette

1. How to address people in business situations

There are two common ways of addressing people in addition to "Mr.", "Miss", and "Ms." in business situations.

The first is to address the title. When using the title, we should use the surname or full name. British and American given names usually come first and then surnames. For example, Mr. William Jones, we should call Mr. Jones instead of Mr. William.

微课：商务场合
常用称呼

The second is to address people of higher status "Your Excellency", professor, judge, lawyer, doctor, and other positions because they are highly respected in the society.

In some English speaking countries, it is traditional for a woman to change her last name when she gets married. However, not all women do. You can safely ask, "Are you going by the same name?" This question gets trickier when a woman gets divorced or becomes a widow. Some women will change their name back to their maiden name. If you don't know the woman well, wait for her to tell you if her name has changed.

2. Guidelines on business addressing etiquette

Many feel uncomfortable asking the question, "What should I call you?" There will always be some people and some professions that require more formality than others.

微课：商务称呼
礼仪注意事项

1）Asking the question

If you are unsure of what to call someone, it's best to use a formal address or simply ask one of these questions:

What should I call you?

Can I call you [first name]?

Is it okay if I call you [Mr. ...]?

2）Answering the question

If they seem unsure about how to pronounce your name, or you want them to call you something more casual, help them out:

Please call me...

You can call me...

3）Formal titles in English

In business situations, use formal titles unless the people you meet tell you otherwise.

Here are the formal titles English speakers use:

Sir (adult male of any age).

Ma'am (adult female — North American).

Madam (adult female).

Mr. + last name.

Mrs. + last name (married woman who uses her husband's last name).

Ms. + last name (married or unmarried woman; common in business).

Miss + last name (unmarried woman).

Dr. + last name.

Professor + last name.

Occasionally you may have a close relationship with someone. At some point this person may give you permission to use his or her first name.

3. Etiquette taboos on business addressing etiquette

1）Using the wrong terms of address

Misunderstandings mainly refer to the wrong judgments about the addressee's age, generation, marital status, and relationship with others. For example, it's misunderstanding to call an unmarried woman "Mrs. ...".

微课：商务
称呼禁忌

2）Using vulgar titles

In interpersonal communication, some titles should not be used in formal occasions. For example, titles such as "brothers" "friends" "buddies", etc. seem to be vulgar.

3）Using nickname

For those with ordinary relationships, don't nickname them by yourself, let alone address them by the nickname you hear from others.

3.1.2   Business Greetings Etiquette

Greeting etiquette around the world and even among different industries varies. Be prepared to adjust your greeting slightly based on circumstance when necessary.

1. Common greetings in Asian countries

1）China

The easiest way to say hello in China is with "ni hao". A way to show more respect to elders and superiors is to use "nin hao" instead.

微课：东方礼节

Handshakes are the standard greeting. The grip tends to be lighter than the Western handshake and is also sustained for longer.

In formal situations, people bow slightly or nod politely to greet one another formally.

If seated, the Chinese will stand up out of respect when they are introduced to someone.

2）Japan

The easiest way to say hello in Japan is with the standard greeting of "konnichiwa".

In Japan, people greet each other by bowing. A bow can range from a small nod of the head to a deep bend at the waist. A deeper, longer bow indicates respect and conversely a small nod with the head is casual and informal.

3）India

In many parts of India and during formal occasions, it is common for people to greet with the traditional Hindu greeting of "Namaste". This is accompanied with a nod of the head or a bow depending on the status of the person you are greeting.

4）Thailand

In both a formal and informal situation, Thai people greet each other with the word "sawadee" followed by "ka" for females and "krub" for males.

Thai people don't always shake hands by default. Instead, they offer a friendly "wai", a prayer-like gesture with the hands placed together in front of the chest, fingers pointing upward, head slightly bowed forward.

2. Common greetings in Western countries

1）U.S.A.

A handshake is the most common greeting when meeting someone for the first time or in professional settings.

微课：西方礼节

Many people hug in informal situations or to greet close friends and family.

2）UK and Germany

The most common greeting is a handshake with direct eye contact.

Men usually greet women first and wait for them to extend their hand.

Close friends may hug to greet and younger people may kiss one another on the cheek.

3）France, Italy, Portugal

These three nations share a very affectionate greeting.

When you meet a friend or a person you know, you give each other two kisses on the cheeks, in France as many as three.

When introducing yourself to someone new, a simple handshake is enough.

3. English greetings

（1）When you greet someone you know but seldom see, use one of these greetings:

How are you doing?

How is everything going?

What's new?

What's up?

（2）When you greet your acquaintances you haven't seen for a while, use one of these greetings:

微课：英语
问候语

How are you?

How have you been?

Glad to meet you again.

Long time no see.

（3）When you meet your friend unexpectedly, use one of these greetings:

What a pleasant surprise!

Fancy seeing you here.

（4）When you are introduced to others, use one of these greetings:

How do you do?

Hello.

（5）When you greet someone you don't know and want to attract his (her) attention, use one of these greetings:

Excuse me, Sir/Madam.

Just a minute, Sir/Madam.

（6）If you greet someone close to you, use one of these informal greetings:

Hello, old chap.

Hi there, Jim.

Small world, isn't it?

What brings you here today?

4. Taboos on business greetings etiquette

In a professional setting, don't impose hugs on anyone. When we meet clients, handshakes are definitely the golden standard.

Waving your full arm side to side in many countries is recognized as saying "hello"or "goodbye". However, in East Asian countries it is considered overly demonstrative. Additionally in some European countries, as well as Japan and Latin America, it can be confused with a "no" or general negative response. In India, it means "come here".

微课：商务问候
注意事项

Curling the index finger, or four fingers toward you as a gesture of inviting somebody to come closer, can be mistaken for "good bye" in southern Europe. In Philippines and East Asia, curling the index finger is used only to beckon dogs.

Pointing directly to someone or something using index finger in Europe is considered impolite. In China, Japan, Latin America and Indonesia, it has very rude connotations. In many African countries, the index finger is used for pointing only at inanimate objects.

3.1.3　Business Introduction Etiquette

Making introductions is particularly important in business settings as they give you an aura of being confident, prepared, and in control, establish a rapport of respect and get relationships off on the right foot.

1. Introducing yourself

A self-introduction is as simple as saying, "Hi, we haven't met. I'm _____." as you extend your hand for the common handshake.

微课：介绍自己

If you're approaching someone you are familiar with, you could make your introduction a bit friendlier by using his name, "Mr. Robinson, my name is _____. It's a pleasure to meet you."

When introducing yourself in business settings, apart from your name you should consider the following:

（1）your role or title.

（2）your business, trade, or industry.

（3）a brief description of your business.

（4）a "memory hook" (quick, ear-catching phrase that people are likely to remember).

The length of your introduction will depend on the circumstances of the introduction. It shouldn't need to be long, and it's possible to combine certain elements, such as your business and your benefit statement.

2. Introducing others

When you introduce people, the most important part can be to figure out who should be introduced to whom, based on rank and authority.

微课：介绍他人

（1）Introducing business associates of different levels.

Introduce the person of lower rank to the person of higher rank, regardless of age or gender.

Example: "Mr. Manager, I would like to introduce Jean Junior from Human Resources."

（2）Introducing a business associate of any rank and a client.

Introduce the business associate to the client, regardless of rank, age, or gender.

Example: "Mr. Client, please meet our Managing Director, Greg Manning."

（3）Introducing two business associates of equal rank.

Introduce the person that you don't know as well to the person you know better.

Example: Let's say your manager, Greg Manning is meeting the manager of the Singapore office, Mary Lim. "Greg, I'd like you to meet the manager of the Singapore Office, Mary Lim."

（4）Introducing a man and a woman.

Introduce the man to the woman.

Example: "Mary, this is Kevin Jones, who has been setting up the music for this event."

（5）Introducing a younger person and an older person (of the same gender).

Introduce the younger person to the older person.

Example: "Mr. Mature, I'd like you to meet my friend Shireen. She's my friend from university."

3. Guidelines on business introduction

Introduce people in business based on rank, not gender or age.

In business, the client, guest or visitor outranks the boss or co-worker and should be introduced first.

Always smile and maintain eye contact.

微课：介绍注意事项

Do not call a person by his or her first name when meeting or being introduced for the first time. Use their title and last name until invited to be on a first-name basis.

Do have an "elevator pitch" prepared. When introducing yourself, have a one-sentence elevator pitch at the ready so you don't hesitate when someone asks, "What do you do?"

微课：介绍禁忌

 Extended Reading

Scan the QR code, read the passage about "The Do's and Don'ts of Business Introductions and Greeting Etiquette" and finish the following tasks.

拓展阅读：商务介绍和问候的注意事项

After-reading tasks

When you finish reading the text above, finish the following tasks.

Task 1 Read the statements and decide whether they are true or not. Mark "T" for true and "F" for false.

（1）Texting professional contacts is generally considered quite informal and not recommended.（　　）

（2）It's much safer to use the standard Ms. for all women in formal business greetings. (　　　)

（3）In creative industries in the United States, immediately going to a last-name basis when conducting business introductions is common. (　　　)

（4）Keep your business greetings in voicemail to the basics: Your name, the purpose of your call and how to reach you. (　　　)

（5）When meeting clients, handshakes are the golden standard. (　　　)

Task 2　Critical thinking

Share your experience of addressing and greeting a foreign friend for the first time.

 Basic Knowledge Test

Read the statements and decide whether they are true or not. Mark "T" for true and "F" for false.

（1）Generally, you can call others by their family name or full name by putting the Mr. or Ms. in front. This is the general address most widely used in company, hotels, stores, restaurants, and other places. (　　　)

同步测试：汉语版 –M3T1 判断正误

（2）Handshakes are the standard greeting. The grip in Asian countries tends to be lighter than the Western handshake and is also sustained for longer. (　　　)

（3）When introducing business associates of different levels, we should introduce the person of higher rank to the person of lower rank, regardless of age or gender. (　　　)

（4）Do not call a person by his or her first name when meeting or being introduced for the first time. Use their title and last name until invited to be on a first-name basis. (　　　)

（5）British and American given names usually come first and then surnames. For example, Mr. William Jones, we should call Mr. William instead of Mr. Jones. (　　　)

 **Case Study**

• Case 1

Xiaowang, a foreign trade businessman was booking a birthday cake for his foreign client and asking the assistant in the cake shop to write a greeting card. After receiving the order, the assistant asked Xiaowang, "Sir, is your friend married or not? How should I address her, Miss White or Mrs. White?" Xiaowang didn't know the answer yet. Thinking she doesn't look young and must be married, Xiaowang

微课：小姐还是太太

said to the assistant: "Please call her Mrs. White." After the cake was made, the assistant delivered the cake to the designated place and knocked on the door. A lady opened the door. The assistant asked politely: "Excuse me, may I ask if you are Mrs. White?" The lady was stunned and said unhappily: "No, I am not!" Then she closed the door. The assistant was confused and called Xiaowang to confirm the address and room number. She knocked on the door again and said, "Sorry, Mrs. White, this is your cake!" The lady yelled, "I told you that you are wrong. There is only Miss White, no Mrs. White!" With a "bang", the door closed loudly.

Discussion: Why was Xiaowang's foreign client angry when she was addressed "Mrs. White"?

• Case 2

Michael, an Englishman, was invited to the home of his French friend, Craig. As soon as they met, Craig gave Michael a warm hug and kissed him twice on the cheek, which made Michael feel very embarrassed. During their conversation, Michael always said "thank you" and "please", which made his enthusiastic French friend Craig feel awkward. After a few words, Michael left Craig's home in a hurry.

Discussion:

（1）Why did Michael feel embarrassed?

（2）Why did Craig feel awkward?

 Skills Training Tasks

Business Addressing, Greetings and Introduction Etiquette

Xixi was employee from Qingdao Brandl and International Co., Ltd.. In a reception task, Xixi accompanied Mr. Tang, her department manager, to meet with their client, Mr. Smith, the purchasing manager from Wonderland Import and Export Trading Company.

Scan the following QR codes to complete the tasks.

3.1 任务工作单　　　3.1 任务实施单　　　3.1 任务检查单　　　3.1 任务评价单

 Curriculum Ideology and Politics

Introducing China to the World — *China and the World in the New Era*

China published a white paper, titled "China and the World in the New Era," to help the international community better understand China's development, on the occasion of the 70th anniversary of the founding of the People's Republic of China (PRC). Issued by the State Council Information Office, the white paper systematically introduced China's achievement and path of development, as well as where China is going. Over the last 70 years the PRC has witnessed profound changes and achieved a miracle of development unprecedented in human history under the leadership of the Communist Party of China (CPC).China now has an impact on the world that is ever more comprehensive, profound and long-lasting, and the world is paying ever greater attention to China. "In this new era, China will not waver in its commitment to forging ahead on the path of socialism with Chinese characteristics, pursuing mutual learning and mutually beneficial cooperation, and working together with the rest of the world," said the white paper. In the future, China will embrace the world in a more open and inclusive manner, engage in more interactions with other countries, and bring more progress and prosperity, it said.

（Source: China Daily）

Discussion: What is your understanding of "China will embrace the world in a more open and inclusive manner, engage in more interactions with other countries, and bring more progress and prosperity."?

Chinese Etiquette

Chinese names(xing ming) are different from Western ones. The family names (surnames) come first and given names come last. People usually ask each other's "xing ming" when they meet. If they share the same family name, they believe that their ancestors were relatives 500 years ago. The family of Confucius is an example of Chinese family names. A young man can trace his family line to an ancestor who lived 2,500 years ago. It is like a tree: leaves, branches and roots are connected by the family name. There are supposedly more than 20,000 family names in China. The secret of where your ancestors came from and what they did are concealed in "xing ming".

（Source: Hello, China）

Task 2

Business Handshaking and Card Exchange Etiquette

◎ Learning Objectives

■ Moral Objectives

• To cultivate students' values of civility and courtesy.

• To establish good social image, respect others and build self-confidence and esteem.

• To strengthen the cultural confidence from the development of China's High-speed Railway.

■ Knowledge Objectives

• To get familiar with the basic requirements and significance of business handshaking and business card exchange etiquette.

• To grasp the basic rules of business handshaking and business card exchange in international business activities.

■ Ability Objectives

• To be able to correctly shake hands with others, receive and give business cards in different business occasions and situations.

 Lead-in: Case Study

Situation: Allen, director of Marketing of Carson International is meeting his client Kate at his office for the first time.

Allen: (Stand up and extend his right hand) Hi Kate. It's nice to meet you. I'm Allen, Director of Marketing.

Kate: (Shake hands with Allen for 3-4 seconds) It's a pleasure to meet you, Allen. Here's my card.

Allen: (Accept the card with two hands, read it for a while and then put it in the bag) Thank you. And here's mine.

Kate: (Accept the card with two hands and read it carefully) Thanks, Allen. By the way, is this your new logo?

Allen: Yes, we just changed it recently.

Kate: It's very memorable. I like it.

Allen: Thank you. Now, would you like something to drink?

Kate: Yes, please. A green tea would be great.

Allen: It'll just be a minute.

Kate: Thank you.

Discussion: What business handshaking and card exchange etiquette can you learn from the dialogue?

 Basic Knowledge

3.2.1　Business Handshaking Etiquette

A proper handshake should: convey confidence; respect all the rules of etiquette; avoid

微课：恰当的
握手

awkwardness and embarrassment.

There are three steps to be followed:

Extend your right hand and grip the other person's hand. Make sure that both hands are pushed all the way in to meet Palm to palm and your thumbs are facing straight up.

Shake just a couple of times in a vertical motion. The range of motion is 2 or 3 inches. The motion is extended from the shoulder, through the elbow, and straight through to your hand.

End the handshake cleanly, before the introduction is over. If you want to count, a good handshake is held for 3 or 4 seconds.

微课：商务握手
注意事项

For most business settings, pay attention to the following rules to avoid awkwardness and appear confident whenever you shake hands.

Do stand up. If you're sitting down, get up to shake hands. It's a sign of respect and puts you on the same level as the other person.

Do respect authority and age. The person in the higher position of authority or age should be the one to initiate a handshake. For example, the interviewer at a job interview, a senior manager in a company meeting, etc.

Don't use two hands. In business, it's best to use just one hand. Usually your right. The two-handed shake is reserved for politicians.

Do be aware of your other hand. Most importantly, keep it visible. Just keep it relaxed at the side of your body.

Do smile. A handshake is a gesture of respect, sympathy, and appreciation. A sincere smile should go along with that. It shows you're happy to be where you are.

Don't look away. Eye-contact is important during a handshake. If you avoid looking at someone when you shake their hands they'll think you're not confident or you don't think the other person deserves a proper handshake.

Do say their name. Greet the person first to get their attention and then offer your hand. It's a smart idea to repeat the person's name. Say something like, "It's great to meet you, Derek. " It will help you remember the name later on.

Don't "hold hands". Your handshake should end before the verbal introduction or saying-goodbye ends.

Generally speaking, handshakes are pretty universal. There are only a few cultural differences. But if you're in a new place, it's best to just check about local customs.

🔗 Knowledge Related

Handshake Types

The Hand Hug: The "handhug" is a popular type of handshake often used by politicians. This shake which involves the covering of the clenched hand shake with the left hand, communicates warmth, friendship, trust and honesty.

> The Crusher: This painful handshake is a favorite shake of aggressive people. This shake is said to display confidence and power.
>
> The Queen's Fingertips: This handshake greeting is most commonly observed in male-female encounters. Usually the female presents her outstretched hand and the recipient grasps only a few digits of the right hand.
>
> The Please Keep Back: This handshake is usually extended when one of the parties is not too excited about the greeting. He or she may feel intruded upon or inconvenienced and the handshake will communicate the discomfort.

3.2.2　Business Card Exchange Etiquette

1. Business card receiving etiquette

If you are sitting when receiving a card, stand up.

微课：接收
名片礼仪

Use right hand to receive cards. In China, it is best to use both of your hands to receive business card.

Always make a comment about a card when you receive it. Pay attention to the logo, the business name or some other piece of information. This shows that you value the card and the giver.

Avoid writing irrelevant information on somebody else's business card during the exchange. If you really need to write some reminder on the card, do it later out of sight.

Don't place others' cards at random on the table or other locations. This is disrespectful and you may forget to take it.

Never play with others' business cards.

2. Business card giving etiquette

Always leave home or office with plenty of business cards so that you won't miss one single opportunity.

微课：递送
名片礼仪

Keep your cards protected by a case from wear and tear. Never give tainted or crumpled ones because they will leave poor first impression.

Don't give business cards from back pockets. This is rude.

Always remember where to find your business cards. Looking for them by going through all pockets or every nook and cranny of a briefcase wastes others' time and loses credibility immediately.

Remember to update your card in time especially the change of contact information. It is unprofessional to give cards on which you have crossed off some lines and written in the new information.

Hand them out with discretion. If you don't value your own card, receivers won't, either.

3. Business card etiquette in different cultures

When doing business abroad it is important to understand the local culture and etiquette. An important aspect of etiquette is exchanging business cards. Below we have provided you with a few examples of international business card exchange etiquette.

1）Business card etiquette in the UK

Business card etiquette is relaxed in the UK and involves little ceremony.

It is not considered bad etiquette to keep cards in a pocket.

Business cards should be kept clean and presentable.

Do not feel obliged to hand out a business card to everyone you meet as it is not expected.

微课：不同文化
名片礼仪

2）Business card etiquette in India

If you have a university degree or any honour, put it on your business card.

Always use the right hand to give and receive business cards.

Business cards need not be translated into Hindi as English is widely spoken within the business community.

3）Business card etiquette in Japan

Business cards are exchanged with great ceremony.

Invest in quality cards.

Make sure your business card includes your title. The Japanese place emphasis on status and hierarchy.

Business cards are always received with two hands but can be given with only one.

During a meeting, place the business cards on the table in front of you in the order people are seated.

When the meeting is over, put the business cards in a business card case or a portfolio.

4）Business card etiquette in the Middle East

Exchanging business cards in the Middle East is slightly less ritualistic than in Japan, but there is one thing to bear in mind. When presenting your card to someone else, make sure you do it with your right hand and not your left.

Extended Reading

Scan the QR code, read the passage about "How To Use Business Cards As A Marketing Tool" and finish the following tasks.

拓展阅读：如何
将名片作为营销
工具

After-reading tasks

When you finish reading the text above, finish the following tasks.

Task 1   Read the statements and decide whether they are true or not. Mark "T" for true and "F" for false.

（1）Business cards are an expensive way to promote a service or business. （   ）

（2）If you want to promote a business, it is important to always have business cards with you when you participate in different meetings. （   ）

（3）If your business cards don't look good, your acquaintances will be hesitant to hand them over when the opportunity arises. (   )

（4）A good business card is to make the people who receive it spend as much time as possible looking at it and remembering the company or person who gave it to them. (   )

（5）At a large company, the most important thing for your business cards to transmit is knowledge. (   )

Task 2　Critical thinking

Share with others your experience concerning good manners or bad manners on the handshaking etiquette.

Basic Knowledge Test

Read the statements and decide whether they are true or not. Mark "T" for true and "F" for false.

（1）Don't place others' cards at random on the table or other locations. This is disrespectful and you may forget to take it. (   )

（2）If you're sitting down, get up to shake hands. It's a sign of respect and puts you on the same level as the other person. (   )

（3）Don't give business cards from back pockets. This is rude. (   )

（4）The person in the lower position of authority or age should be the one to initiate a handshake. (   )

（5）Make sure your business card includes your title. The Japanese place emphasis on status and hierarchy. (   )

同步测试：汉语
版 –M3T2 判断
正误

Case Study

Joe Girard was considered the best car salesman in the world. In 1973, he was able to sell 1,425 cars in one year, a record he held until 2017. What is the secret to his success? Girard understood that he wasn't just selling cars, he was selling himself too. Whenever he met someone on the street or in the shop, he would give his business card immediately. When he went to a restaurant, he gave the waiter a bigger tip along with his business card. What's more, he didn't even let go of the opportunity to watch sports games to sell himself.

微课：名片的
重要性

He threw out his business cards like snowflakes when people were cheering. On 2002 National Achievers Congress in Beijing, Joe Gillard was invited to give a speech. Before his speech, the staff had put his business cards on every chair. He seemed to be not satisfied with it. In the process of his speech, he scattered business cards to the crowd. To him, business opportunities were everywhere.

Discussion: According to the above case, what is the importance of business card?

Skills Training Tasks

Business Handshaking and Card Exchange Etiquette

Brandland International Co., Ltd. is located at the international harbor city, Qingdao. From taking shape at the beginning in 2002, to now a professional manufacturing export enterprise in stationery, furniture and home decoration area, Brandland production base covers more than 200,000 square meters, including the workshop occupying above 100,000 square meters. The personnel of high quality and strong competence makes a well-organized and innovative team. With wisdom and creativity, this elite group manages tens of production lines, consisting of above 200 advanced equipment both at home and abroad.

Kevin Wang, sales manager of Qingdao Brandland International Co., Ltd., is meeting his client from Egypt, Mr. Kayna, the purchasing manager and his secretary, Ms. Razek from Wonderland Import and Export Trading Company. After addressing and greeting each other, shaking hands and exchanging business card, the Egyptian guests are asking for some basic information about the company, such as its history, size, business scope, production line, etc.

Please notice that Ms. Razek is a typical Arab woman of Egypt.

Scan the following QR codes to complete the tasks.

3.2 任务工作单   3.2 任务实施单   3.2 任务检查单   3.2 任务评价单

Curriculum Ideology and Politics

China's New Business Card — China's High-speed Railway

China is leading the way with the scope and sophistication of its rail networks and rolling stock. For example, a suspended train in Qingdao runs at 70 km/h, while in Chongqing, the train is running through blocks of high-rising buildings. It's a phenomenon much covered in the Western media.

But the most amazing part is it's leading worldwide in operations and management. China's high-speed passenger railway network has extended to 40,000 kilometers, which could circle all around the earth. And the high-speed passenger train shuttling between Beijing and Shanghai is operated on the world's busiest route - with an annual passenger volume of one hundred million and a departure every 3 minutes during the busiest time. Despite challenging operation times, trains in China usually score perfectly for punctuality!

The efficiency and safety of the train lines in China have been guaranteed by the world's most advanced train control and operating system. More than 4,100 trains are under surveillance 24h a day. Besides running conditions, bridge tracks, running speeds and even the axle temperatures are all real-time monitored.

Today, China has expanded its railway business to other countries. CRRC, the world's largest supplier of rail transit equipment, has provided rolling stock for more than one hundred countries and regions. The number continues to rise. Wherever you are in the world, there's a good chance your train rides is a "Made in China" carriage!

(Source: China Daily)

Discussion: What is the most amazing part of China's High-speed Railway?

 Chinese Etiquette

Every culture has its rules on how to act, and China is not different. In China, to greet someone, you nod your head, or you bow slightly. Handshakes are also common, but you should wait for your Chinese partner to initiate the motion. In addition, as opposed to those found in Western society, Chinese people do not enjoy being touched by strangers. Don't touch someone unless you absolutely have to. Finally, from the perspective of Confucianism, the elders are to be respected in every situation by those who are younger. You should always acknowledge the elders first and show the most respect to them.

Task 3

Business Communication Etiquettes

🎯 Learning Objectives

■ Moral Objectives

- To prepare students the awareness of intercultural communication and cultural confidence.
- To develop students' awareness of respecting different culture and to create a good professional image.

■ Knowledge Objectives

- To master the basic procedures and etiquette requirements of telephone, e-mail and cross-border e-commerce platform communication.
- To know the cultural differences between China and Western countries and get familiar with communication skills.

■ Ability Objectives

• To be able to conduct smooth and proper communication by telephone, e-mail and cross-border e-commerce platform.

Lead-in: Case Study

Situation: Xiaoli is working as an assistant manager in Qingdao Brandland International Trade Co.. Recently, the company is preparing for a new product launch. A lot of cooperative clients were coming to attend the ceremony. One day, Xiaoli received a phone call.

Xiaoli: Hello.

Client: Hello, this is the secretary of the president of Goodgo Corporate. Is Mr. Wang here?

Xiaoli: Mr. Wang is in a meeting.

Client: When is it convenient for Mr. Wang to answer the phone?

Xiaoli: I'm not sure, you can call him later.

Client: Is it okay if I call in an hour?

Xiaoli: You may have a try. It's not for sure.

Xiaoli hung up the phone and went back to her own business without informing Manager Wang of the call. Later, the client contacted Mr. Wang through a private phone and communicated the problem in time, thus avoiding losses on both sides.

After learning the whole incident, Mr. Wang criticized Xiaoli seriously. He told Xiaoli that telephone etiquette represents the image of the company, and if one person behaves rudely, the whole company may suffer possible losses.

Discussion:

(1) Xiaoli conducted improper telephone etiquette. Can you list the mistakes she had made?

(2) Are there any other rules for people to follow when they make phone calls in the office?

Basic Knowledge

In the information society, a variety of modern communication tools emerge one after another. Among them, telephone, e-mail and cross-border e-commerce platforms have become effective tools for business people to obtain and deliver information.

3.3.1 Telephone Etiquette

1. Etiquette for making a call

1）Choose the right time and environment

When you make a business call, it is important to choose the right

微课：电话
使用礼仪

environment and time of day for the call. A call with noisy background is very rude and may affect the communication.

Usually, the best time to make a call is either at a mutually agreed time or at a time that is convenient for the other party. For business calls, it is advised to make during office hours. Even personal calls should avoid the time when the other party is resting. Hence, try not to call before 8 am or after 10 pm, and it is also best not to disturb the other party at lunch **and dinner** times. If it is an international call, take into account the time difference of the other party.

2）Be prepared to make the call

It is necessary to check the other party's company telephone number, company name and the name of the speaker before you make a business call. If you accidentally dial a wrong number, it is better to admit the mistake and apologise to the other party immediately.

Rehearse the main points of the call in advance. Generally speaking, you can use the "5W1H" rule when planning your call, i.e. When, What, Where, Why and How. Once the call has been made, try to be as focused and concise as possible.

In addition to having the necessary reference documents and information before the call, you should also prepare blank paper and a pen to take down important information.

3）Be polite and concise

When you get on the phone, you are supposed to greet the other party before revealing yourself, including your name, company and reason for the call. For example, "Good morning, this is Li Ming, assistant manager of Qingdao Brandland International Trade Co." Then, you may quickly explain the reason for the call and ask the other party if they are free now. If the person thinks the time is suitable, you need to estimate the time and make clear the purpose quickly. For example, "Mr. James, I would like to discuss product shipping with you and it will take about five minutes."

Use polite language during the conversation, such as "hello", "please", "thank you", etc. The tone of your voice should be gentle; the speed of your voice should be moderate and you must speak clearly.

4）Behave appropriately

It is better to sit in a dignified position and keep body straight when you make a phone call. If you are lying on your stomach or back , you will reveal yourself through the way your are talking, even if the other person cannot see you.

Don't hold the phone under your neck or walk around with the phone in your arms, as these rude manners can be heard by the other party.

2. Etiquette for answering a call

1）Answer the phone politely and promptly

When the phone rings, it is best to answer it within three rings to avoid giving the person a bad impression. When you receive a call from outside the company, you should state the name of the company and your name, e.g. "Good morning, this is Hengxin Foreign Trade Company. I am the secretary of Manager Li. How can I help you?" If the other party does not immediately get to the point, you can take the initiative to ask for advice, "May I ask which one you are looking for?"

2）Listen carefully and give positive feedback

As the other party answers the phone, we should listen carefully to what the other is saying during the call and give positive feedback by answering in a timely manner. When you do not hear clearly or do not understand, tell the other party immediately so as to avoid misunderstandings.

3）Transfer calls in a standard way

If you are asked to transfer a call, tell the person to "wait a moment" and cover the phone with your hand. Then, gently call out to the person who is wanted. If you need to leave your seat to find someone, inform the person calling, "Can you hold on for a couple of minutes? I'll go and find him for you." If you have trouble finding the person you are looking for, you should tell the person, "I am sorry, he is not in the office at the moment. Would you like to leave your name and phone number and I will pass on the message for you."

4）Make a careful record

If the person the other party is looking for is not available, you can make a record of the call for him or her. It is a good idea to repeat the information to the caller to avoid missing or misunderstanding. You can prepare some cards next to the phone to make a more detailed record of the call immediately.

Common phone record sheets are shown in the following Figure 3-1.

来电时间	月　日　时　分		来电人		联系电话	
来电内容						
领导指示					指示人	
处理结果					记录人	

交班人：		接班人：		日期／时间：
交接事项：（值班、值宿）				
电话记录				
时间		来电人		来电事宜
备注：				

Figure 3-1　Common Phone Record Sheets

3. Etiquette for using mobile phone

1）Carry your mobile phone

Businessmen should carry their mobile phones with them and keep them within easy reach. Men's mobile phones should preferably be carried in an inside coat pocket or briefcase of a suit. Women's mobile phones should be kept in their handbags. Do not hang your mobile phone on your body or keep it in your hand at all times.

微课：手机
使用礼仪

2）Taboos for using mobile phones

Try to turn your mobile phone off or put it on vibrate or silent mode when attending business meetings, parties and celebrations. It is also inappropriate to take mobile phone calls in places such as theatres, cinemas and restaurants. If you must answer a phone call, do so in a low voice after finding a private place, or use text messaging to communicate.

Avoid using strange and exaggerated music as your ringtone. Also, as a personal item, we usually do not borrow others' mobile phone.

3.3.2　E-mail Etiquette

1. Etiquette for writing e-mails

1）Be clear on the subject

A blank subject is considered to be rude in an e-mail. A clear subject allows the reader to quickly understand what the e-mail is about. The subject of an e-mail should not be too long. You can use capital letters, characters, etc. to highlight the subject and get the recipient's attention in a moderate way.

2）Be concise

The body of the e-mail should be concise and well-written. If the other party does not know you, you should first identify yourself and the company you represent. When writing the content of the e-mail, try to avoid out-of-the-ordinary words and unusual characters. After the e-mail is completed, you should check it carefully to avoid typos or ambiguities.

Use marks such as 1,2,3,4 in the body of the e-mail to make things clear. If the things conveyed in the mail is complex, it is best to break it up into paragraphs and keep each paragraph short and concise.

3）Use attachments appropriately

If the e-mail contains an attachment, you are supposed to inform recipient to view it in the body of the message. Attachments should be entitled with a meaningful name that summarises the content of the attachment and is easy for the recipient to manage after downloading. The attachments should be limited within four, and should be compressed into one file if there are more than four. If the attachment is a special format file, it is better to mention the way of properly opening it in the body of the text so as not to cause trouble.

4）Choose the proper signature file

It is not advisable to have too many signatures at the end of an e-mail. The signature file may include name, title, company, telephone, fax, address, etc. However, there should not be too many lines. The content is generally limited to fewer than 4 lines. When using signature files, they should be simplified for internal staff or familiar customers.

2. Etiquette for receiving and sending e-mails

1）Notify recipients of important e-mails for checking

When the recipient is away on a business trip or has a computer breakdown, it may affect the timely processing of e-mails. For important business e-mails, after sending the e-mails, you must call to confirm whether the recipient has received and read the e-mails to avoid delays of important matters.

2）Reply to e-mails in a timely manner

It is essential to reply promptly to e-mails received from others as a sign of respect for them. The ideal response time is within two hours, especially for urgent and important e-mails. If the matter is complicated and you can not reply immediately, you should at least inform the other party in time that the e-mail has been received and is being discussed and dealt with.

3）Pay attention to network security

Be conscious of network security when using e-mail. Don't click on unfamiliar e-mails in case your computer may get a virus. Do not use e-mail to spread false information or gossip. Do not use e-mail to pass on confidential information, as it is not safe and may let out in some way.

知识链接：
钓鱼邮件

3.3.3　Communication Etiquette in Cross-border E-commerce

Today, with the rapid development of cross-border e-commerce, many small foreign trade orders are conducted and paid for online. The international trade e-commerce platform with the closest communication with foreign customers is the Aliexpress platform, which brings together buyers from 220 countries and regions around the world, and where customer service is a very important aspect.

微课：跨境电商
沟通礼仪

1. Etiquette for customer service pre-sales communication

1）Product enquiries from buyers

As a customer service agent, you should sincerely treat every customer who comes to you with an enquiry about stock, price, size, colour, etc. Firstly, you should thank the clients for their enquiry and answer their questions promptly. Secondly, express that you are happy to answer the person's questions. Finally, end the communication politely.

2）Buyers' requests for discounts

When you receive a request for a bargain from a customer, it is advised to make a clarification depending on the situation. It is best not to give the buyer the impression that the discount has been agreed because the shop already has a promotion, but instead lead the buyer to believe that the discount has been granted because a certain number of purchases have been made.

When communicating with customers, express your appreciation for their message, state clearly the link between the discount and the quantity of purchases, and show that you are happy to answer their questions. Finish with an appropriate use of well-wishes.

3）Encourage customers to buy wholesale

When you communicate with a customer who needs a small quantity for an order, try to figure out if they are likely to buy in large quantities. A more attractive price should be quoted in time to prompt the clients to place a large order. When communicating, first thank the customers for their interest in the product. Then identify the type of customer by his or her offer and answer the questions in a timely and professional manner. Finally, give a rather attractive wholesale price to facilitate cooperation.

2. Etiquette for customer service in-sales communication

1）Unpaid orders

When dealing with unpaid orders, start by expressing your gratitude to the customer for placing the order. At the same time, express your agreement with the customer's choice of products allowing them confidence in the product. Then, from the customer's point of view, remind them that timely payment can avoid stock-outs and ensure delivery.

2）Paid orders

When dealing with paid orders, first express your appreciation to the customer for choosing this product. Take the initiative to communicate with the customer about the quality of the product, delivery and logistics information, estimate the arrival time and inform the buyer, so that the buyer is psychologically prepared to wait. At the same time, you should actively follow up on the logistics information of the product so that the customer feels valued.

3）Order out of stock

If a customer has placed an order but the product is out of stock, first thank the customer for choosing this product. Then inform the customer of the current out-of-stock situation and propose several solutions. Apologise sincerely for any inconvenience caused to the customer and try to get his forgiveness.

 Knowledge Related

Communication for Orders out of Stock

Dear Customer,

Thanks for your order. However, the product you selected has been out of stock. Would you consider the similar items below?

If you don't need any other items, please apply for canceling the order. And please choose the reason of "buyer ordered wrong product". In such case, your payment will be returned in 7 business days. Sorry for the trouble and thanks so much for your understanding.

3. Etiquette for after-sales communication

1）After-sales communication skills in normal situation

After the product has been shipped, the customer should be informed of the relevant shipping information and given an waiting time interval for the transaction.

At the time of product entry, inform the customer of the progress of the delivery of the goods. Apologise to buyers if there is cargo congestion. If the product needs to be declared at customs, the buyer can be informed here to prepare in advance.

Remind customers during the delivery process not to miss information and to keep their mobile phones on. At the same time, customers can be reminded to give you positive feedback.

Finally, express your gratitude to the buyer for the positive feedback. You can also recommend hot products in response to buyers' purchase intentions and guide them to continue placing orders.

2）Communication skills in case of disputes

The most common after-sales problem is that the customer has not received the goods. The main reasons for this problem are: no information on the waybill number, the parcel is still in transit, the parcel is detained by customs, the wrong address is sent and the original parcel is returned. In these situations, we should explain to customers and appease them. Extend the delivery time for orders with logistics problems.

知识链接：售后
沟通注意事项

If the customer is not satisfied with the product, we should take the initiative to apologise and try to communicate promptly and effectively to offer possible solutions.

Extended Reading

Scan the QR code, read the passage about "Customer Service Phone Etiquette" and finish the following tasks.

拓展阅读：客服
电话礼仪

After-reading tasks

When you finish reading the text above, finish the following tasks.

Task 1　Read the statements and decide whether they are true or not. Mark "T" for true and "F" for false.

（1）When you are able to explain your company's policy on your own, it's helpful to offer a standardized document to build credibility for your argument. （　　）

（2）If the customer is unwilling to hang up, explain how you need to get back to work which is more important for you. （　　）

（3）When customers demand to speak to your manager, you can certainly ask your manager for advice but make sure he or she is actively participating in the conversation with the customer. （　　）

（4）Tools like shared screens and virtual assistants provide hands-on support and guide customers through each step of the troubleshooting process. （　　）

（5）While you should give each customer your utmost attention and dedication to their problem, be mindful of how long you're on the phone with a customer. （　　）

Task 2　Critical thinking

（1）Have you ever experienced the same situation in the passage?

（2）Can you gave any other advice about these situations?

 Basic Knowledge Test

Read the statements and decide whether they are true or not. Mark "T" for true and "F" for false.

（1）When you make a business call, it is important to choose the right environment and time of day and take time difference into consideration. （　　）

（2）You don't have to sit in a dignified position and keep your body straight when making a phone call. （　　）

同步测试：汉语版 –M3T3 判断正误

（3）When you write an e-mail, attachments should be named with a meaningful name that summarises the content of the attachment and is easy for the recipient to manage after downloading. （　　）

（4）We should be conscious of network security when using e-mail. It is safe to click on unfamiliar e-mails. （　　）

（5）When buyers ask for a discount, it is better to lead the buyer to believe the discount has been granted because a certain quantity of purchases have been made. （　　）

 Case Study

Zhang Ming works for a cross-border e-commerce company as a business specialist and is responsible for handling different customer requests. A U.S. customer, Joey Corners, has placed an order for a product on the Aliexpress platform but delayed payment. Zhang Ming communicated with him as follows.

Dear Joey Corners,

We have noticed that you haven't made the payment yet. This is a friendly reminder to you to complete the payment transaction as soon as possible. Instant payments are very important; the earlier you pay, the sooner you will get the item.

If you have any problem making the payment, or if you don't want to go through with the order, please let us know. We can help you to resolve the payment problems or cancel the order.

Looking forward to hearing from you soon.

Discussion:

（1）Is Zhang Ming's communication with the client proper and polite?

（2）If you were Zhang Ming, how would you communicate with the client?

 Skills Training Tasks

Task: practicing making a phone call

Basic information:

Situation: You are the salesman of Qingdao Brandland International Trade Co., and your company is going to hold a ceremony to launch new product. Many important guests are invited to attend this ceremony and the invitation letters have been sent. You are responsible for making phone calls to make sure these guests have received invitation.

Now, you are going to call Mr. James, the CEO of Goodgo company, who happens to be in China right now. Mr. James' secretary will answer the phone call.

Information about the ceremony:

Hosting place: Central hall of Yizhong Crown Hotel

Time: December 3th, 2023

Theme: new product launch

Practice requirement:

Students do the role play and work in pairs to practise making phone calls by conducting the proper etiquette.

Before making a call	Prepare paper and pen to take notes.
When making a call	Greet the person you are calling. Inform the other your name and company. Make clear your intention of call. Express gratitude.
After making a call	Organize the information.

Scan the following QR codes to complete the tasks.

3.3 任务工作单　　　3.3 任务实施单　　　3.3 任务检查单　　　3.3 任务评价单

 Curriculum Ideology and Politics

The Importance of Cyber Security

From 5th to 11th September, the 2022 National Cyber Security Awareness Week was launched nationwide. Organizing Cyber Security Awareness Week and enhancing national cyber security awareness and skills is an important part of the country's cyber security efforts. General Secretary Xi Jinping has repeatedly stressed the importance of cyber security awareness and put forward specific requirements for strengthening cyber security awareness.

In the Internet Age with overloaded information, a variety of entertainment methods not only broaden people's horizons, but also bring a lot of laughter to people. With fingertips pointing and drawing and screens zooming in and out, the internet not only takes away the day, but also quietly brings security risks. The most common issues around us, such as copyright disputes, theft of original videos and leakage of personal privacy, are commonplace in our lives.

It is important to attach great importance to cyber security. General Secretary Xi Jinping stressed that network security and informatization is a major strategic issue concerning national security and national development, and the working life of the public, and that we should start from the international and domestic trends, make a general layout, coordinate all parties, innovate and develop, and strive to build China into a strong network country. Towards the goal of the basic popularization of network infrastructure, significant enhancement of independent innovation capacity, comprehensive development of the information economy, and strong protection of network security, we will continue to move forward.

(Source: https://www.cznews.gov.cn/newweb/zhuanti/wangluoanquan/2022-09-13/72140.html)

Discussion:

(1) Have you ever experienced network fraud?

(2) How to maintain cyber security?

 ## Chinese Etiquette

Traditional Letter Etiquette: "Respect Others and Self-Effacement"

The Chinese people is a nation of etiquette, and correspondence is as much about rhetoric and grammar as it is about etiquette.

The use of honorific titles to address each other in correspondence shows respects. This can be done by using the ancient titles, such as "Jun" or "Gong", or by adding the word respect to the title. For example, some elders of a certain academic standing whom we admire greatly are usually referred to as a "*** Gong".

The ancient principle of "self-effacement and respect for others" is expressed in the letter by the use of respectful terms for others and modest terms for oneself. In the body of the letter, you should use a modest title when addressing your relatives. The salutation is used to address the other party and people and things related to them. At the end of the letter, the recipient of the letter is wished a good day by using words such as "Good day" and "I wish you progress".

(Sources: https://epaper.gmw.cn/wzb/html/2016-01/12/nw.D110000wzb_20160112_4-05.htm)

模块 3
商务交往礼仪

模块导读

　　商务交往礼仪是对外商务活动中人们交流情感、建立友谊和开展各种活动的桥梁和纽带。见面问候和介绍礼仪是否规范、握手和递送名片是否得体，各种通信手段是否有效利用很大程度上都直接影响商务活动的成败。良好的商务交往礼仪不仅能展现个人的魅力和形象，更能帮助商务人士在商务活动中获得对方的尊重和信任。了解商务交往礼仪的重要意义和基本礼仪，掌握各种规范和技巧，是商务人士必备的能力和素质。

任务 1

商务称呼、问候及介绍礼仪

◎ 学习目标

■ **素养目标**
- 培养"文明礼貌"的礼仪修养。
- 具备良好的社交形象，尊重他人并自尊自信。
- 具备文化自信，把中国介绍给世界。

■ **知识目标**
- 了解称呼、问候和介绍礼仪在商务活动中的重要性。
- 掌握见面时商务称呼、问候和介绍的基本原则。

■ **能力目标**
- 能够根据不同交际场合、情景和对象，在交往中恰当地称呼、问候和介绍他人。

情境导入

情境：美国人伊丽莎白·达尔是来中国教授国际关系理论课的副教授。她年轻、未婚、漂亮。一天，她第一次见到学生莉莉。

莉莉：您好。很高兴认识您。我是王莉莉，您国际关系理论课的学生。我可以问您的名字吗？

伊丽莎白：你好。我叫伊丽莎白·达尔。很高兴认识你。

莉莉：不好意思，请问我该怎么称呼您？达尔小姐还是伊丽莎白。我听说美国儿童可以直呼父母和祖父母的名字，从而拉近彼此之间的距离。

伊丽莎白：（笑了笑）确实是这样，但是我更喜欢别人称呼我为教授。

讨论：从本段对话中我们可以学到什么？

 知识储备

3.1.1 商务称呼礼仪

1. 商务场合常用称呼

在商务场合中，常见的称呼除"先生""小姐""女士"外，还有两种方式。

一是称呼职位，用职位称呼，要用姓或全名。英美人名通常名在前、姓在后，如 Mr. William Jones，我们应该称呼 Mr. Jones 而不是 Mr. William。

二是对地位较高的人称呼"阁下"，教授、法官、律师、医生等职位因为在社会中很受尊重，可以直接作为称呼。

在一些讲英语的国家，女性结婚后冠夫姓是一种传统。然而，并非所有的女性都这样做。你可以这样问："您还是用原来的姓吗？"当女性离婚或丧偶时，这个问题变得更棘手。有些女性会把姓氏改回之前的。如果你不了解，等她告诉你她的姓氏是否有变化即可。

2. 商务称呼礼仪注意事项

许多人在问"我该怎么称呼您？"时会感到不自在。称呼某些人士和职业时更需要注重礼节。

1）询问问题

如果你不确定该怎么称呼别人，最好使用正式的称呼，或者这样问：

我该怎么称呼您？

我能叫您［名］吗？

我可以叫您［……先生］吗？

2）回答问题

如果对方不会念你的名字，或者你希望他们称呼你随意些，可以这样说：

请叫我……

您可以叫我……

3）英文中的正式称呼

在商务场合，除非对方告诉你，否则请使用正式的称呼。

下面是讲英语的人使用的正式称呼：

先生（任何年龄的成年男性）。

女士（成年女性——北美）。

女士（成年女性）。

姓＋先生。

姓＋夫人（冠夫姓的已婚女性）。

姓＋女士（已婚或未婚女性；商业中常见）。

姓＋小姐（未婚女性）。

姓＋医生／博士。

姓＋教授。

在某些时刻遇到关系比较近的人，可以直呼其名。

3. 商务称呼禁忌

1）使用错误的称呼

误会主要指对被称呼人的年龄、辈分、婚否以及与其他人的关系做出了错误判断。例如，将未婚女性称为"夫人"就属于误会。

2）使用庸俗低级的称呼

在人际交往中，在正式场合切勿使用某些称呼。例如，"兄弟""朋友""哥们儿"等称呼就显得庸俗低级。

3）使用绰号作为称呼

对于关系一般者，切勿自作主张给对方起绰号，更不能随意以道听途说来的对方的绰号称呼对方。

3.1.2 商务问候礼仪

世界各地甚至不同行业之间的问候礼仪各不相同，在必要时需要根据具体情况进行调整。

1. 东方礼节

1）中国

在中国，最简单的问候方式就是说"你好"。对长辈和上级表示尊重可以用"您好"。

握手是标准的问候。东方的握手往往比西方更轻，而且持续时间更长。

在正式场合，人们会微微鞠躬或礼貌地点头以示正式的问候。

如果坐着，中国人在被介绍给他人时会出于尊重而站起来。

2）日本

日本最简单的问候方法是说"konnichiwa"（空尼几哇，意为你好）。

在日本，人们互相鞠躬致意。鞠躬的范围从头部的小点头到腰部的深弯。较深、较长的鞠躬表示尊重；反之，稍微点头表示随意和非正式。

3）印度

在印度许多地方和正式场合，人们通常用印度传统"合十礼"来打招呼。同时根据对方的地位点头或鞠躬。

4）泰国

在正式和非正式场合，泰国人用"sawadee"（萨瓦迪，意为你好）这个词互相问候，女性在后面用"ka"（卡），男性用"krub"（可拉不）。

泰国人不总是握手，而是做一个祈祷式的手势，双手并拢放在胸前，手指向上，头微微前倾。

2. 西方礼节

1）美国

握手是第一次见面或在商务场合最常见的问候方式。

许多人在非正式场合拥抱或问候亲密的朋友和家人。

2）英国和德国

最常见的问候方式是握手和直接的眼神交流。

男性通常会先和女性打招呼，等她们先伸出手后再握手。

亲密的朋友可以拥抱问候，年轻人可以亲吻对方的脸颊。

3）法国、意大利、葡萄牙

这三个国家的问候充满深情。

当遇到朋友或认识的人时，会亲吻对方脸颊两次，法国人会亲吻三次。

当向新朋友介绍自己时，简单的握手就足够了。

3. 英语问候语

（1）若是问候自己认识但又不经常见面的人，可以使用下面的问候语：

你好吗？

一切都好吗？

有什么新鲜事吗？

近来怎么样？

（2）若是问候熟人，但又有一段时间未见面了，可以使用下面的问候语：

你好吗？

最近怎么样？

很高兴又见到了你。

好久不见了。

（3）若是问候意外见到的朋友，可以使用下面的问候语：

真没想到在这儿见到你。

真没想到会在这儿见到你。

（4）若是经人介绍彼此认识，可以使用下面的问候语：

您好！（较正式）

你好！（较随便）

（5）若是与不认识的人打招呼，想引起他（她）的注意，可以使用下面的问候语：

对不起／请问／劳驾，先生／女士。

等一下，先生／女士。

（6）若是问候与自己关系密切的朋友，可以使用非正式用语：

老朋友，你好!

吉姆，你好!

又见面了。

今天是什么风把你吹来了?

4. 商务问候注意事项

职场中不要随意拥抱别人。与客户会面时，握手绝对是标准礼仪。

挥舞手臂在许多国家表示"你好"或"再见"。而在东亚国家，这个姿势会被认为过于夸张。在一些欧洲国家或地区、日本和拉丁美洲国家或地区，还可能会被混淆为"不"或否定答复。在印度，挥舞手臂的意思是"来这里"。

将食指或四个手指向内卷曲表示邀请某人走近，在欧洲南部地区可能会被误认为是"再见"。在菲律宾和东亚地区，卷曲食指是用来招呼狗的手势。

在欧洲国家或地区，用食指直接指着某人或某物被认为是不礼貌的。在中国、日本、拉丁美洲国家或地区和印度尼西亚，它有着非常粗鲁的含义。在许多非洲国家，食指只用来指向无生命的物体。

3.1.3　商务介绍礼仪

介绍在商务场合尤其重要，因为它能营造一种自信、准备充分和一切尽在掌控的氛围，同时使双方建立一种相互尊重的融洽关系，并建立良好的关系。

1. 介绍自己

自我介绍很简单，可以说："您好，初次见面。我的名字是＿＿＿＿＿＿。"同时握手。

如果面对一个熟悉的人，你可以称呼他的名字使介绍更加友好，"罗宾逊先生，我的名字是＿＿＿＿＿。很高兴见到您。"

商务环境下，除了姓名，还应介绍:

(1) 角色或头衔。

(2) 业务、贸易或行业。

(3) 业务简介。

(4) 一个"记忆钩"(人们能快速记住你的引人注目的话语)。

介绍时间长短取决于介绍的环境。介绍不需要太长，可以合并某些内容，如业务和优势介绍。

2. 介绍他人

当介绍他人时，最重要的是根据职级和权威，弄清楚应该向谁介绍谁。

(1) 介绍不同级别的商业伙伴。

不论年龄或性别，将级别低的人介绍给级别高的。

例如："经理先生，我想向您介绍人力资源部的朱聂尔·吉恩。"

(2) 介绍任何级别的商业伙伴和客户。

无论其职级、年龄还是性别，都要将业务伙伴介绍给客户。

例如："客户先生，这是我们的董事总经理曼宁·格雷格先生。"

(3) 介绍两个同等级别的商业伙伴。

把不认识的人介绍给你更了解的人。

例如：假设你的经理曼宁·格雷格正在会见新加坡办事处的经理利姆·玛丽。"格雷格，这是我们新加坡办事处的经理利姆·玛丽。"

（4）介绍一位男士和女士。

把男士介绍给女士。

例如："玛丽，这是琼斯·凯义，他一直在为这项活动准备音乐。"

（5）介绍一个年轻的人和年长的人（同性别）。

把年轻的人介绍给年长的。

例如："麦卓先生，这是我的朋友希琳。她是我大学的朋友。"

3. 介绍注意事项

在职场中根据职级而不是性别或年龄进行介绍。

商务场合中，客户、客人或访客的位置要高于老板或同事，因此要优先了解情况。

始终微笑并保持眼神交流。

第一次见面或者第一次被介绍时不要直呼对方的名字。对方允许称呼名字前应使用头衔和姓氏。

准备好你的"电梯游说"。介绍自己时，请准备好一句话的"电梯游说"（用极具吸引力的方式简明扼要地阐述自己的观点）。这样当有人问"您是做什么工作的"时，就可以毫不犹豫地回答。

 同步测试

扫码做题。

同步测试：汉语版－M3T1 判断正误

案例分析

• **案例 1**

有一次，一位外贸职员小王为他的外国客户预订生日蛋糕，并要求写一份贺卡。蛋糕店小姐接到订单后，询问小王说："先生，请问您的朋友是小姐还是太太？"小王也不清楚客户是否结婚了，但想想对方的年龄，应该是太太吧，于是就跟店员说："写太太吧"。蛋糕做好后，店员把蛋糕送到指定的地方，敲开门，只见一位女士开门，店员有礼貌地询问："您好，请问您是怀特太太吗？"女士愣了愣，不高兴地说："咦，错了！"然后就把门关上了。蛋糕店店员糊涂了，打电话向小王确认，地址和房间号码都没错。店员于是再次敲开门，说道："没错，怀特太太，这正是您的蛋糕！"谁知这时，这位女士大叫道："告诉你错了，这里只有怀特小姐，没有怀特太太！""啪"的一声，门被大声地关上了。

讨论：为什么被称呼为"怀特夫人"时，小王的外国客户会生气？

• **案例 2**

一位英国人迈克尔应法国朋友克瑞格的邀请来到他的家中做客，一见面，法国朋友克瑞格就给了迈克尔一个热情的拥抱并在他的脸颊上亲吻了两下，迈克尔对此表现得很不自然。两人坐下来喝茶闲聊时，迈克尔时不时地对克瑞格说"谢谢"和"请"之类的话，这让热情的法国朋友克瑞格感觉很别扭。最后两人闲聊了几句后，迈克尔便匆匆离开了克瑞格的家。

讨论：

（1）迈克尔感到尴尬的原因是什么？

（2）克瑞格感到尴尬的原因是什么？

 **实训项目**

掌握商务称呼、问候、介绍礼仪

1. 实训目的

通过训练，掌握商务称呼、问候、介绍礼仪。

2. 实训内容

（1）背景资料：西西是青岛贝来国际贸易有限公司的一名员工。在一次接待任务中，西西陪同她的部门经理汤先生去会见他们的客户，来自明门进出口贸易公司的采购经理史密斯先生。

（2）以小组为单位，练习商务称呼、问候和介绍礼仪；分享身边案例，掌握称呼、问候和介绍礼仪。

3. 实训要求

（1）采取"组内异质，组间同质"的原则，将学生分为若干小组，每组 3～4 人。

（2）每组提交一份商务称呼、问候、介绍礼仪实训报告，内容包括本案例展示以及生活中称呼、问候和介绍礼仪的注意事项和禁忌。

（3）每组讲解和展示本组的工作成果。

4. 实训考核

（1）评价方式：采取小组自评、小组互评、教师评价、企业导师评价四维评价方式，总评成绩 = 小组自评×20% + 小组互评×20% + 教师评价×30% + 企业导师评价×30%。

（2）评价指标：从素质目标、知识目标、能力目标 3 方面进行评价。

3.1 任务工作单　　　3.1 任务实施单　　　3.1 任务检查单　　　3.1 任务评价单

 **思政课堂**

向世界介绍中国——《新时代的中国与世界》

在中华人民共和国成立 70 周年之际，国务院新闻办公室发布《新时代的中国与世界》

白皮书。白皮书系统介绍中国的发展成就、发展道路、发展走向，深入阐述中国与世界的关系，以增进国际社会对中国发展的了解和理解。白皮书指出，70年来，在中国共产党领导下，中国发生了翻天覆地的变化，创造了人类历史上前所未有的发展奇迹，中国对世界的影响，从未像今天这样全面、深刻、长远；世界对中国的关注，也从未像今天这样广泛、深切、聚焦。当前，中国发展进入了新时代。白皮书指出，新时代的中国，走中国特色社会主义道路的决心不会改变，与其他国家互学互鉴、合作共赢的决心不会改变，与世界携手同行的决心不会改变。未来之中国，将以更加开放包容的姿态拥抱世界，同世界形成更加良性的互动，带来更加进步和繁荣的中国和世界。

（资料来源：http://www.scio.gov.cn/ztk/dtzt/39912/41838/index.htm?eqid=c2058afe00025213 00000002644744f2，http://www.scio.gov.cn/ztk/dtzt/39912/41838/41841/Document/1665420/1665420.htm）

讨论：党的二十大报告指出"传播好中国声音，展现可信、可爱、可敬的中国形象"。你会从哪些方面向世界介绍中国？

🤝 中华礼仪

和西方人的习惯不一样，中国人的姓名是姓在前，名在后。在两个中国人见面的时候会问起对方的姓氏，倘若同姓，两人就会很高兴地说："咱们500年前是一家。"孔子家族是中国姓氏的标本，它可以让一个青年人一代代追溯到2500年前的祖先。这就像一棵大树，从一片叶子到根茎，联系他们之间关系的就是姓。据说，中国有2万个姓氏。祖先从哪里来？为什么来到这里？他们是干什么的？这些秘密都藏在姓名里。

任务 2

商务握手与交换名片礼仪

◎ 学习目标

■ **素养目标**

• 培养"文明礼貌"的礼仪修养。

• 具备良好的社交形象，尊重他人并自尊自信。

• 从中国高铁飞速发展的案例中增强文化自信。

■ **知识目标**

• 了解商务握手和交换名片礼仪在商务活动中的基本要求和意义。

• 掌握见面时握手、交换名片的基本原则。

■ **能力目标**

• 能够根据不同交际场合、情景和对象，得体恰当地握手、接收和递送名片。

 情境导入

情境：卡森国际公司的市场总监艾伦在办公室第一次会见客户凯特。

艾伦：（起身站立，伸出右手）您好凯特，很高兴见到您。我是营销总监艾伦。

凯特：（与对方握手3～4秒）很高兴见到您，艾伦。这是我的名片。

艾伦：（双手接过名片，阅读后放进包里）谢谢您，这是我的名片。

凯特：（双手接过名片，仔细阅读）谢谢。这是贵公司的新标识吗？

艾伦：对，我们刚换的。

凯特：这个标识让人过目不忘，我很喜欢。

艾伦：谢谢您。现在，您想喝点什么吗？

凯特：是的。一杯绿茶就很好了。

艾伦：请稍等。

凯特：谢谢您。

讨论：从对话中你学到哪些商务握手和交换名片礼仪？

知识储备

3.2.1 商务握手礼仪

恰当的握手应该：传递信心；尊重所有的礼节；避免尴尬和不自然。

握手时要遵循的3个步骤：

伸出右手，握住对方的手。确保双方的手掌贴在一起，拇指朝上。

垂直摇动几次。动作幅度是2英寸或3英寸。从肩膀延伸到肘部，然后一直延伸到手。

在介绍结束之前，干净利落地结束握手。从时长的角度考虑，3秒或4秒的握手最佳。

对于大多数商务场合，请注意以下规则，以避免尴尬，并在握手时显得自信。

请站起来。如果是坐着的，请起身握手。握手时与对方处于同一个高度是尊重对方的表现。

要尊重权威和年龄。处于较高职权或年龄的人应该先伸手握手。例如面试中的面试官、公司会议中的高级经理等。

不要用两只手。商务场合最好用一只手握手。通常用右手。双手握手一般用于政治家。

请注意另一只手。最重要的是，另一只手放在明显的位置上，在身体一侧保持放松。

请微笑。握手是一种表示尊重、赞同和感激的姿态。应该伴随一个真诚的微笑。表明你很高兴来到这里。

不要移开视线。握手时眼神交流很重要。如果握手时不看对方，对方会认为你不自信，或者你认为对方不值得握手。

一定要说出对方的名字。首先问候对方以引起注意，然后伸手握手。重复对方的名字是一个好主意。例如，"很高兴见到你，德里克。"这能帮助你记住对方的名字。

不要长时间握手。握手应该在口头介绍或告别结束前结束。

一般来讲，握手是非常普遍的，有较少的文化差异。但如果到一个新地方，最好了解一下当地的习俗。

 知识链接

握 手 类 型

手的拥抱："手的拥抱"是政治家经常使用的一种握手方式。这种握手方式是用左手捂住紧握的手，表达温暖、友谊、信任、诚实。

粉碎者：这是进取心强的人最喜欢的握手方式。通常认为，这种握手方式体现了自信和力量。

女王的指尖：这种握手方式在男女会面中最为常见。通常女性伸出手来，男性只握住女性的右手手指。

生人勿近：这种握手方式通常是双方中的一方对会面和问候不热情的情况。在不方便或不想被打扰时，握手的时候就会表露出这种不适。

3.2.2　商务名片礼仪

1. 收名片礼仪

如果收到名片时是坐着的，请站起来。

用右手接受名片。在中国最好用双手。

收到名片时记得发表评论。注意标志、企业名称和其他信息。这表明你重视名片和对方。

在交换过程中，避免在别人的名片上写不相关的信息。如果确实需要在名片上写一些提醒内容，请稍后再做。

不要随意把别人的名片放在桌上或其他地方。可能会忘记带走，这是不尊重对方的表现。

不要随意摆弄别人的名片。

2. 递送名片礼仪

离开家或办公室时随身携带足量的名片，确保不会错过任何一个机会。

用名片夹保护名片不被磨损。不要给别人污损或弄皱的名片，会给对方留下不好的第一印象。

不要从后口袋里拿出名片。这是不礼貌的。

记住在哪里可以找到名片。翻遍公文包的每个口袋或角落寻找名片都会浪费别人的时间，失去信誉。

记得及时更新名片，尤其是变更联系方式后。不要在名片上划掉一些信息并写上新信息。给别人这样的名片是不专业的。

慎重地分发名片。如果不珍惜自己的名片，那么接收者也不会珍惜。

3. 不同文化名片礼仪

在国外做生意时，了解当地的文化和礼仪非常重要。礼仪的一个重要方面就是交换名片。下面是一些国际名片交换礼仪的示例。

1）英国名片礼仪

英国的商务名片礼仪轻松，不拘礼节。

把名片放在口袋里不会被认为失礼。

名片应该保持干净和美观。

不需要把名片发给见到的每一个人。

2）印度名片礼仪

如果有大学学位或任何荣誉，请写在名片上。

总是用右手递送和接收名片。

名片不需要翻译成印度语，因为英语在商业界被广泛使用。

3）日本名片礼仪

名片的交换非常有仪式感。

购买质量好的卡片。

确保名片上有你的头衔或职位。日本人重视地位和等级。

接受名片总是用双手，但可以用一只手递送。

在会议期间，按照人们就座的顺序，将名片放在面前的桌子上。

会议结束后，把名片放在名片夹或文件夹里。

4）中东国家或地区名片礼仪

与日本相比，在中东国家或地区交换名片的仪式感稍弱一些。但有一点请记住，给对方递送名片时，确保用右手而不是左手。

 同步测试

扫码做题。

同步测试：汉语版–M3T2 判断正误

案例分析

乔·吉拉德被认为是世界上最优秀的汽车推销员。1973 年，他一年内就能卖出 1425 辆汽车，这一纪录一直保持到 2017 年。他成功的秘诀是什么？乔·吉拉德有一个习惯：只要碰到一个人，他马上会把名片递过去，无论是在街上还是在商店。去餐厅吃饭，他给的小费每次都会比别人多一点点，同时主动放上名片。他甚至不放过看体育比赛的机会来推广自己，当人们欢呼的时候，他把名片像雪花般撒出去。2002 在北京举行的全国成才大会上，乔·吉拉德应邀发表演讲，在他演讲之前，工作人员就已经把他的名片摆放在每一张椅子上，他似乎还嫌不过瘾，演讲过程中，不时将名片一把一把地往人群中撒。他认为生意的机会遍布于每一个角落。

讨论：从以上案例来看，名片的重要性是什么？

实训项目

掌握商务握手和交换名片礼仪

1. 实训目的

通过训练，掌握商务握手和交换名片的礼仪。

2. 实训内容

（1）背景资料：青岛贝来国际有限公司位于国际港口城市青岛。从 2002 年年初初具规模，到现在成为文具、家具、家装领域的专业制造出口企业。贝来生产基地占地 20 多万平方米，其中车间占地 10 多万平方米。高素质、胜任力强的人才构成了一支组织严密、富有创新精神的团队。凭借智慧和创造力，这个精英集团管理着数十条生产线，包括 200 多台国内外先进设备。

青岛贝来国际贸易有限公司销售经理王凯文正在会见他的埃及客户明门进出口贸易公司采购部经理卡纳先生及秘书拉泽克女士。在相互问候、握手和交换名片后，埃及客人询问有关该公司的一些基本信息，如历史、规模、业务范围、生产线等。

（2）以小组为单位，练习商务握手和交换名片礼仪；分享身边案例，掌握商务握手和交换名片礼仪。

3. 实训要求

（1）采取"组内异质，组间同质"的原则，将学生分为若干小组，每组 3～4 人。

（2）每组提交一份商务握手和交换名片礼仪实训报告，内容包括本案例展示以及生活中握手和交换名片礼仪的注意事项和禁忌。

（3）每组讲解和展示本组的工作成果。

4. 实训考核

（1）评价方式：采取小组自评、小组互评、教师评价、企业导师评价四维评价方式，总评成绩 = 小组自评×20% + 小组互评×20% + 教师评价×30% + 企业导师评价×30%。

（2）评价指标：从素质目标、知识目标、能力目标 3 方面进行评价。

3.2 任务工作单　　　3.2 任务实施单　　　3.2 任务检查单　　　3.2 任务评价单

 **思政课堂**

中国的新名片——中国高铁

中国在铁路网络和铁路车辆的规模和复杂程度方面，正在领跑全世界。例如，青岛的一列悬挂式单轨列车以时速 70km 的速度运行，而在重庆，列车可以在林立的楼宇间穿梭。这些都被多家西方媒体报道过。

中国铁路最令人惊叹的是它处于世界领先地位的运营和管理能力。中国所有铁路构成的快速客运网已超过 4 万千米，足以绕地球一圈。而往返于北京和上海的高铁列车，是世界上发车最密集的线路之一，每年客运旅客 1 亿人次，最短 3 分钟发车一次。尽管运行时间很短，但中国的铁路列车，几乎从来不晚点！

中国铁路线路的高效和安全由世界上最先进的列车控制和运营系统保证。每天 24 小时实时监控 4100 多趟列车，除了列车运行状况，桥梁轨道状况、行驶速度甚至每趟列车的车轴温度都被实时监控。

如今，中国铁路的业务不仅仅局限于国内。中国中车是世界上最大的轨道交通设备供应商，已为 100 多个国家或地区提供了铁路车辆，并且这个数字在继续上升。不论你在世界的哪个角落，都有可能坐在中国制造的车厢里！

讨论： 党的二十大报告指出"建成世界最大的高速铁路网、高速公路网，机场港口、水利、能源、信息等基础设施建设取得重大成就"。本案例中展现的中国高速铁路最令人惊叹的部分是什么？

中华礼仪

每种文化都有自己的行为准则，中国也不例外。在中国，跟别人打招呼时，或者点个头，或者微微鞠个躬。握手也很常见，但要等到中国朋友先伸手才可以。另外，与西方社会的做法截然相反，中国人不太喜欢被陌生人触碰。所以不要轻易地触碰别人，除非万不得已。最后一点，根据儒家思想的观点，老人在任何情况下都应该受到年轻人的尊敬。你应该以老人为先，并对他们表示出最大的敬意。

任务 3

商务通信礼仪

◎ 学习目标

■ **素养目标**
- 具备跨文化沟通意识，树立文化自信。
- 尊重不同文化，塑造良好职业形象。

■ **知识目标**
- 掌握电话、电子邮件和跨境电商沟通基本流程和礼仪规范。
- 认识中西方差异，熟悉沟通技巧。

■ **能力目标**

• 能够流畅恰当地进行电话、电子邮件和跨境电商平台沟通。

 情境导入

　　情境： 小丽就职于青岛贝来国际贸易有限公司，工作岗位为经理助理。最近，贝来公司正在准备新产品发布会。不少合作客户要来参加典礼。这天，小丽接到了一个电话。

　　小丽： 你好。

　　客户： 你好，我是古德购公司的总裁秘书。请问王经理在吗？

　　小丽： 王经理在开会。

　　客户： 请问王经理什么时候方便接电话？

　　小丽： 不清楚，你过会儿再打电话吧。

　　客户： 那我一小时后再打电话可以吗？

　　小丽： 你试试吧。也不一定。

　　小丽挂断电话后，继续忙自己的事情，也没有告知王经理这次通话。后来，对方客户通过私人电话联系到王经理，及时沟通了问题，避免了双方损失。

　　王经理得知事情经过，非常严肃地批评了小丽。他告诉小丽，电话礼仪是公司的门面，一人失礼，整个公司都有可能蒙受损失。

　　讨论：

　　（1）小丽未能展现良好的电话礼仪，列举她犯了哪些错误。

　　（2）在办公室中，还有哪些电话礼仪？

 知识储备

　　在信息化社会中，多种多样的现代化通信工具层出不穷。其中，电话、电子邮件以及跨境电商平台已经成为商务人士获取、传递信息的有效工具。

3.3.1　电话礼仪

1. 拨打电话礼仪

1）选择合适的时间和环境

　　在拨打商务电话时，一定要选择合适的通话环境和时间。通话背景中有嘈杂的声音是非常不礼貌的，会影响通话质量。

　　通常最佳的通话时间，一是双方约定的时间，二是对方方便的时间。打公务电话，最好是在上班时间。即使是私人电话，也应避开对方休息的时间。尽量不要在早上8点之前或晚上10点之后，也最好不要打扰对方午餐和晚餐的时间。如果是国际电话，要考虑对方的时差。

2）做好拨打电话的准备

拨打业务电话前应核对对方公司的电话号码、公司名称以及接话人姓名。如果不小心打错了，要向对方表示歉意。

通话前提前计划通话要点。一般来说，构思通话内容时，可以借鉴"5W1H"法则，即 When（什么时候）、What（什么事情）、Where（什么地点）、Why（为什么）、How（怎么说）。电话拨通后，尽可能突出重点，力求谈话简洁。

通话前除了准备必要的参考文件和资料，还需要准备空白纸张和笔，以便随时记录重要信息。

3）言语礼貌，内容紧凑

电话接通后，应先向对方问好，再自报家门，包括姓名、公司和通话原因等。例如："早上好，我是青岛贝来国际贸易有限公司经理助理李明。"接下来迅速解释你打电话的原因，并询问对方是否有时间进行会谈。如对方认为时间合适，应迅速预估一下时间并表达目的。例如："詹姆斯先生，我想跟您讨论一下产品运输问题，大约需要 5 分钟。"

通话过程需使用礼貌用语，如"您好""请""麻烦您""多谢"等。语调温和，语速适中，吐字清楚。

4）举止得体

打电话时要坐姿端庄，身体挺直。趴着、仰着或高架双腿，即使对方看不见你，也会从声音中有所察觉。

通话时不要把电话夹在脖子下，或者抱着电话随意走动，这些失礼的举止，对方也能够听出来。

2. 接听电话礼仪

1）礼貌、及时地接听电话

电话铃声响起时，最好在三声之内接听，避免让打电话的人产生不良印象。接到公司外部电话时，应报上公司名称和自己的姓名。例如："早上好，这里是恒信外贸公司，我是李经理的秘书，请问有什么可以帮您？"如果对方没有马上进入正题，可以主动请教："请问您找哪位？"

2）仔细聆听并积极反馈

作为接听电话者，在通话过程中，要仔细聆听对方的讲话，并及时作答，给对方积极的反馈。在听不清楚或不明白时，要马上告诉对方，以免发生误解。

3）规范地代转电话

如果对方请你代转电话，应告知对方"稍等片刻"，并用手轻捂话筒，然后轻声叫接电话的人。如果需要起身离开座位去找人，应告诉对方："您可以稍等两分钟吗？我去找他。"如果未能找到要找的人，应向对方说明："很抱歉，他现在不在公司，要不您留下名字和电话号码，我为您转达。"

4）认真做好电话记录

如果对方想要找的人不在，应为其做好电话记录。记录完最好向来电话的人重复一遍，核对信息，以免遗漏或记错。可以准备一些电话记录卡放在电话旁边，以便更详细地做好电话记录。常见的电话记录单如图 3-1 所示。

来电时间	月 日 时 分		来电人		联系电话	
来电内容						
领导指示					指示人	
处理结果					记录人	

交班人：		接班人：		日期/时间：
交接事项：（值班、值宿）				
电话记录				
时间		来电人		来电事宜
备注：				

图 3-1　常见的电话记录单

3. 手机使用礼仪

1）手机的携带

商务人士应将手机随身携带并放在方便拿取的地方。男士的手机最好放在西装的内侧衣袋或公文包中。女士的手机要放在手袋内。切勿把手机挂在身上，也不要总放在手里。

2）使用手机的禁忌

在参加商务会议、宴会、庆典时应尽量将手机关闭或调成振动、静音状态。在剧院、电影院、餐厅等场所接打手机电话也不合适。如必须通话，应避开众人后压低声音通话，也可采用微信文字等方式进行联络。

来电铃声的选用尽量避免怪异和夸张的音乐。同时，手机作为私人物品，不要随意向他人借用。

3.3.2　电子邮件礼仪

1. 电子邮件书写礼仪

1）主题要明确

在使用电子邮件时，空白主题是失礼的行为。明确的主题可以让阅读者快速了解邮件涉及的内容。电子邮件的主题不宜过长。可以使用大写字母、字符等来突出主题，引起收件人的注意，但应适度。

2）语言流畅，内容简洁

邮件正文要简明扼要，行文通顺。若对方不认识自己，首先应标明自己的身份以及代表的企业。在书写邮件内容时，要尽量避免生僻字和异体字。邮件完成之后应仔细检查，避免有错别字或引起歧义之处。

邮件正文多用 1、2、3、4 之类的标记，以明确事项。如果事情复杂，最好分成几个段落进行说明，同时保持每个段落简短、干练。

3）恰当使用附件

如果邮件中带有附件，应在正文里面提示收件人查看。附件文件应以有意义的名字命名，能够概括附件内容，方便收件人下载后管理。附件数量不宜超过 4 个，数目较多时应压缩成一个文件。如果附件是特殊格式的文件，应在正文中说明正确的打开方式，以免影响使用。

4）选择合适的签名档

邮件结尾签名信息不宜过多。签名档可包括姓名、职务、公司、电话、传真、地址等信息。但行数不宜过多，一般在 4 行之内。在使用签名档时，对公司内部人员或熟悉的客户，签名档应该进行简化。

2. 电子邮件收发礼仪

1）重要邮件通知收件人查收

收件人出差不在或计算机发生故障时，有可能影响电子邮件的及时处理。如果是比较重要的商务邮件，在发完邮件以后，一定要打电话确认一下收件人是否收到并阅读了电子邮件，以免耽误重要事宜。

2）收到邮件及时回复

收到他人邮件后，及时回复是必不可少的，这是对他人的尊重。理想的回复时间是两个小时内，特别是一些紧急的重要邮件。如果事情复杂，无法及时确切回复，至少应该及时通知对方邮件已经收到，正在商讨处理等。

知识链接

"钓鱼"邮件

"钓鱼"邮件是指利用伪装的电子邮件欺骗收件人获得重要信息或传播恶意程序的电子邮件，其危害性不容小觑。

3）注意网络安全

在使用电子邮件时要自觉维护网络安全。不要随意点开陌生邮件，以防计算机感染病毒。不要弄虚作假，切勿使用电子邮件传播虚假信息或散布流言蜚语。不要利用电子邮件传递机密资讯，其安全性往往难以保证。

3.3.3 跨境电商平台沟通礼仪

在跨境电商发展突飞猛进的今天，很多外贸小额订单实现了在线交易和在线支付。在国际贸易电子商务平台中与国外客户交流最密切的是速卖通 Aliexpress 平台。Aliexpress 汇集了全球 220 个国家和地区的买家，客户服务是其非常重要的环节。

1. 客服售前沟通礼仪

1）买家产品咨询

速卖通客服经常会收到客户针对产品有关存货、价格、尺码、颜色等信息的咨询。作为客服人员应真诚地面对每一位前来咨询的客户。首先要感谢对方的咨询，及时解答对方的问题。其次要表现出很乐意回答对方的问题。最后要有礼貌地结束交流。

2）买家要求折扣

在收到客户讨价还价要求的时候，应根据不同的情况做出说明。最好不要让买家觉得是店铺已经有促销活动所以同意给折扣，而是引导买家相信是购买数量达到了一定数量才获得了折扣。

在与客户沟通时要感谢对方的留言，告知对方折扣与购买数量的关系，同时表示很愿意解答对方的疑问。最后要适当地运用祝福语。

3）鼓励客户批发

在遇到需要小额数量的订单客户时，要善于发现其是否有大量购买的可能性。应及时报出一个较为诱人的价格，促使对方下大订单。在沟通时，首先要感谢对方对产品感兴趣。其次通过对方的报价判断客户的类型，及时专业地解答客户提出的问题。最后给出一个相当诱人的批发价格，促成合作。

2. 客服售中沟通礼仪

1）未付款订单

在处理未付款订单时，首先要对客户的下单表示感谢。同时，对客户选择的产品表示认同，让客户对产品产生信心。然后从客户的角度出发，提醒及时付款能避免缺货，确保发货。

2）已付款订单

处理已付款订单时，同样首先要对客户选择本产品表示感谢。主动与客户沟通产品的质量、发货与物流信息，预估到达时间并告知客户，让客户有等待的心理准备。同时，应积极跟进产品的物流信息，让客户感觉到对他的重视。

3）订单缺货

如果客户已经下单，但是产品缺货，首先感谢客户选择本产品。然后告知客户目前缺货的现状，提出几种解决方案。对给客户造成的不便要诚恳道歉，并尽可能取得客户的原谅。

✐ 知识链接

订单缺货沟通

亲爱的客户：

非常感谢您的订单。但抱歉的是，您选择的产品目前没有存货了。您能否考虑一下其他的类似款。

（略）

如果您不需要其他产品，您可以申请取消订单。麻烦您选择理由——"买家选错产品"。这种情形下，货款会在7个工作日内返还给您。对于给您造成的不便非常抱歉，希望您能谅解。

---

3. 客服售后沟通礼仪

1）一般情况下的售后沟通技巧

在产品发货后，应及时告知客户相关货运信息，给客户一个初步的交易等待时间。

在产品入库的时候，告知客户货物的交付进度。如果遇到货物拥堵的情况，对客户表示歉意。产品如需报关，可以通知客户提前做准备。

在运输过程中提醒客户注意不要错过收件信息，保持手机开机。同时，可以提醒客户给你好评。

最后，对客户的好评表示感谢。你也可以针对客户的购买意向，推荐热销产品，引导客户继续下单。

2）有争议情况下的沟通技巧

最常见的售后问题是客户没有收到货。造成该问题的主要原因有运单号查不到信息、包裹仍在运输途中、包裹被海关扣留、发错地址、包裹原件退回。遇到这种情况，首先要对客户做好解释和安抚沟通工作，争取客户谅解。针对物流不正常的订单应及时延长收货期。

若客户对产品不满意，应主动道歉，并做到及时有效的沟通，提出解决方案。

 ## 同步测试

扫码做题。

同步测试：汉语
版－M3T3 判断
正误

 ## 案例分析

张明就职于某跨境电商公司，职位为业务专员，负责处理不同的客户诉求。美国客户乔伊·康纳斯在速卖通平台下单了某产品，但迟迟没有付款。张明与其沟通如下。

亲爱的乔伊·康纳斯：

我们已经注意到你还没有付款。这是对你的友好提醒，请尽快完成付款交易。即时付款是非常重要的；越早付款，你就可能越早得到物品。

如果你付款有任何问题，或者你不想继续下订单，请告诉我们。我们可以帮助你解决付款问题或取消订单。

期待你的来信！

讨论：

（1）张明与客户的沟通是否得体、礼貌？

（2）如果你是张明，你会如何与客户沟通？

 ## 实训项目

练习接打电话礼仪

1. 实训目的

通过实训，掌握接打电话的礼仪。

2. 实训内容

（1）情境：你是青岛贝来国际贸易有限公司的销售员，公司要举行一个新产品的发布仪式。许多重要的客人被邀请参加这个仪式，邀请信已经发出。你负责打电话确保这些客人收到了邀请。

（2）任务：现在，你要给 Goodgo 公司的 CEO 詹姆斯先生打电话，目前他恰好在中国。接电话的是詹姆斯先生的秘书，你们将对接詹姆斯先生出席仪式的相关信息。

关于仪式的信息如下。

主办地点：颐中皇冠酒店的中央大厅。

时间：2023年12月3日。

主题：新产品发布会。

（3）注意事项：

打电话前	准备好笔和电话记录单
打电话中	向对方问好 表明公司和自己身份 说明打电话目的 表示感激
打电话后	整理相关信息

3. 实训要求

（1）采取"组内异质，组间同质"的原则，将学生分为若干小组，每组4～6人。

（2）学生进行角色扮演，以小组为单位，用正确的礼仪练习打电话。

（3）每小组合作轮流展示接打电话礼仪。

4. 实训考核

（1）评价方式：采取小组自评、小组互评、教师评价、企业导师评价四维评价方式，总评成绩＝小组自评×20%＋小组互评×20%＋教师评价×30%＋企业导师评价×30%。

（2）评价指标：从素质目标、知识目标、能力目标3方面进行评价。

3.3 任务工作单	3.3 任务实施单	3.3 任务检查单	3.3 任务评价单

 思政课堂

网络安全的重要性

2022年9月5日至11日，国家网络安全宣传周在全国范围内开展。举办网络安全宣传周、提升全民网络安全意识和技能，是国家网络安全工作的重要内容。习近平总书记曾多次强调网络安全意识的重要性，并对强化网络安全意识提出具体要求。

在信息过载的互联网时代，多种多样的娱乐方式不仅让人们开阔了眼界，也给人们带来不少欢声笑语。指尖点点画画，屏幕放大缩小，网络不仅带走了一天的时光，也悄无声息地带来了安全隐患。最常见的版权纠纷、原创视频被盗用、个人隐私泄露等问题，在生活中屡见不鲜。因此，要高度重视网络安全。

习近平总书记强调，网络安全和信息化是重大战略问题，要从国际国内大势出发，总体布局，统筹各方，创新发展，努力把我国建设成为网络强国。向着网络基础设施基本普及、自主创新能力显著增强、信息经济全面发展、网络安全保障有力的目标不断前进。

讨论：党的二十大报告指出要"健全网络综合治理体系，推动形成良好网络生态"。网络安全至关重要。你有没有经历过类似网络诈骗？作为新时代的大学生，应该怎样维护网络安全？

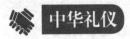
中华礼仪

传统书信礼仪：自谦而敬人

中华民族是礼仪之邦，人们相互通信来往，既讲究修辞、文法，又讲究礼仪。

书信中以敬称称呼对方表明尊重。可以用古代的爵称，如君、公等，也可在称谓前加敬字。例如，对于我们非常敬仰的有一定学术地位的长者，一般称某公。

古人"自谦而敬人"的做人原则在书信中表现为对别人用敬称，对自己用谦称。书信的正文中，在称谓自己的亲属时应使用谦称。敬辞则用在称呼对方及和对方有关的人和事上。书信结尾时，要用"即颂近安""祝你进步"之类祝词对收信人表示祝愿。

Module 4
Seating and Interpersonal Space Etiquette

 Profile of the Module

Both verbal and non-verbal behaviors play a vital role in business activities such as business negotiation, cross-border trade, international exhibition and so on. Seating arrangements have the power to make or break deals, relationships, and even event goals. When meeting any customer or business contact, let that person set a comfortable personal space. If the person's tendency to move in close or stay removed physically doesn't correspond with your personal space preference, accept the fact that you're not going to be working in your comfort zone.

 **Task 1**

Seating Etiquette

 Learning Objectives

■ Moral Objectives
  • To cultivate students' attitude of "being polite and observing".
  • To establish cultural self-confidence and maintain China's image.

■ Knowledge Objectives
  • To get familiar with the importance of seating etiquette in business activities.
  • To grasp the basic principles of business conference seating, business bus seating and other seating arrangements.

■ Ability Objectives

• To be able to arrange business seats according to the etiquette principle of precedence.

Lead-in: Case Study

Situation: Xiaoliu, secretary of Xijie Logistics International, together with Mr. Ding, the sales manager, Mrs. Wang, public relation manager and Mr. Chen, interpreter, is going to pick up business patterns from Malaysia Import and Export Trading company. Xiaoliu has arranged the seats as follows：Xiaoliu sits on the passenger seat and the manager on the right back seat. Mr. Ding, the sales manager, the right back seat of the second row, Mrs. Wang, public relation manager, the left back seat and Mr. Chen, interpreter, the right back seat of the third row.

Discussion: Is the seating arrangement OK?

Basic Knowledge

4.1.1   Rules of Seating Arrangements

Seating arrangements have the power to make or break deals, relationships, and even event goals. "Much of getting what you want comes down to where (event attendees) sit." says Brian Lee, Chief of Product Management at Lifehack. The following are the basic rules of seating arrangements:

微课：会议座次
安排

The guest side comes first. In the case of bilateral exchanges, the guest side will be taken precedence.

Ranking. People of higher ranks take precedence over people of lower ranks.

Equality and fairness. Both ranks and equality should be considered in seating arrangement.

Which seat is superior?

"Front side"is superior to"Back side".

"Center" is superior to"Side".

"Right side" is superior to "left side " in international practice, while it is quite the opposite in China. In China's business or government affairs occasions, such as holding meetings, arranging venues, and arranging seats on the rostrum, the protocol of "left side being superior to right side" is applicable.

知识链接：中国
"以左为尊"
历史渊源

4.1.2   Seating Arrangements in Business Occasions

Seating arrangements in a business meeting can make a big difference to the conversation in the meeting room. When you arrange seats for a business meeting, it's important to consider the needs of the attendees. The type of seating arrangements will depend on the number of attendees in the meeting, and whether it is a formal or informal meeting. These factors will often dictate the style of table and the way in which you seat your guests.

1. Bilateral meetings

It is international practice to arrange the seats of the host and the guest in a position facing the door.

"right side" is superior to "left side" in international practice, while "left side" is superior to "right side" in Chinese practice. Whether the guest side sits on the right side or the left side varies with the situation.

2. Small-sized meetings or negotiation meetings

1）Rectangular meeting tables—the table is put with the long side against the door

微课：小型会议
座次安排

The guest side: facing the door; "the right" is superior to "the left" in the international practice.

The host side: with the back to the door; "the left" is superior to "the right" according to the Chinese practice.

The international and Chinese customary seating arrangements for the table with the long side against the door are shown in Figures 4-1 and 4-2.

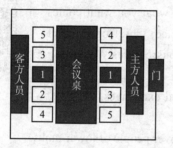

Figure 4-1　Seating Arrangements for the Table with the Long Side against the Door (International Practice — "Right" Side is Superior to "Left" Side)

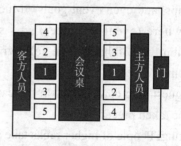

Figure 4-2　Seating Arrangements for the Table with the Long Side against the Door (Chinese Practice — "Left" Side is Superior to "Right" Side)

2）Rectangular meeting tables—the table is put with the short side against the door

The guest side: in the right; the host side: in the left.

The seating protocol: "left" is superior to "right" in China, "right" is superior to "left" in international practice.

If there are some other signs for reference in the conference room, such as the national flag, national emblem or particularly exquisite screen decorations on the wall opposite the door, then their right side is superior, and the left side of the door is superior.The international and Chinese customary seating arrangements for the table with the short side against the door, and that with the podium, national flag, national emblem, etc. as reference are shown in Figure 4-3 to Figure 4-5.

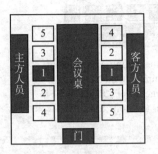

Figure 4-3   Seating Arrangements for the Table with the Short Side against the Door (International Practice — "Right" Side is Superior to "Left" Side)

Figure 4-4   Seating Arrangements for the Table with the Short Side against the Door (Chinese Practice — "Left" Side is Superior to "Right" Side)

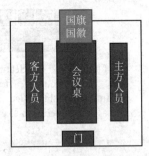

Figure 4-5   Seating Arrangements for the Table with the Short Side against the Door (with the Podium, National Flag, National Emblem, etc. as Reference)

3) Round meeting tables

Round tables indicate no order of precedence and so are far better if you want to resolve disputes. The shape of a round conference table helps to encourage the engagement of all attendees. The nature of a round table doesn't imply any form of leader or chair. This means it is far more conducive to conversation.

A round table, also referred to as a "round table meeting", is a consultative meeting format for equality and dialogue. It is a meeting where participants sit around a round table. In the practice of international conferences, the seats of the President and representatives of various countries are not distinguished in terms of seniority or inferiority, which can avoid conflicts in other seating arrangements where some representative seats are in the front or center, while

知识链接：圆桌会议历史渊源

others are in the back or side. Seating arrangements of the round table better reflect the principle of equality and the spirit of consultation among all countries.

3. Seating arrangements of large business meetings

Large business meetings are usually held in auditoriums. Some very important attendees will sit on the rostrum, and some under it.

Chinese meeting: "left" is superior to "right". The most important sits in the middle, the second important sits on his left side, and the third important on his right side.

International meeting: "right" is superior to "left". The host side sits on the left and the guest side on the right.

The international customary arrangements for seating positions for even and odd numbers on the podium are shown in Figure 4-6 and Figure 4-7, while the Chinese customary arrangements for that are shown in Figure 4-8 and Figure 4-9.

4. Seating arrangements of vehicles

Basic rules of seating arrangements of vehicles:

The back seats are priority seats. But if the driver is the host himself, then the passenger seat

Figure 4-6　The Seating Arrangement for the Podium — Even Numbers (International Practice — "Right" Side is Superior to "Left" Side)

Figure 4-7　The Seating Arrangement for the Podium — Odd Numbers (International Practice — "Right" Side is Superior to "Left" Side)

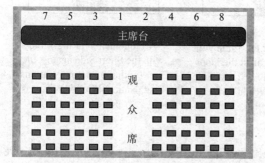

Figure 4-8　The Seating Arrangement for the Podium — Even Numbers (Chinese Practice — "Left" Side is Superior to "Right" Side)

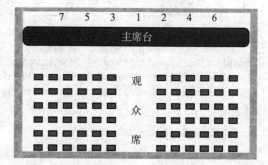

Figure 4-9　The Seating Arrangement for the Podium — Odd Numbers (Chinese Practice — "Left" Side is Superior to "Right" Side)

is the priority seat.

The right seat is superior to the left one, with the middle seat the least priority.

Some seats need to be vacant in case of being crowded. Two or at most three people except the driver will be seated in a car with five seats, and four or at most five people except the driver will be seated in a business car with seven seats.

微课：乘车座次安排

1）Seating arrangements of 5-seater vehicles

The back seats are priority seats. The right back seat is the first priority, and then comes to the left back seat. The passenger seat comes last. If the host would like to drive himself, then the passenger seat will be the first priority, followed by the right back seat and the left back seat. The seating arrangements of 2-row 5-seater vehicles with the driver and the host driving the car are shown in Figure 4-10 and Figure 4-11.

微课：五座轿车座次安排

2）Seating arrangements of 7-seater vehicles

The right back seat in the second row is the first priority, and then comes to the left back seat, followed by the right back seat and the left back in the third row. The passenger seat comes last.

If the host would like to drive himself, then the passenger seat will be the first priority, followed by the right back seat and the left back seat in the

微课：七座商务车座次安排

second row, the right back seat and the left back seat in the third row. The seating arrangements of 3-row 7-seater vehicles with the driver and the host driving the car are shown in Figure 4-12 and Figure 4-13.

Figure 4-10   The Seating Arrangement of 2-Row 5-Seater Vehicles (with the Driver Driving the Car)

Figure 4-11   The Seating Arrangement of 2-Row 5-Seater Vehicles (with the Host Driving the Car)

Figure 4-12   The Seating Arrangement of 3-Row 7-Seater Vehicles (with the Driver Driving the Car)

Figure 4-13   The Seating Arrangement of 3-Row 7-Seater Vehicles (with the Host Driving the Car)

5. Precedence of a group photo

"Front" is superior to "back"; "center" is superior to "side"; "left side" is superior to "right side" in China; "right side" is superior to "left side" in international practice. The group photos of odd and even guests with the left as the top priority are shown in Figure 4-14 and Figure 4-15.

6. Precedence of taking the elevator

If there is an elevator operator in the elevator car, the escort should be the last to come in and go out, with the guest and the superior coming in and going out first.

If there is no elevator operator in the elevator car, the escort should be the first to come in and press the button and the last to go out, with the guest and the superior coming in later and going out first.

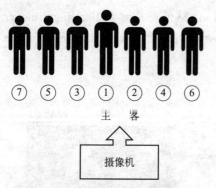

Figure 4-14　Odd Guest Group Photo Positions with Left as the Priority

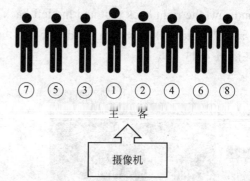

Figure 4-15　Even Guest Group Photo Positions with Left as the Priority

 ## Extended Reading

Scan the QR code, read the passage about "Seating Arrangements in a Business Meeting" and finish the following tasks.

After-reading tasks

When you finish reading the text above, finish the following tasks.

Task 1　Read the statements and decide whether they are true or not. Mark "T" for true and "F" for false.

（1）Seating arrangements are vital to business interaction. （　　）

（2）The rectangular table is far more conducive to conversation. （　　）

（3）Seating all on the same side of the table but a few spaces away from each other can sometimes avoid conflicts since they can avoid eye contact. （　　）

（4）Seating arrangements vary from area to area. （　　）

（5）Gender determines seating arrangements for business lunches and dinners. （　　）

Task 2　Critical thinking

Share your experience of seating arrangements.

Basic Knowledge Test

Read the statements and decide whether they are true or not. Mark "T" for true and "F" for false.

（1）If the host would like to drive himself, then the passenger seat will be the first priority. （　　）

（2）If there is an elevator operator in the elevator car, the escort should be the last to come in and go out. （　　）

（3）The rule of "right side being superior to left side" applies to all areas. （　　）

（4）In order to show respects to guests, the guest side will be arranged to sit facing the door. （　　）

（5）If there are some other signs for reference in the conference room, such as the national flag, national emblem or particularly exquisite screen decorations on the wall opposite the door, then their right side is superior. （　　）

Xijie Logistics International is going to have a meeting with representatives from Malaysia Kuala Lumpur Import and Export Trading company. Xiaoliu, the secretary of Xijie Logistics International has arranged the seats as follows: Xijie Logistics International, as the host side, sits facing the door, with the general manager in the middle, the Liaison Department manager and Interpreter on the general manager's left and right respectively. Xiaoliu sits on the Interpreter's right. Malaysia Kuala Lumpur Import and Export Trading company, as the guest side, sits with the back to the door, with the CEO in the middle, the Liaison Department manager and the clerk on the CEO's left and right respectively, as shown in Figure 4-16.

Discussion: Is the seating arrangement OK?

Figure 4-16　Seating Arrangement of China and Malaysia Sides

 Skills Training Tasks

The Seating Arrangement of Meetings and Vehicles

CJ Logistics International will meet with representatives of Malaysia Kuala Lumpur Import and Export Trading Company. Business activities such as talks, visits and banquets will be held during the three days of visit.

The representatives of Malaysia Kuala Lumpur Import and Export Trading Company: Hassimi Abu Hasan, President; Siti Kartom Kamarudin, Manager of the Public Relations Department; Noorsham Tan Kofli, staff member of the Public Relations Department.

The participants of CJ Logistics International are: Wang Qiang, General Manager; Li Hua, Manager of the Public Relations Department; Liu Wei, Secretary; Zhang Li, translator.

Scan the following QR codes to complete the tasks.

4.1 任务工作单　　　4.1 任务实施单　　　4.1 任务检查单　　　4.1 任务评价单

 Curriculum Ideology and Politics

In 1946, the Far East International Military Tribunal tried 28 Japanese Class-A war criminals headed by Tojo Hideki. The judges of the 10 participating countries had an extremely heated debate over the seating arrangement. The Chinese judge is supposed to be seated on the left of the President, but due to China's weak national strength, this is denied by powerful countries. In this case, Mei Ruao, the only Chinese judge in court, launched a witty verbal battle with the foreign powers. First of all, he explained positively that the row of seats should be arranged according to the order of signatures of the recipient countries when Japan surrendered, which is the only correct protocol. Then he smiled and said, "Of course, if you do not agree with this protocol, we might as well find a weight gauge to arrange seats according to the size of our weight, with the heavy one in the middle and the light one at the end of the table." Judges of all countries could not help laughing. The President smiled and said, "Your suggestion is very good, but it only applies to boxing matches." Judge Mei then replied, "If you don't arrange your seats according to the order of signatures of the recipient country, you should arrange your seats according to our weight. In this way, even if I am at the end of the table, I will feel at ease and explain to my country. Once they think it is inappropriate for me to sit at the end of the table, they can replace me with a much fatter one." This remark triggered laughter, and Judge Mei finally sat down on the appropriate seat, as shown in Figure 4-17.

Discussion:

（1）Why does Judge Mei attach so much importance to the seating arrangement?

（2）What does Judge Mei's argument reflect?

 Chinese Etiquette

In ancient China there was a piece of furniture known as an Eight Immortals table, a big square table with benches for two people on each side. If there was a seat facing the entrance, then the right hand seat facing the entrance was for the guest of honor. If there was no seat facing the entrance door (presumably if the meal was outside or there were two or more doors of equal importance), then the right hand seat facing east was the seat of honor. The seats on the left hand side of the seat of honor were, in order of importance, second, fourth, sixth and eighth and those on the right were third, fifth and seventh.

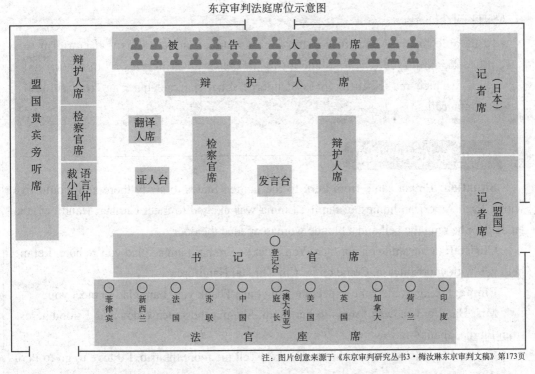

Figure 4-17   Tokyo Trial Seating Arrangement and Delegation List

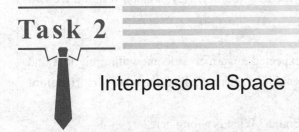

Interpersonal Space

◎ Learning Objectives

■ Moral Objectives

- To cultivate students' respectfulness and confidence.
- To possess an international vision and spread traditional Chinese culture.

■ Knowledge Objectives

- To get familiar with the concept and importance of interpersonal space.
- To grasp the basic rules of interpersonal space.
- To master the interpersonal space difference under the cross-cultural communication background.

■ Ability Objectives

- To be able to carry out cross-cultural communication activities that conform to international etiquette norms according to the basic principles of interpersonal space distance and the differences of interpersonal space distance in cross-cultural communication.

 ## Lead-in: Case Study

Situation: Emma came from Peru to the United States to study there and would live with a local American homestay family. Emma was excited to meet Christal Handford, the landlady. She rang the bell and a blonde woman opened the door.

Christal: (a big smile on her face) You must be Emma! I am so glad you're here. Let me help you with your suitcase. Come on in. I'm Christal Handford.

Emma: (being excited and expecting a big hug) Thank you. I am glad to meet you.

Mrs. Handford showed Emma to her room. She put the suitcase down and stood across from Emma, about 4 feet away.

Christal: (crossing her arm in front of her) Tell me more the trip. I'd love to go to Peru someday.

Emma: (feeling estranged) It is a nice trip. Welcome to Peru and I would love to show you around then.

Christal: You must be very tired after the long journey. Have a good rest and we will have dinner together then.

Emma: Thank you. See you then.

Emma was a little disappointed. She expected a warmer welcome with a big kiss and hug instead of just standing there, on the other side of the room. It seemed that Mrs. Handford was cold to her.

Discussion: Is Mrs. Handford cold to Emma? What is wrong here?

 ## Basic Knowledge

4.2.1 Interpersonal Space

Proxemics is nonverbal communication that involves space. The word Proxemics derives from the same Latin root as proximity, implying that one dimension of space is how close or distant two or more people are located. The distance individuals maintain between themselves and others can be defined as "interpersonal space"(IPS). This distance can be modulated both by situational factors and individual characteristics. When others violate our IPS, feelings

微课：人际空间
距离概述

知识链接：人际
空间学

of discomfort rise up, which urges us to move farther away and reinstate an appropriate interpersonal distance.

Each individual acts as though he/she was surrounded by a thin bubble of space that should not be penetrated. A personal space bubble is an imaginary bubble around yourself to represent the comfortable distance between you and other people or objects. Each person has varying comfort levels of personal space bubbles.

 Knowledge Related

Interpersonal bubble

"Interpersonal bubble" simply means that there is an invisible "bubble" around people, which represents your "boundary". If no one else intrudes within your "bubble" range, you will feel safe. On the contrary, it will make people feel uneasy, even angry.

When people are forced by a building, a room, or other constraints to stand at a distance closer than their culture would suggest appropriate for conversation, they seldom talk. For example, have you observed communication among people on a crowded elevator? They generally avoid eye contact, remain silent, and tense their bodies. Touching another person, even accidentally, is embarrassing and leads to an apology.

Initial studies in proxemics were conducted by Hall (1966), who theorized that people managed their social distance from one another as a way of regulating how much sensation or stimulation they received from other people.

With that initial theory, Hall further categorized social distances into four general types, as shown in Figure 4-18. Those four distances have served as the general categories for subsequent proxemics evaluations as well (Hans & Hans, 2015). Thus, in the US, research generally supports the following four social distances and meanings:

Public Distance (12 to 25 Feet): The least intimate distance, usually reserved for public speaking, to show power, or to feel secure and safe. This distance mostly limits individuals to seeing one another and speaking loudly.

Social Distance (4 to 12 Feet): Used for more formal interactions, while still keeping others at a safe distance. This spacing allows individuals to see and hear each other better but still prevents them from coming into contact with each other.

Personal Distance (1.5 to 4 Feet): This is the personal space or "bubble" that is generally for acquaintances and friends. At this distance, individuals can speak quietly without being overheard and observe each other's nonverbal communication clearly. Furthermore, individuals are also close enough to reach out and touch each other socially too (e.g. a pat on the hand, handshake, touch on the elbow, etc.).

Intimate Distance (Less than 1.5 Feet): This space is kept for romantic partners, family, and close friends. Primarily, this is used for more intimate touching, either of a friendly nature (e.g. hugging) or for romance (e.g. kissing). Also, at this distance, individuals are likely to be able to smell each other too.

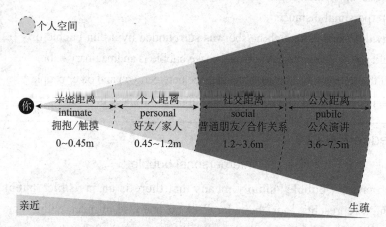

Figure 4-18　The Four Distances of Interpersonal Communication (Edward Hall)

4.2.2　Cultural Differences in Interpersonal Space

Interpersonal space varies from culture to culture. When a European American talks with a Latin American, the former feels that the Latin American is uncomfortably "pushy" or trying to be intimate, while the Latin American perceives the person from the United States as cold and remote. Arabic people from the Middle East do not feel that someone is friendly unless they are standing close enough to smell the garlic on the other's

微课：人际空间
距离文化差异

breath. Clearly, there are strong cultural differences in perception of the appropriate space between people involved in the interpersonal communication. Often this nonverbal dimension is unconscious. In Saudi Arabia, for example, if a stranger moves close to you to converse, you might find yourself unconsciously backing away. In the Middle East, social distance is closer than it is in the United States, so as you back up, your conversational partner may attempt to move closer once again. It's like an awkward dance down a sidewalk, with one party retreating and the other advancing as the conversation progresses. People from cold climate regions need a greater distance to communicate with others than people from tropical regions, so Nordic people need a greater interpersonal space. Therefore, the distance that is regarded as intimate in Germany and Britain is regarded as social in Mediterranean countries such as France, Italy, Greece and Spain. Nordic people think that the comfortable distance of southern Europeans is close, while southern Europeans will feel alienated because the distance required by northern Europeans is too large. Some regions and countries can be defined as "intimate distance" culture, where people are closer to each other and have more body language. "Intimate distance" culture areas include Arab countries, Latin America, southern Europe (especially Italy), Western Europe such as France, etc.

Other regions and countries belong to "social distance culture", and people keep a greater distance from each other when they talk. "Social distance culture" areas include East-South Asian countries (especially China, Japan, Thailand and the Philippines), Western European countries, especially the United Kingdom and the Netherlands, Central European countries, especially

Germany, North American countries such as the United States and Canada, and Australia. The interpersonal distance in some countries is shown in Figure 4-19.

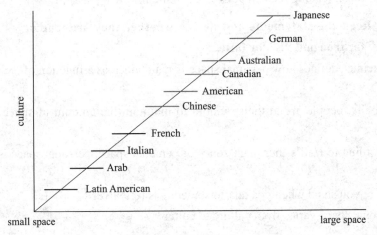

Figure 4-19 Interpersonal Distance in Some Countries

People belonging to "intimate distance culture" keep a smaller distance than those belonging to "social distance culture". At the same time, they often face each other directly, gaze at each other, have more physical contact, and speak louder. On the contrary, people belonging to "social distance culture" keep a larger distance in communication and have fewer body languages.

The major countries and characteristics of "Intimate Distance Culture" and "Social Distance Culture" are shown in Table 4-1.

Table 4-1 The Major Countries and Characteristics of "Intimate Distance Culture" and "Social Distance Culture"

Region/Features	Countries of "Intimate Distance Culture"	Countries of "Social Distance Culture"
Regions	Countries or regions such as Latin America and Southern Europe (especially Italy), as well as France and Arab countries in Western Europe	Southeast Asian countries (especially China, Japan, Thailand, and the Philippines), Western European countries (especially the UK and the Netherlands), Central European countries (especially Germany), North American countries or regions such as the United States and Canada, and Australia
Features	Lack of queuing habits and traditions, closer communication distance, and more body language	Maintain a greater distance from the other party during the conversation, consciously queue up in order, and view sorting behavior as a manifestation of civilized cultivation

Extended Reading

Scan the QR code, read the passage about "Understanding Personal Space Across Cultures" and finish the following tasks.

After-reading tasks

When you finish reading the text above, finish the following tasks.

拓展阅读：人际
空间文化差异

Task 1　Read the statements and decide whether they are true or not. Mark "T" for true and "F" for false.

（1）Proxemics defines how personal space is maintained as a function of one's culture. （　　）

（2）Actually, people are at their random to maintain the amount of space between each other. （　　）

（3）According to Hall's four main zones of personal space, personal space is the closest of all. （　　）

（4）Where you stand when you talk to someone is reflexive. （　　）

（5）Personal space varies from culture to culture. （　　）

Task 2　Critical thinking

What is the cultural difference concerning personal space? What is your comfortable zone? How do people show their respect to others concerning personal space in China?

 Basic Knowledge Test

Read the statements and decide whether they are true or not. Mark "T" for true and "F" for false.

（1）When others violate our interpersonal space, we will feel uncomfortable. （　　）

（2）Interpersonal space varies from culture to culture. （　　）

（3）People from Arab countries prefer closer interpersonal space than people from America. （　　）

同步测试：汉语
版 –M4T2 判断
正误

（4）Each person has varying comfort levels of personal space bubbles. （　　）

（5）Each individual acts as though he/she was surrounded by a thin bubble of space that can be penetrated. （　　）

 **Case Study**

• Case 1

What's the problem ?

A young Danish couple moved from Denmark to Australia to work there. In order to integrate into local life as soon as possible, they joined a club sponsored by the local Chamber of Commerce. They not only actively participated in various activities of the club, but also actively communicated with members of the club. But a few weeks later, the Chamber of Commerce received complaints from other members. Some female members complained that the new Danish man was trying to seduce them. At the same time, some male members also complained to the Chamber of Commerce that the new Danish woman always expressed in a nonverbal way that she was willing to have a closer relationship with them.

The Chamber of Commerce explained to the Danish couples other members' complaints. They felt astonished and complained, "What?!" So what's the problem?

Discussion: What caused the misunderstanding? How to avoid misunderstanding regarding "intimate distance"?

• Case 2

A British businessman and a UAE businessman were chatting at a cocktail party. The UAE businessman kept leaning forward, trying to stand closer, but the British businessman felt embarrassed to be so close, so he kept moving back until he got to the door. The British businessman had no way to go back, so he had to say: "Sorry, I really have no way to go back, please don't go forward."

Discussion: What can we learn from the story?

 Skills Training Tasks

The following are the different requirements of office room and personal space. You can fill in the blank choosing from China, United States, Germany, France, Japan and Arab.

(1) When people are conversing, they generally prefer the face-to-face arrangement of chairs placed at right angles to one another. _____

(2) People prefer the side-by-side arrangement; this preference may be related to the customs of avoiding direct eye contact in the culture. _____

(3) Top-level executives would occupy a position in the middle of an office area with subordinate located around them. The purpose of this arrangement is to help them stay informed of activities and to maintain control over the work area. _____

(4) People do not consider private office appropriate. In the business firms only executives of the highest rank have private offices and they also have desks in large work area. _____

(5) Office doors are closed. It would be unthinkable to just barge into an office without first knocking at the doors, both the boss's and the secretary's, and waiting for "come in". An office is a private workplace that one does not enter uninvited. _____

(6) An office is a meeting place. The businessperson in this region thinks nothing of having several different persons in the office at the same time and doing business with them simultaneously. Western businessmen, who might be offended by the informality and lack of privacy and total attention, may have a hard time coping, but the businessman here sees nothing wrong with the arrangement. _____ .

Scan the following QR codes to complete the tasks.

4.2 任务工作单

4.2 任务实施单

4.2 任务检查单

4.2 任务评价单

 Curriculum Ideology and Politics

Deng Xiaoping Kisses a Child During His Visit to the United States

People in different countries have great differences in political systems, customs and values, but there are similarities in emotional expression that transcends national boundaries and nations. After the founding of PRC, there was little contact between China and the United States, and Americans often have a stereotype about the leaders of the Communist Party of China. But when Deng Xiaoping warmly embraced the child and leaned over to kiss the child who sang songs at the Kennedy Center for the Performing Arts, many American audiences were moved to tears. At that moment, they saw a grandpa next door sharing his genuine feelings. After watching the performance, Senator Laksert, who has been strongly opposed to establishing diplomatic relations with China, said: "We were defeated by them—no one can vote against children singing Chinese songs. Deng and his wife seem to love people from the bottom of their heart; he really charmed the audience and TV viewers."

Discussion: Is it common to kiss children in public in China? What can we learn from Mr. Deng's diplomacy?

 Chinese Etiquette

Chinese people don't like physical proximity as much as Westerners do. cheek to cheek, kissing, and hugging between men and women are not acceptable in China which values the social distance between different genders. Instead, they pay attention to the distance between people to show "respect". Fist and palm salute is the meeting etiquette that best reflects the Chinese humanistic spirit. This distance not only emits elegance, but also conforms to modern health requirements.

模块 4
位次空间礼仪

模块导读

言语和非言语行为在商务谈判、跨境贸易、国际展览等商务活动中都起着至关重要的作用。座次安排有助于达成或打破交易、关系甚至活动目标。当与任何客户或业务联系人会面时，让他们设置一个舒适的个人空间。如果此人靠近或远离身体的倾向与你的个人空间偏好不符，那么你得接受这样一个事实：与此人的交往中，你不能处于一种舒适的个人空间距离舒适区域状态。

任务 1

位次礼仪

学习目标

- **素养目标**
  - 培养"讲礼和守礼"的处事态度。
  - 树立文化自信，维护国家形象。

- **知识目标**
  - 了解位次排序礼仪在商务活动中的重要性。
  - 掌握商务会议座次、商务乘车座次等座次安排基本原则。

- **能力目标**
  - 能够根据位次排序礼仪原则，安排商务会议、商务乘车等位次。

情境导入

> **情境：**希杰物流国际公司秘书小刘要去接马来西亚进出口贸易公司贸易伙伴。销售部经理丁先生，公关部经理王女士和翻译陈先生同行。小刘是这样安排座次的：小刘坐在副驾驶位，销售部丁经理坐在第二排右座，公关部王经理坐在第二排左座，翻译陈先生坐在第三排右座。
>
> **讨论：**案例中秘书小刘的这种座次安排是否合适？

 知识储备

4.1.1　座次安排原则

座次安排关乎交易、关系甚至活动目标的成败。生活妙招产品管理主管布莱恩·李表示："你想要什么，很大程度上取决于（活动参与者）坐在哪里。"座次安排的基本原则有以下三点。

客为尊原则。如果是双边交往，主方会把客方安排在尊位。

职位高低原则。职位从高到低，位次从尊到卑。

平等公平原则。位次排序一方面强调等级，另一方面强调平等。

哪种座位为尊位呢？

前与后相比，前为尊。

中间与旁边相比，中为尊。

根据国际惯例，左与右相比，右为尊，而在中国恰恰相反，左为尊。在中国的商务或政府事务场合，如举行会议、安排场地、在主席台上安排座位等，都适用"左为尊"的礼节。

4.1.2　商务场合位次安排

商务会议中的座位安排可以对会议室中的对话产生很大的影响。当考虑为商务会议安排座位时，重点是考虑与会者的需求。座位安排的类型将取决于参加会议的人数，以及它是一个正式或非正式的会议。这些因素往往会决定会议桌的不同类型和你为客人安排座位的方式。

1. 双边会见

根据国际惯例，会见时，一般要将主人和主宾的座位安排在面向出口的位置。

根据国际惯例，"以右为尊"，客方人员坐在主方的右侧。中国惯例以左为尊，所以为"主右客左"。安排会见位次时，可以按照国际惯例，也可以按照中国惯例。

2. 小型会议/会谈（谈判）

1）矩形会议桌：横桌式

会谈桌从进门的角度看是横向摆放，为"横桌式"。客方人员面门而坐，主方人员背门而坐。国际惯例中"右"尊于"左"，客方在主方右边。中国惯例中，座位安排上"左"尊于"右"，客方在主方左边。横桌式国际惯例与中国惯例座次安排如图4-1、图4-2所示。

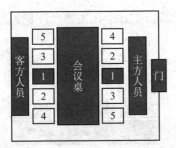 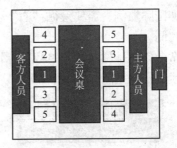

图 4-1　横桌式会谈座次安排（国际惯例—右为尊）　图 4-2　横桌式会谈座次安排（中国惯例—左为尊）

2）矩形会议桌：竖桌式

会议桌的窄边面向门口，这种摆放为"竖桌式"。客方居右，主方居左。座位安排原则：中国惯例中，以左为尊；国际惯例中，以右为尊。如果会谈室有一些标志可供参考，如正对门的墙壁上有国旗、国徽或特别精美的屏风装饰物等，那么它们的右边为尊，门口左边为尊，为客。竖桌式国际惯例、中国惯例以及以主席台、国旗、国徽等为参照物座次安排如图 4-3～图 4-5 所示。

  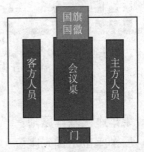

图 4-3　竖桌式会谈座次安排（国际惯例—右为尊）　　图 4-4　竖桌式会谈座次安排（中国惯例—左为尊）　　图 4-5　竖桌式会谈座次安排（以主席台、国旗、国徽等为参照物）

3）圆桌会议

圆桌表示没有先后顺序，因此，如果你想解决一个问题，圆桌的效果要好得多。会议桌的形状应该有助于鼓励所有与会者的投入。圆桌的性质并不意味着有任何形式的领导或主持。这意味着它更有利于交谈。

圆桌也指"圆桌会议"，是指一种平等、对话的协商会议形式，是一个与会者围圆桌而坐的会议。在国际会议的实践中，主席和各国代表的席位不分上下尊卑，可避免其他排座方式出现一些代表席位居前、居中，另一些代表居后、居侧的矛盾，能更好地体现各国平等原则和协商精神。

3. 大型会议座次安排

大型会议一般在礼堂举办，较为重要的与会者将坐在主席台上，有些人则坐在主席台下。

根据中国惯例，需要遵循"左"优于"右"的礼节。最重要的坐在中间，第二重要的坐在左边，第三重要的坐在右边。

根据国际惯例，需要遵循"右"优于"左"的礼节，主方坐在主席台左侧，客方坐在主席台右侧。

主席台就座排位双数及单数国际惯例安排见图4-6、图4-7，主席台就座排位双数及单数中国惯例安排见图4-8、图4-9。

图4-6　主席台就座排位法——双数
（国际惯例—右为尊）

图4-7　主席台就座排位法——单数
（国际惯例—右为尊）

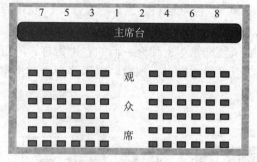

图4-8　主席台就座排位法——双数
（中国惯例—左为尊）

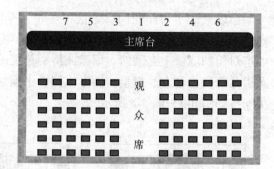

图4-9　主席台就座排位法——单数
（中国惯例—左为尊）

4. 乘车座次

乘车座次基本原则：

后排座位是优先座位。但如果主人是司机，那么副驾驶座位就是优先座位。

右侧座位优于左侧座位，中间座位排在最后。

安排乘车人数时，需要留出空位，不要太满。除司机外，五座汽车最多安排2~3人，七座汽车最多安排4~5人。

1）五座轿车座次安排

后排座位是优先座位。后排右座为一号位，后排左位为二号位，前排副驾为三号位。如果是主人开车，那么一号座变成前排副驾的位置，二号座为后排右座，三号座为后排左座。双排五座轿车专职司机开车及主人开车座次安排如图4-10、图4-11所示。

2）七座轿车座次安排

第二排的右后座优先，其次是左后座，再次是第三排右后座和左后座，最后是副驾驶座位。如果是主人开车，那么副驾驶座位优先，其次是第二排右后座和左后座，最后是第三排右后座和左后座。三排七座轿车专职司机开车及主人开车座次安排如图4-12、图4-13所示。

5. 合影位次

在国内活动中进行合影排位时，遵循中国惯例"居中为上、居左为上、居前为上"。在涉外活动中，则遵循国际惯例"居中为上、居右为上、居前为上"。以左为尊时单数及双数来宾合影位次如图4-14、图4-15所示。

图 4-10　双排五座轿车座次安排　　　　　图 4-11　双排五座轿车座次安排（主人开车）
　　　　　（专职司机开车）

图 4-12　三排七座轿车座次安排（专职司机开车）　　图 4-13　三排七座轿车座次安排（主人开车）

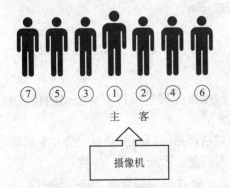

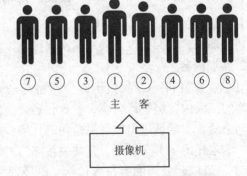

图 4-14　以左为尊时单数来宾合影位次　　图 4-15　以左为尊时双数来宾合影位次

6. 乘坐电梯位次

如果轿厢里有电梯操作工作人员，引导员要后进后出，让客人和尊者先进先出。如果轿厢里无电梯操作工作人员，陪同人员应先行进入电梯按按钮，最后一个出轿厢，让客人和尊者后进先出。

 同步测试

扫码做题。

同步测试：汉语
版 –M4T1 判断
正误

 案例分析

希杰物流国际公司将与马来西亚吉隆坡进出口贸易公司代表会面。希杰物流国际公司的秘书小刘安排了座次：希杰物流国际公司作为东道主，面朝门而坐，总经理坐在中间，外联部经理和翻译分别坐在总经理的左右，他本人坐在翻译的右边。马来西亚吉隆坡进出口贸易公司作为客方，坐在门后，CEO坐在中间，外联部经理和外联部工作人员坐在CEO的左右，具体安排如图4-16所示。

讨论： 案例中的座位安排合适吗?

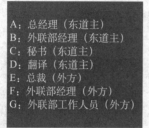

A：总经理（东道主）
B：外联部经理（东道主）
C：秘书（东道主）
D：翻译（东道主）
E：总裁（外方）
F：外联部经理（外方）
G：外联部工作人员（外方）

图4-16　双方会谈座次安排

 实训项目

会议及乘车座次安排

1. 实训目的

通过训练，掌握会议及乘车座次安排原则。

2. 实训内容

（1）背景资料：CJ物流国际公司将与马来西亚吉隆坡进出口贸易公司的代表会面。在访问的三天内，将举行会谈、参观和宴会等商务活动。

马来西亚吉隆坡进出口贸易公司的代表：总裁哈西米·阿布·哈桑、公共关系部经理西蒂·卡尔托姆·卡马鲁丁、公共关系部门工作人员努尔沙姆·谭·科利。

CJ物流国际公司的参与者包括：总经理王强、公共关系部经理李华、秘书刘伟、翻译张丽。

（2）以小组为单位，完成以下任务。假设你是CJ物流国际公司的秘书刘伟，你需要完成以下任务并制订详细的接待计划，包括以下内容。

① 制订详细的接待计划和时间表。

② 代表CJ物流国际公司派车前往机场，接马来西亚吉隆坡进出口贸易公司代表。包括安排接客人的车辆、人员以及安排汽车座次。

③ 双方将举行会谈。安排会议地点，重点是座次安排。

3. 实训要求

（1）采取"组内异质，组间同质"的原则，将学生分为若干小组，每组4~6人。

（2）每组提交一份座次安排表。

（3）每组讲解和展示本组的工作成果。

4. 实训考核

（1）评价方式：采取小组自评、小组互评、教师评价、企业导师评价四维评价方式，总评成绩 = 小组自评 ×20% + 小组互评 ×20% + 教师评价 ×30% + 企业导师评价 ×30%。

（2）评价指标：从素质目标、知识目标、能力目标 3 方面进行评价。

4.1 任务工作单　　　4.1 任务实施单　　　4.1 任务检查单　　　4.1 任务评价单

 思政课堂

1946 年，远东国际军事法庭审判以东条英机为首的 28 名日本甲级战犯。10 个参与国的法官因排定座次展开了异常激烈的争论。中国法官理应排在庭长左边的那把椅子，但是由于当时中国的国力不强而被各强权国否定。在这种情况下，唯一出庭的中国法官梅汝璈与列强展开了一场机智的舌战。他首先从正面阐述：排座位应按日本投降时各受降国的签字顺序排列，这是唯一正确的原则。接着他微微一笑说："当然，如果各位同仁不赞同这一方法，我们不妨找个体重器来，依体重的大小排座，体重者居中，体轻者居旁。"各国法官听了，忍俊不禁。庭长笑着说："您的建议很好，但它只适用于拳击比赛。"梅法官接着回答："若不以受降国签字顺序排座，那就按体重排座。这样纵使我置末座而心安理得，并且对我的国家也有所交代。一旦他们认为我坐在边上不合适，可以换另一名比我胖的来。"这一回答引得法官们大笑起来，梅法官终于坐到了应坐的座位上，如图 4-17 所示。

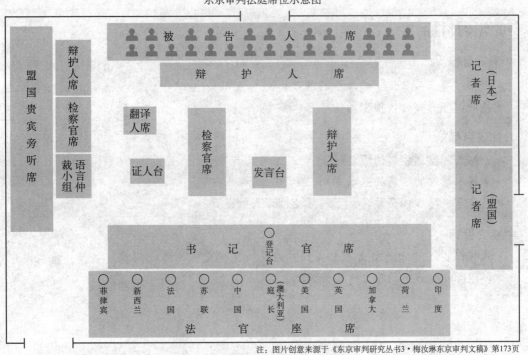

注：图片创意来源于《东京审判研究丛书3·梅汝琳东京审判文稿》第173页

图 4-17　东京审判座次安排及代表团名单

（资料来源：《民主与法制》周刊 2021 年第 39 期）

讨论：党的二十大报告指出"面对外部讹诈、遏制、封锁、极限施压，我们坚持国家利益为重、国内政治优先，保持战略定力，发扬斗争精神，展示不畏强权的坚定意志，在斗争中维护国家尊严和核心利益"。本案例中梅法官为什么如此重视东京审判时的座位安排？梅法官的据理力争反映了什么？

中华礼仪

在中国古代，有一种被称为八仙桌的家具，这是一张大方桌，两边各有两个人的长椅。如果有一个面向入口的座位，那么面向入口的右手座位是给主宾的。如果没有面向入口门的座位（假设用餐在外面，或者有两个或多个同等重要的门），那么面向东面的右手座位就是贵宾座位。贵宾座左侧的座位按重要性排序为第二、第四、第六和第八位，右侧的座位为第三、第五和第七位。

任务 2

人际空间距离

◎ 学习目标

■ **素养目标**
- 培养"尊重与自信"的处事态度。
- 具备国际视野并传播中国传统文化。

■ **知识目标**
- 了解人际空间距离的重要性。
- 掌握人际空间距离的基本原则。
- 熟练掌握跨文化交际背景下人际空间距离的差异。

■ **能力目标**
- 能够根据人际空间距离基本原则，以及跨文化交际人际空间距离差异，进行符合国际礼仪规范的跨文化交际活动。

情境导入

> **情境:** 艾玛从秘鲁到美国学习,她将住在美国人克里斯托·汉德福德家里。她按了门铃,一个金发女人开了门。
>
> **克里斯托:**(脸上露出灿烂的笑容)你一定是艾玛! 在这里见到你很高兴。让我帮你拿手提箱。进来吧。我是克里斯托·汉德福德。
>
> **艾玛:**(激动地期待着一个拥抱)谢谢。我很高兴见到你。
>
> 汉德福德太太带艾玛去了她的房间。她放下手提箱,站在艾玛对面,大约 4 英尺远。
>
> **克里斯托:**(在她面前交叉手臂)告诉我更多的旅行的事情吧。我希望有一天能去秘鲁。
>
> **艾玛:**(感觉疏远)这是一次不错的旅行。欢迎去秘鲁,届时我很乐意带你参观。
>
> **克里斯托:** 长途旅行后你一定很累。好好休息,然后我们可以一起吃晚饭。
>
> **艾玛:** 谢谢。到时候见。
>
> 艾玛有点失望。她期待着一个热烈的吻和拥抱,而不是站在房间的另一边。看来汉德福德太太对她有点冷淡。
>
> **讨论:** 为什么艾玛会觉得汉德福德太太对她有点冷淡?

知识储备

4.2.1 人际空间

人际空间学是一种涉及空间的非言语交流。Proxemics 一词源自与邻近度相同的拉丁词根,意思是空间的一个维度是两个或两个以上的人之间的距离。个人与他人之间保持的距离可以定义为"人际空间"(IPS)。这种距离受到情境因素和个人影响。当其他人违反我们的"人际空间"时,不适感会上升,促使我们远离并调整到合适的人际距离。

每个人都表现得好像他 / 她被一个不应该被穿透的薄薄的空间泡包围。个人空间气泡是人们自己想象出来的一种气泡。它环绕在自己周围,代表你和其他人或物体之间感到舒适的距离。每个人都有不同的个人空间泡泡舒适度。

🔗 知识链接

"人际泡泡"

简单地说,"人际泡泡"就是人的周围有一个看不见的"泡泡",它代表着你的"边界"。如果没有其他人闯入你的"泡泡"范围,你会感到安全。反之,它会让人感到不安,甚至愤怒。

当人们被建筑物、房间或其他限制所迫,站在比他们的文化所表明的更近的距离进行交谈时,他们很少说话。例如,你有没有观察到拥挤的电梯里人们之间的交流? 他们通常避免眼神接触,保持沉默,并且身体紧张。触摸另一个人,即使是不小心,也会令人尴尬,并需要道歉。

霍尔（1966年）对空间关系学进行了初步研究，他认为人们管理彼此之间的社会距离，是用来调节他们从他人获得的感觉或刺激的一种方式。

根据最初的理论，霍尔进一步将社会距离分为四种类型，如图4-18所示。这四个距离也作为后续的概率学评估的一般类别。因此，在美国，研究通常支持以下四种社交距离和含义。

公众距离（12~25英尺）：最不亲密的距离，通常为公开演讲、展示权力或感到安全的距离。这种距离主要限制了人们彼此之间的交流和大声说话。

社交距离（4~12英尺）：用于更正式的互动，同时保持与他人的安全距离。这种间距允许个体更好地看到和听到对方，但仍阻止他们接触。

个人距离（1.5~4英尺）：这是个人空间或"泡泡"，通常留给重要的人和朋友。这个距离个人可以安静地说话而不被偷听，并清楚地观察彼此的非言语交流。此外，个体之间也足够亲密，可以在社交场合相互接触（如拍手、握手、触摸肘部等）。

亲密距离（小于1.5英尺）：这个空间是为浪漫伴侣、家人和亲密朋友保留的。主要用于更亲密的接触，无论是友好的性质（如拥抱）还是浪漫的性质（如亲吻）。而且，这个距离个体也可能闻到彼此的气味。

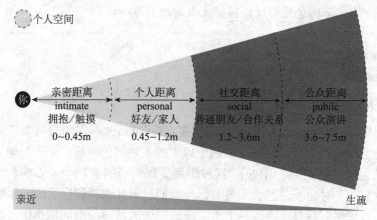

图 4-18　人际交流四种距离（爱德华·霍尔）

4.2.2　人际空间文化差异

人际空间因文化而异。当一个欧裔美国人与一个拉丁美洲人交谈时，前者会觉得拉丁美洲人"咄咄逼人"或过于亲密，而拉丁美洲人则认为来自美国的人冷酷而有距离感。来自中东的阿拉伯人认为，只有距离近到能够闻到对方呼吸中的大蒜味，才算得上友好。显然，参与人际交往的人之间对适当空间的感知存在着强烈的文化差异。通常这种非语言层面是无意识的。例如，在沙特阿拉伯，如果一个陌生人靠近你交谈，你可能会发现自己不知不觉地后退。在中东国家或地区，社交距离比美国更近，所以当你后退时，你的谈话伙伴可能会再次试图缩小差距。随着对话地进行，一方后退，另一方前进。来自寒冷气候区域的人们在与他人交流时所需的距离比来自热带地区人们所需的距离要大，所以北欧人就需要较大的交际距离。因此，在德国、英国被视为亲密的距离，在法国、意大利、希腊、

---

① 　1英尺＝0.3m。

西班牙等地中海沿岸国家却被视作普通的交际距离。北欧人认为南欧人的舒适距离较近，而南欧人却会因北欧人所需的距离太大而感到疏远。一些地区和国家可以被定义为"近体性文化"，即人们之间的距离更近，肢体语言也更多。"近体性文化"地区包括阿拉伯国家、拉丁美洲、南欧（尤其是意大利）、西欧（如法国）等。

其他地区和国家属于"非近体性文化"，人们在交谈时保持更大的距离。"非近体性文化"地区包括东亚国家（尤其是中国、日本、泰国和菲律宾）、西欧国家（尤其英国和荷兰）、中欧国家（尤其是德国）、北美国家（如美国、加拿大）和澳大利亚。部分国家人际空间距离如图 4-19 所示。

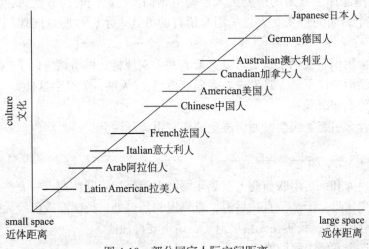

图 4-19 部分国家人际空间距离

属于"近体性文化"的人们在人际交流时使用比非近体性文化的人们更近的距离。同时，往往直接面对面，互相注视和身体接触较多，说话声音也更大。而"非近体性文化"则相反，交流距离更远，且肢体语言更少。

"近体性文化"和"非近体性文化"主要国家及特征如表 4-1 所示。

表 4-1 "近体性文化"国家与"非近体性文化"国家及表现

区域 / 表现	"近体性文化"形态的国家	"非近体性文化"形态的国家
区域	拉丁美洲、南欧（特别是意大利）等国家或地区，西欧中的法国以及阿拉伯国家	东南亚国家（特别是中国、日本、泰国、菲律宾），西欧国家（特别是英国、荷兰），中欧国家（特别是德国），美国、加拿大等北美洲国家或地区和澳大利亚
表现	缺少排队的习惯与传统，交流时距离更近，有更多的肢体语言	对话时与对方保持更远的距离，自觉按序排队，把排序行为看作文明教养的表现

 同步测试

扫码做题。

同步测试：汉语
版 –M4T2 判断正误

案例分析

• 案例 1

出了什么事

一对年轻的丹麦夫妇因为工作关系从丹麦移居到澳大利亚。为了尽快融入当地的生活，他们参加了当地商会发起的一个俱乐部。他们不但非常积极地参加俱乐部的各种活动，还热情主动地与俱乐部的会员交流。但几周以后，出现了一些小问题，一些女会员向商会的组织者抱怨那个新来的丹麦男人想勾引她们。与此同时，一些男会员也向商会组织者抱怨，那个新来的丹麦女人总是用非语言的方式表示，她愿意同他们发生更亲密的关系。

之后，商会组织者找到了这对丹麦夫妇，并委婉地将这件事情告诉了他们。两人听完商会组织者的话后惊诧不已。丹麦夫妇委屈地抱怨："天呐，怎么会这样？"

这究竟是怎么回事呢？

讨论： 是什么引起了误会？如何避免"亲密距离"误会？

• 案例 2

一名英国商人和一名阿联酋商人在鸡尾酒会上闲聊，阿联酋商人一直往前靠，但是英国商人觉得距离太近，于是一直往后退，直到退到门口处，英国商人已经无路可退，只好尴尬地说："不好意思，我实在无路可退了，请不要再往前了。"

讨论： 从这个案例中我们能学到什么？

实训项目

人际空间距离文化差异

1. 实训目的

通过训练，掌握人际空间距离文化差异。

2. 实训内容

（1）背景资料：人际空间距离文化差异大，以下是对办公室和个人空间的不同要求。你可以从中国、美国、德国、法国、日本和阿拉伯国家中选择。

① 当人们交谈时，他们通常更喜欢面对面的椅子，椅子彼此成直角放置。_____
_____。

② 人们更喜欢并排排列；这种偏好可能与文化中避免眼神直接接触的习惯有关。
_____。

③ 高层管理人员将占据办公区中央的一个位置，下属位于他们周围。这种安排的目的是帮助他们了解活动并保持对工作区域的控制。_____。

④ 人们认为私人办公室并不合适。在商业公司中，只有最高级别的高管才有私人办公室，而且他们在大的工作区域也有办公桌。_____。

⑤ 办公室门关闭。如果不敲老板和秘书的门，然后等着听"进来"，就冲进办公室，这是不可想象的。办公室是一个私人工作场所，任何人不得擅自进入。_____。

⑥ 办公室是一个会议场所。这个地区的商人认为在办公室里同时与几个人做生意不是什么大事。西方商人可能会因为这样做不正式、缺乏隐私和全面关注而感到愤怒，他们可能很难应对，但这个地区的商人认为这种安排没有任何问题。＿＿＿＿＿＿＿＿。

（2）以小组为单位，分析此案例中不同人际空间距离的文化差异以及产生文化差异的原因。

3. 实训要求

（1）采取"组内异质，组间同质"的原则，将学生分为若干小组，每组 4~6 人。

（2）每组提交一份人际空间距离文化差异实训报告，内容包括文化差异原因及具体分类。

（3）每组讲解和展示本组的工作成果。

4. 实训考核

（1）评价方式：采取小组自评、小组互评、教师评价、企业导师评价四维评价方式，总评成绩 = 小组自评×20% + 小组互评×20% + 教师评价×30% + 企业导师评价×30%。

（2）评价指标：从素质目标、知识目标、能力目标 3 方面进行评价。

| 4.2 任务工作单 | 4.2 任务实施单 | 4.2 任务检查单 | 4.2 任务评价单 |

思政课堂

邓小平访问美国期间亲吻唱歌的孩子

各国人民在政治制度、风俗习惯和价值观念等方面差异巨大，但在情感抒发和表达上却有超越国界和民族的相通之处。中华人民共和国成立以后，中美之间交往很少，美国人对于中共领导人往往留有刻板的印象。但是，当邓小平在肯尼迪表演艺术中心热情拥抱并俯身亲吻了唱歌的孩子，在场的不少美国观众感动得流下了眼泪。那一刻，他们看到的是一位和他们有着一样真情实感的邻家爷爷。一直强烈反对同中国建交的参议员拉克泽尔特在看了这场演出后说："我们被他们打败了——谁也没法投票反对孩子们唱中国歌曲。邓和他的夫人看来真的爱人民；他确实令在场的观众和电视观众倾倒。"

（资料来源：http://dangshi.people.com.cn/n1/2020/0219/c85037-31595084.html）

讨论：党的二十大报告指出"以文明交流超越文明隔阂、文明互鉴超越文明冲突、文明共存超越文明优越"。本案例中邓小平的外交行为体现了什么？

中华礼仪

中国人不像西方人那样喜欢身体接近，男女之间的贴面、亲吻、拥抱礼在讲究"男女大防"的中国更是行不通。中国人讲究以人和人之间的距离来表现出"敬"意。拱手礼是最能体现中国人文精神的见面礼节，这种距离不仅散发着典雅气息，而且比较符合现代卫生要求。

Module 5
Business Activities Etiquette

 Profile of the Module

Business etiquette is essentially about building relationships with colleagues, clients or customers. Etiquette, and in particular business etiquette, is simply a means of maximising your business potential by presenting yourself favourably. By improving your business etiquette you automatically improve your chances of success. A key to being successful in business internationally is to understand the role of culture in international business. No matter which industry you are in cultural differences will have a direct impact on your profitability. Improving your level of knowledge of international cultural difference in business can aid in building international competencies as well as enabling you to gain a competitive advantage.

Task 1

International Exhibition Etiquette

◎ Learning Objectives

■ Moral Objectives
- To cultivate students' respectfulness and confidence.
- To cultivate students' values of civilization, harmony, patriotism, friendship.
- To strengthen the concept of green exhibition and sustainable development.

■ Knowledge Objectives
- To get familiar with the importance of international exhibition etiquette.
- To grasp the basic rules of international exhibition etiquette.

- To grasp do's and don'ts for organizing and participating in international exhibitions.

■ **Ability Objectives**

- To be able to organize international exhibitions.
- To be able to do a good job of exhibition invitation, exhibition services and exhibition follow-up.

Lead-in: Case Study

Situation: A Chinese foreign trade company engaged in textile business went to 2017 Dubai Commodity Fair. They brought the best-selling fabrics suitable for the Middle East market, hoping to attract more customers at this exhibition. It is the first time for Flora, one of the Chinese foreign trade company staff to attend the Dubai Commodity Fair.

Customer: (a big smile on his face) Hi, I am from Dubai International Trading Co., Ltd, and I am quite interested in your product.

Flora: (a smile on her face and eye contact with the customer) Welcome to our booth. Our company has been engaging in textile business for 20 years and the products are quite popular in Dubai. This is the sample of our bestsellers in Dubai and this is my business card.

Customer: (holding the business card with two hands and coming closer to have a look at the product) Nice to meet you, Flora. This is my business card. I want to know more about the product.

Flora took the business card with two hands, have a look at it and then put it in the bag. But just then, she smelt a strong perfume. It is too strong for her to tolerate. Flora frowned and put on a mask.

Flora: (wearing the mask) This is the pamphlet of our products including the price, designs, etc.

Customer: (taking the pamphlet hesitantly) OK, I will have a look at it.

The customer left the booth, embarrassedly and disappointedly. Flora wondered what was going on.

Discussion: Why did the customer leave the booth embarrassedly and disappointedly?

Basic Knowledge

5.1.1　Exhibition Invitation Etiquette

1. Categorize invited customers

Only by classifying the customer groups can we have a clear target and carry out effective invitation work. In general, the customer base is divided into the following three categories.

Class A: target customers. There is a good foundation for cooperation, and the purchase intention is strong.

Class B: potential customers. The transaction has not been completed yet, but there are many e-mail inquiries in the early stage.

Class C: ordinary customers. There were several e-mails but no inquiry.

Class A customers are professional purchasers of the exhibition and have a great intention to sign agreements. Class B customers belong to potential stocks, so you need to introduce the company and products in detail and express sincerity and intention of cooperation. Class C customers are general visitors to the exhibition, who can be briefed on the company and products.

2. Different ways of pre-exhibition invitation

The pre-exhibition invitation generally adopts various ways such as electronic invitation, public release, telephone invitation, etc. Different invitation methods can be adopted for different customers.

E-mail: one of the most extensive ways to invite customers. You need to choose the right time to send one-to-one messages to targeted customers, instead of sending e-mails in groups.

Public release: the release of enterprise exhibition information in major social media software such as LinkedIn, Facebook, Twitter, etc. Proper use of social software can improve the marketing effect. When publishing content through social software, you must pay attention to the uniqueness and timeliness of the published content.

Telephone: For extremely important customers, in addition to sending an electronic invitation, you can also directly enhance the communication effect through telephone invitation.

3. A trade show invitation e-mail

1) Trade show invitation e-mail writing tips

（1）Be concise

The most important thing is to answer the following fundamental questions in your e-mail: who, when, where, why.

（2）Be prompt

As a general rule, we advise you to contact your local customers about 6 weeks in advance and your international customers up to 2 months before the event so they can organize travel and accommodations.

2) Trade show invitation template

The sample trade show invitation is specifically addressed to a long-standing customer, but you can adapt it to any type of event or customer by using all tips above. You can also design it according to your customers' customs and taboos. For example, if you send the invitation card to your Russian customers, avoid using the color of yellow which is taken as ominous for Russians.

Dear [client's name]:

We are very grateful that you've been a loyal customer for [number of years].

In the near future, our company will be taking part in the [name of trade show], which will take place on [date] in [city].

We would love to invite you to visit us at the [exhibit number] booth. You should find this event interesting because [personal reason].

As a thank you for coming to see us, our team will present you with an amazing gift on entry and you will be entered into a prize contest for a free trial of [your product]. We'd be delighted if you decide to join us.

Spaces are limited, so please confirm your presence before [date] so that we can send you your free access card.

For more information, feel free to contact [person in charge's name] at [phone number] or by e-mail via [e-mail address].

You can also find more information on our website: [web address].

Hope to see you soon at our event.

[Signature]

[Job title].

[Company's logo].

5.1.2   Trade Show Booth Etiquette

1. Basic rules for the stand

Firstly, you should have an appropriate stand design. Make your space cozy and familiar. Set up a cozy space where visitors can not only see your products and get to know your brand, but also relax, chat, and possibly connect to Wi-fi and charge their phones. Another great idea could be to offer coffee and cookies to your visitors.

微课：国际会展
服务礼仪

Secondly, keep the stand tidy. Do not eat or drink at your booth or have cups, bottles and used plates around your booth. Keep your area free of food and drink debris.

2. Basic trade show booth etiquette rules for staff

1）Staff roles and sales script

Besides the sales script or elevator pitch, company representatives in a trade show booth should be prepared to answer basic questions or know where to obtain more information. The booth should also always be managed by at least one person who has expertise or authority, and that person should provide support for staff and attendees at all times.

Knowledge Related

Elevator Pitch

An elevator pitch (or elevator speech) is a 30-to-60-second summary of yourself or an idea that you share with a certain audience, typically a boss or interviewer. It is named as such since it should be short and compelling enough that you can introduce yourself during an elevator ride. The elevator pitch is a way to share your credentials and expertise quickly with individuals who don't know anything about you.

There are three main questions to answer with an elevator pitch: "Who am I?", "What do I do?" and "What's my ask?"

2）Dress to impress

Some companies have corporate apparel (e.g., polo shirts, sport coats, dress shirts, etc.) while others give employees some direction on personal attire regarding colors and clothing style. Here's our handy tips on what to wear at an exhibition:

Dress according to the market and environment you exhibit in.

Never underdress, always put effort into your appearance.

If you have a uniform, use it.

Use personality and individual items to stand out from the crowd.

Choose comfortable clothing and shoes.

3）Greet and engage

After being initially drawn in by the booth or brand itself, the customers may stay for your staff. The following body language tips will help convey a professional and approachable demeanor:

微课：会展互动

Stand up and greet attendees in front of the booth.

Smile and make eye contact with attendees from all directions.

Do not cross arms or legs; keep hands out of pockets.

Avoid fidgeting and leaning against booth walls and furniture.

Do not eat or chew gum in the trade show exhibit.

Do not send text messages, browse or make phone calls.

5.1.3　Trade Fair Follow-up Etiquette

1. Basic rules for follow-up etiquette

1）Be prompt

Follow up within 24 hours. If the exhibition is on Friday, follow up on Monday. Get in before your competition does. The sooner you follow up with your leads the better the chance of turning them into sales.

2）Be specific

（1）Who are you? No one wants a "Dear Sir / Madam". Use their names to address the customers.

（2）Where do we meet? Always add the name of the exhibition into the subject header and the e-mail text.

In the follow-up e-mail, you can add a photo of your exhibition stand.

3）Contact your potential customers by various ways

Call or interact via LinkedIn or send a number of e-mails during the weeks after the event – this is your golden window of opportunity.

2. Trade show follow-up e-mail templates

Make sure your B2B e-mail marketing strategy template is:

Timely (consider automated e-mail follow-up for some sends, but don't sound like a robot!).

In appropriate length (enough to be on your leads' minds, but not enough to annoy them).

Customized.

Not sales-just friendly-not pushing.

1）'Was nice to meet you'

Suggested subject line: It was nice to meet you at [trade show name]!

Hi [lead name],

It was nice meeting you at [trade show name] the other day. It was fun chatting with you about [fun personal element you learned about the lead.]

I'm sure you're busy after being gone for the show, so I'll reach out next week after you're able to get caught up and we can take it from there.

Thank you,

[your name]

2）Request a follow-up chat

Suggested subject line: Let's catch up on [pain point]!

Hi [lead name],

Thanks for stopping by my booth for a chat at [trade show name], it was so nice to meet you.

[Give them a reminder of what your company does or any offers / promotions that are going on for your company that they may be interested in.]

I would love to set up a quick call with you to answer any questions and talk about the next steps.

Do you have any free time within the next week for a 15-minute call?

Thank you,

[Your Name]

After sending follow-up chat emails, it is a great time to use the HubSpot meetings tool to connect.

3）Send educational resources

Suggested subject line: Resources to help with [pain point].

Hi [lead name],

I hope you enjoyed [trade show name], it was nice to meet you! Thanks for stopping by our booth and your interest in [your company name.]

It was nice to discuss [reference conversation/ services that you may have discussed] with you, and I thought it might be helpful to send along some digital resources to answer any further questions [links to relevant resources on your company's website.]

I would love to have a quick call with you to talk about this further! Do you have any free time within the next week for a 15-minute call?

Thank you,

[Your Name]

In this post-event follow-up e-mail template, you're using content marketing to provide information and make the other party happy. This could be a blog post, FAQ page, or any other resource that you think is relevant.

4）Soothe their pain points

Suggested subject line: How can I help [company name]?

Hi [lead name],

It was great chatting with you at [trade show name], I hope you enjoyed the rest of the show!

I'm sure fixing [their company's pain point] is something that is important to you, so I wanted to reach out to further talk about how [your company's service] can help you out with this as soon as possible!

I would love to set up a quick call with you to answer any questions and chat about the next steps.

Do you have any free time within the next week for a 15-minute call?

Thank you,

[Your Name]

5）The bigger, more urgent offer

Suggested subject line: Don't forget [offer promotion]!

Hi [lead name],

It was nice to meet you at [trade show name] last week!

Just wanted to remind you that you signed up for [insert promotion details], and I don't want you to miss out on the chance to take advantage of this offer!

If you have any questions about the [promotional offer] or [your company's name] services in general, I'm happy to chat further!

Feel free to schedule a call with me over the next week right on my calendar!

Thank you,

[Your Name]

 Extended Reading

Scan the QR code, read the passage about "Exhibition Etiquette：The Do's and Don'ts" and finish the following tasks.

拓展阅读：展览礼仪：该做的和不该做的

After-reading tasks

When you finish reading the text above, finish the following tasks.

Task 1   Read the statements and decide whether they are true or not. Mark "T" for true and "F" for false.

（1）Body language, dress, tone of voice and eye contact are all important in exhibition. (   )

（2）Giving away freebies can help build immediate connection between you and your target audience. (   )

（3）To communicate effectively, it is OK for you to be pushy or domineering. (   )

（4）It is important to make sure that stand staff are well-trained to be quite familiar with products. (   )

（5）It's essential to listen to what the attendees are telling you. (   )

Task 2   Critical thinking

What exhibition rules are mentioned in the passage? What other exhibition rules should we also pay attention to?

 Basic Knowledge Test

Read the statements and decide whether they are true or not. Mark "T" for true and "F" for false.

（1）For potential leads, it is not necessary to call them in addition to e-mails. (   )

（2）The pre-exhibition invitation needs to be as concise as possible. (   )

（3）Exhibition staff can eat or chew gum in the trade show exhibit to relax. (   )

同步测试：汉语版–M5T1 判断正误

（4）The sooner you follow up with your leads, the greater chance of turning them into sales. (   )

（5）When communicating with potential leads, be friendly rather than pushy. (   )

Case Study

Lucy was going to attend RosUpack one week later. She sent pre-exhibition invitation e-mails to leads in mass two days before the expo. The following is the e-mail (She used yellow color as the background color). She went to the expo, only to find few customers came to the booth and they had little potential of reaching a deal.

> Dear Sir or Madam,
>
> We sincerely invite you to visit our booth at the RosUpack from June 6th to June 9th, 2022. Our booth number is 2A62.
>
> It will be great pleasure to meet you at the exhibition. We look forward to cooperation with you further.

Discussion: Explain the reason why lucy failed to attract leads to her booth.

Skills Training Tasks

International Exhibition Etiquette

Situation: You are the sales manager of Brandland and your team is going to attend U.S. National Stationery Show two months later. The basic information are as follows:

Basic information about the expo:

Hosting City: New York, U.S.A.

Exhibition Hall: Javits Convention Center (655 West 34th Street New York, NY 10001-1188 U.S.A)

Time: February 5th～8th, 2023

Booth No.: Hall B2 101

Basic information about the attendees and products

Exhibitor: Brandland

Attendees: Lily, business assistant; Sean, Sales Manager; Tom, General Manager

The Top Attraction: the latest product "green writing board" launched by the company. (Features: camphor pine wood frame imported from Russia: environmental-friendly, light-weight, corrosion-resist, moisture-resist, and elegant); the company launched a promotional activity "5% discount with a turnover of more than $ 500,000" for this exhibition.

Scan the following QR codes to complete the tasks.

5.1 任务工作单   5.1 任务实施单   5.1 任务检查单   5.1 任务评价单

Curriculum Ideology and Politics

China, Doer of Green Exhibition

On July 25, 2022, the opening ceremony of "The 2nd China International Consumer Products Expo" was held in Haikou. It promotes the concept of "green exhibition and low carbon exhibition", highlights green and low carbon exhibition, issues green exhibition guidelines, practices the green and low carbon concept in all aspects of operation, construction, transportation and catering. It strives to create a benchmark for environmental protection and energy saving exhibitions and highlights social responsibility. In the construction phase, the booth construction unit, the exhibition center operator and the official service provider of the Consumer Products Expo signed the Proposal for Green and Low Carbon Exhibition of the 2th Consumer Products Expo, proposing the following initiatives: improve green and low carbon awareness, encourage green and low carbon design, use green and low carbon materials, advocate green and low carbon construction, and jointly create green and low carbon exhibitions. As for service, the organizing committee uses disposable catering utensils made of biodegradable and recyclable materials. The decoration of the restaurant is made of environment-friendly and pollution-free materials. The waiter must wear protective equipment when directly contacting with food. In terms of logistics, green transportation mode is adopted, and frugal and clean fuels are used to achieve energy conservation and emission reduction. In terms of garbage disposal, the Secretariat has effectively implemented the plastic prohibition measures, and at the same time, it will classify and innocuously dispose of the garbage in the exhibition area, and will strictly urge the exhibition hall operator to implement the garbage classification disposal. The trash cans set in the exhibition hall are classified trash ones, laying the foundation for garbage reduction, recycling and innocuous disposal.

Discussion: Why is China proposing Green Exhibition?

Chinese Etiquette

Numbers, shù zì in Chinese Pinyin, have long represented hierarchy order and symbols of nature in China.

According to Chinese tradition, Dao produces One, One produces Two then Two produces Three, and Three produces all. Shù zì represents the basic order of the universe.

The numbers of 3, 5, 6 and 9 have even more mysterious connotations in a classic Chinese works, *the Book of Changes*. The five elements theory summarizes the relationship of five basic energies. Chinese also lay importance to the use of shù zì in designing architectures. Chinese are fond of the mysterious use of shù zì. While digital techniques are well-developed, people never stop trying to solve the puzzles.

(Source:Hello,China)

Task 2

International Business Negotiation Etiquette

 Learning Objectives

■ Moral Objectives

• To cultivate students' respectfulness and confidence.

• To cultivate students' values of civilization, harmony, patriotism, friendship.

• To strengthen students' the cultural confidence.

■ Knowledge Objectives

• To get familiar with the importance of business negotiation etiquette.

• To grasp the basic rules of business negotiation in international business activities.

• To grasp differences in negotiating across cultures.

■ Ability Objectives

• To be able to do a good job before, during and after the bushiness negotiation.

 Lead-in: Case Study

Situation: David Li entered a large exporting company after graduation and he has been promoted to the sales manager recently because of his good performance. Last month, his company negotiated with an important American client on the development of a new product. David was in charge of the negotiation. He had been preparing for the negotiation carefully in previous weeks. The negotiation processed smoothly and the two negotiating parties reached an agreement finally. The two companies decided to sign the contract and held a signing ceremony last Monday. David was responsible for the arrangement of the signing hall. When both parties entered the signing hall, the guest negotiators stopped and left the hall angrily. What was wrong? The host company checked the room setting carefully and found that the national flag of the guest company had been placed on the left side of the signing table.

Discussion: Why were the guest negotiators angry?

Basic Knowledge

5.2.1   Preparation for the Business Negotiations

1. Dress for a negotiation

The way we dress for a business meeting, the way we talk, and even the accessories we wear can influence the other party. Although the clothes we wear are not defining our personality, it's essential to look presentable if we want to gain the respect of our opponents.

知识储备：商务
谈判着装礼仪

2. Arrange the negotiation room

1）Tables

Many rooms have tables in the centre, with chairs around it. Round tables are "fair". Long tables have a place for a "chairperson". Square tables have corners you can sit across.

2）Chairs

Have enough chairs for everyone to sit, but get rid of many extras (unless you want to create a particular effect).

3）Refreshment

Drinks and food may be at hand, to allow for breaks and keeping people comfortable.

3. Other preparations for business negotiation

1）Gather the information of the guest negotiators and their company

Information may include the number of negotiators, their positions, age, gender, even hobbies, and special eating habits, etc..

2）Draft a reception plan and negotiating agenda

Deliver the agenda through e-mail or fax to the guest negotiating party before they arrive. Ask for their advice and make possible revisions. Explain to the guest party if their requirements can not be met.

3）Meet guest negotiators and see them off

Check with the guest negotiators about the time and place they arrive. Send staff to the airport or railway station earlier to wait for the guest party. The level and size for greeting and send-off are determined by 3 factors:

（1）The rank and the purpose of the negotiators;

（2）The relationship between the negotiators;

（3）The usual practice.

The basic rule is to have someone in the same business with the same or similar rank, title and status in charge of the greeting and send-off.

4）Reserve the hotel and arrange accommodations

Choose proper hotel with good meeting facilities and convenient transport. Book enough room for the guest negotiators in case there are more people than expected. Make clear if there are guests who have special dining habits or requirements.

5）Arrange tourist sightseeing and shopping

If time permits, you can prepare some sightseeing plan in case the guests are interested. Ask the guests if they need help when they want to visit around the city.

6）Send small gifts when guest negotiators leave

When doing business with foreigners, do research to understand what gifts are most appropriate, and when they are normally exchanged.

5.2.2 Business Etiquette in the Business Negotiation

1. Greeting

The most common form of greeting in the corporate world is the handshake. However, if you are in countries such as France or Brazil, kisses on the cheek are the norm. If you are in the Middle East, a nod of acknowledgment may be best when greeting someone of the opposite sex.

2. Small talk

It is also common for some professionals to engage in small talk before the negotiations begin and to have short conversations after negotiations have ended for the day. This gives everyone time to become more comfortable with one another and is the gateway to building a lasting business relationship. However, in some countries such as Finland and Germany, small talk is not part of business culture, and meetings start precisely on time. After negotiations, a German or Finnish professional may host a dinner for casual conversation. In places such as Mexico and Saudi Arabia, small talk is expected, but it's best to know which subjects are off-limits. For instance, it is not proper etiquette to discuss the poverty in the country with Mexican professionals, and one should not inquire about the well-being of a female family member in Saudi Arabia.

3. Presentation

Be sure that your presentation is concise, fact-based and easy to follow. Being thoroughly prepared for the presentation and ready to answer any questions is likely to make new clients more at ease when it comes to doing business with you.

4. Deciding on strategy

When you are deciding which negotiation strategy to use, consider the negotiation etiquette of the professionals you are working with is imperative. For example, in the U.S., it is appropriate to use "hard selling" or persuasion to get a businessperson to side with you in the negotiation process. However, in countries like Australia this is inappropriate and could result in the end of a potentially positive business relationship. In the Middle East and parts of Africa, bargaining is common and expected—both sides make offers on an item or service until a satisfactory price is reached.

5. Waiting for a decision

In many companies, the final negotiation decision is made from the top down, meaning that executives will likely have additional meetings to determine the negotiation outcome. Being patient and accommodating during this time shows that you respect the process and are not simply focused on getting "your way". Following up with the negotiation proceedings in the appropriate way, such as sending a short e-mail, will show that you are genuinely interested but don't want to seem too pushy.

🔗 Knowledge Related

Non-verbal Etiquette in Business Negotiation across Cultures

Non-verbal communication conveys meaning from body language. Body language includes eye contact, posture, facial expression and gesture. Due to our cultural differences in non-verbal communication, we can occasionally offend others unintentionally. There are a few examples of differences in non-verbal communication that may vary significantly depending upon cultural background.

Eye Contact: Eye contact is one form of non-verbal communication where the differences are most remarkable. Western cultures mostly consider eye contact to be a positive gesture. It shows respect, attentiveness, confidence and honesty. Other cultures such as Asian, Middle Eastern and Hispanic do not take it positively. Eye contact is taken as rude and even offensive, thus should be avoided at all costs.

Head Movements: In cultures in the Middle East, the head movement for "Yes" is just the opposite of the head movement for "Yes" in almost any other culture. You can imagine how confusing it can be. In such cases expressing "Yes" or "No" in a verbal communicative way would be much easier.

Hand and Arm Gestures: While in some cases a particular gesture means nothing to a representative of another culture, in other cases gestures such as a thumbs up can be interpreted differently. It is taken as an "Okay" sign in many cultures which is not offensive whereas it has a vulgar meaning in others such as Iran and Latin American.

Physical Space: People from different cultures have a different tolerance for physical distance between each other. In Latin America and the Middle East the acceptable distance is much shorter than what most Europeans and Americans feel comfortable with. People have specific personal space which they do not want intruded. In some cultures, even close physical contact between strangers is acceptable.

Touching: Shaking hands is considered to be acceptable in many cultures, even between strangers. Similarly kissing, patting on the shoulder, hugs, embraces or touching other bodily parts aren't. Many people in Asia and other parts of the world are more conservative and such actions are interpreted as an offense or even a violation of one's private space. This is why you should be careful with touching. Touching is considered rude in many cultures.

5.2.3　Differences in Negotiating across Cultures

Successful negotiating across cultures requires agility and an understanding of the nuances of the culture you are dealing with. While the desire to secure the best deal is the same in any negotiation, and the route to achieving this varies greatly between cultures.

知识储备：不同
国家的谈判风格

 Knowledge Related

Classifications of Cultures

In a high-context culture more attention is paid to what's happening in and around the message than to the message itself. Japan and China are some of the best examples of high-context cultures, in addition to Brazil, Argentina, Spain, and many nations throughout Africa and the Middle East.

知识链接：
文化的分类

In a low-context culture is that people pay more attention to the event itself rather than to the context which surrounds the event or the message. Cultures with western European roots rely more heavily on low-context communication. These include Australia, Canada, New Zealand, and the United States, as well as much of Europe, as shown in Figure 5-1.

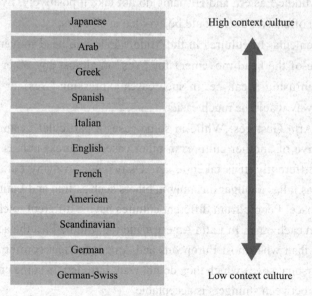

Figure5-1　High Context and Low Context Countries

5.2.4　Signing Ceremony Etiquette after Negotiations

1. Preparation for the signing ceremony

1）Arrange the signing hall

The signing hall will be arranged in accordance with different types of signatures and the customs of different countries. Generally, a rectangular table is set up in the signature hall as a signature table. The tabletop is covered with a tablecloth, and two chairs are placed behind the table as the seats for the signatures of both parties, facing the main entrance. The respective texts are placed in front of the seats, and signed stationery is placed on the top of the texts. A flag stand is placed in the middle of the signing table of the international business negotiation agreement, and the flags of the signatory countries are hung.

2）Make proper seating arrangement

For bilateral signing ceremony, side-by-side seating is the most common. The signing table is placed horizontal to the door and there are two chairs. All participants will be behind the table. The signatories sit in the middle and other staffs stand behind them. The guest should sit on the right side behind the signing table according to international business practices. For multilateral signing ceremonies, the signing table is the same, but there is one chair behind the table. Each signatory will go to the signing table when it is his or her turn and then return to his or her original seat.

3）Prepare the documentation, stationery, national flag and other items for signing

Flag etiquette is very strict and it is essential that flag protocols and rules are followed correctly. National flag of one country should never be flown above another national flag on the same staff as this would suggest superiority, or conversely, inferiority of one flag, or nation, over another. The national flag should never be allowed to drag along the ground. A tattered or faded flag should be removed and replaced with a new flag. Due care and consideration must be taken to ensure that the national flag is always flown the correct way up. As a sign of honor and respect, the national flag of a guest party should be put on the right side on the signing table.

2. The procedure of signing ceremony

（1）Firstly, participants from both parties enter the signing hall at the same time.

（2）Then the signatories take their seats and others stand behind their signatory.

（3）The signatories sign their own copy first.

（4）Then the assistants of both sides pass on the signed copy to the signatory of the other party for signature.

（5）Both parties exchange the signed copy and shake hands.

（6）Then champagne is served to celebrate the signing of the agreement.

（7）A group photo is usually taken in the end.

When taking group photos on international business occasions, the international practice should be followed. The principle of "Right is superior" should be emphasized, that is, the host should be in the middle, the guest of honor should be on his/her right, and the other personnel of both parties should be lined up in order of "host left and guest right". In short, it stresses the right side is superior to the left side.

Extended Reading

Scan the QR code, read the passage about "Dos and Don'ts of Business Negotiating" and finish the following tasks.

拓展阅读　商务
谈判注意事项

After-reading tasks

When you finish reading the text above, finish the following tasks.

Task 1　Read the statements and decide whether they are true or not. Mark "T" for true and "F" for false.

（1）One of the most effective negotiation strategies is preparation. （　　）

（2）The most effective negotiators follow the 80/20 rule: Talk 80% of the time and listen 20% of the time. （　　）

（3）Setting a bottom line will enable you to know when to step back from negotiations and when to move forward. （　　）

（4）The best negotiation tactics are those that focus on developing a mutually beneficial deal for both parties. （　　）

（5）If you go into business negotiations with a open mind, you may miss an unexpected opportunity you would have never thought to consider otherwise. （　　）

Task 2　Critical thinking

（1）What negotiating etiquette rules are mentioned above?

（2）What other rules should we also pay attention to?

Basic Knowledge Test

Read the statements and decide whether they are true or not. Mark "T" for true and "F" for false.

（1）Before the negotiations officially begin, it is essential that you present yourself as friendly and polite to give the impression of trustworthiness. （　　）

（2）Long tables are "fair". Round tables have a place for a "chairperson". Square tables have corners you can sit across. （　　）

同步测试：汉语
版 –M5T2 判断
正误

（3）For bilateral signing ceremony, side-by-side seating is the most common. The signing table is placed horizontal to the door and there are two chairs. All participants will be behind the table. （　　）

（4）Canadians aim for a zero-sum result, meaning one side's loss is the other side's gain. Information is used as power. （　　）

（5）When you are deciding which negotiation strategy to use, consider the negotiation etiquette of the professionals you are working with is essential. （　　）

 **Case Study**

● **Case 1**

When Mr. Kōnosuke Matsushita, the founder of Panasonic Electric Co., Ltd., first made his debut, he was probed by his competitor by greeting, which caused him a great loss. When he first arrived in Tokyo to negotiate with a wholesaler, the wholesaler kindly greeted him and said, "Is this our first-time dealing? I haven't seen you before." Mr. Matsushita respectfully replied, "Yes, this is my first time in Tokyo. I am looking forward to working with you." It was this ordinary greeting that gave the wholesaler important information: Mr. Matsushita is a novice. The wholesaler went on, "Then what is your price?" Mr. Matsushita replied, "the cost is 20 yen per piece, and I am planning to sell at 25 yen." The wholesaler seized the chance and said, "Since it is your first time doing business in Tokyo, why not lower your price to open up new market? How about 20 yen per piece?" There is no doubt that the inexperienced Mr. Matsushita suffered a great loss in this transaction.

Discussion: What accounts for Mr. Matsushita's great loss? What can we learn from this case?

● **Case 2**

A British businessman went to Iran to discuss the details of contract with an Iranian company. During his stay, he respected the traditions of Islam and avoided any political topics in the negotiation with his Iranian business partner. Everything went very well. On the day of signing the contract, he was so happy that he gave his Iranian partner a thumbs up when they both were seated. Almost immediately, his Iranian partner stood up from his seat and left the conference room without saying anything. The British businessman didn't know what happened.

Discussion: Why did the Iranian leave the room looking offended?

 Skills Training Tasks

International Business Negotiation Etiquette

Tian'an Import and Export Company invited United Arab Emirates Khandji Trading Co. for business negotiations. Tianan Import and Export Company is the exporter of electronic products, and the guest, Kanji Trading Company of the UAE, is the importer. The two sides held a business negotiation on a new mobile phone product, mainly focusing on the price, packing, modes of shipment, modes of payment, etc.; they finally reached an agreement and held a signing ceremony.

微课：非言语礼仪

Scan the following QR codes to complete the tasks.

5.2 任务工作单　　5.2 任务实施单　　5.2 任务检查单　　5.2 任务评价单

 Curriculum Ideology and Politics

Deepening Exchanges and Mutual Learning among Civilizations for an Asian Community with a Shared Future

Diversity spurs interaction among civilizations, which in turn promotes mutual learning and their further development. We need to promote exchanges and mutual learning among countries, nations and cultures around the world, and strengthen popular support for jointly building a community with a shared future for both Asia and humanity as a whole.

First, we need to respect each other and treat each other as equals. All civilizations are rooted in their unique cultural environment. Each embodies the wisdom and vision of a country or nation, and each is valuable for being uniquely its own. Civilizations only vary from each other, just as human beings are different only in terms of skin color and the language used. No civilization is superior over others.

Second, we need to uphold the beauty of each civilization and the diversity of civilizations in the world. Each civilization is the crystallization of human creation, and each is beautiful in its own way. The aspiration for all that is beautiful is a common pursuit of humanity that nothing can hold back. Civilizations don't have to clash with each other; what is needed are eyes to see the beauty in all civilizations. We should keep our own civilizations dynamic and create conditions for other civilizations to flourish. Together we can make the garden of world civilizations colorful and vibrant.

Third, we need to stay open and inclusive and draw on each other's strengths. All living organisms in the human body must renew themselves through metabolism; otherwise, life would come to an end. The same is true for civilizations. Long-term self-isolation will cause a civilization to decline, while exchanges and mutual learning will sustain its development. A civilization can flourish only through exchanges and mutual learning with other civilizations.

Fourth, we need to advance with the times and explore new ground in development. For a civilization to endure, efforts must be made to keep it alive and build on its heritage from one generation to the next. More importantly, a civilization needs to adapt itself to the changing times and break new ground. The history of world civilizations tells us that every civilization needs to advance with the times and take in the best of its age in order to develop itself. We need to come up with new ideas to add impetus and inspiration to the development of our civilizations. With these efforts, we will deliver achievements for our civilizations to transcend time and space and have a lasting appeal.

Discussion: What is your understanding of "Uphold the beauty of each civilization and the diversity of civilizations in the world."?

Chinese Etiquette

The Four Books and the Five Classics

The Four Books and the Five Classics were the canonical works of the Confucian culture in the feudal society in ancient China. The Four Books refers to *The Great Learning*, *The Doctrine of the Mean, Confucian Analects and The Works of Mencius*. And The Five Classics includes *The Book of Poetry, The Book of History, The Book of Rites, The Book of Changes*, and *The Spring and Autumn Annals*. The Five Classics got its name during the reign of Emperor Wudi of the Han Dynasty, and there emerged a group of scholars responsible for the interpretation of these classics. The Four Books are short for *The Texts and Annotations of the Four Books*, which were compiled and annotated by Zhu Xi, a Neo-Confucian scholar of the Southern Song Dynasty to establish his own theoretical system or Principles. Collectively called The Four Books and The Five Classics, they cover such a wide range of subjects as literature, history, philosophy, politics, economics, education, moral ethics, geology, arts, science and technology, etc. and are the most important textbooks for the Confucian scholars to disseminate the educational thoughts of the Confucian School and a must for ancient scholars who had to pass the imperial competitive examination to become government officials. In short, they have a far-reaching influence on the way of existence, intellectual quality, moral ethics and esthetic values of the Chinese nation.

模块 5
商务活动礼仪

 模块导读

　　商务礼仪本质上是与同事、客户或顾客建立关系。礼仪，尤其是商务礼仪，仅是一种通过展示自己的优点来最大限度地发挥商业潜力的手段。通过改进商务礼仪，会提升成功的机会。在国际商业中取得成功的关键是理解文化在国际商业中的作用。无论哪个行业，文化差异都会直接影响企业的盈利能力。增加对商业中国际文化差异的了解有助于建立国际竞争力，并使企业获得竞争优势。

任务 1

国际会展礼仪

◎ 学习目标

■ **素养目标**
- 培养"尊重与自信"的处事态度。
- 培养弘扬文明、和谐、爱国、友善等价值观。
- 强化绿色会展与可持续性发展理念。

■ **知识目标**
- 了解国际会展礼仪的重要性。
- 掌握国际会展礼仪的基本原则。
- 掌握组织与参加国际会展的各种注意事项。

■ **能力目标**
- 能够组织展览会。
- 能够得体地完成展前邀请、展中服务以及展会跟进工作。

情境导入

情境：一家从事纺织品业务的中国外贸公司赴 2017 年迪拜商品交易会。他们带去了适合中东市场的畅销面料，希望在这次展会上吸引更多客户。这是中国外贸公司员工弗洛拉首次参加迪拜商品交易会。

顾客：（满脸笑容）嗨，我是迪拜国际贸易有限公司的，我对你们的产品很感兴趣。

弗洛拉：（脸上露出微笑，与顾客眼神交流）欢迎来到我们的展台。我们公司从事纺织业务已有 20 年，产品在迪拜颇受欢迎。这是我们在迪拜的畅销样本，这是我的名片。

顾客：（双手拿着名片，走近看产品）很高兴见到你，弗洛拉。这是我的名片。我想更多地了解产品及其价格。

弗洛拉双手接过名片，看了看，然后把它放进袋子里。但就在这时，她闻到了浓烈的香水味，她无法容忍。弗洛拉皱起眉头，戴上口罩。

弗洛拉：（戴着口罩）这是我们产品的小册子，包括价格、设计等。

顾客：（犹豫地拿着小册子）好的，我会看看的。

这位顾客尴尬而失望地离开了展台。弗洛拉不明白为什么顾客突然离开了。

讨论：为什么顾客失望又尴尬地离开了展台？

知识储备

5.1.1　展前邀请礼仪

1. 对邀约客户进行分类

对客户群进行分类才能做到有的放矢，开展有效的邀约工作。总体来说，客户群分为以下三种。

A 类：目标型客户。已有良好的合作基础，采购意向大。

B 类：潜在型客户。还未成交，但是前期有较多往来邮件并询价。

C 类：普通型客户。前期有零星往来邮件，但是未询价。

A 类客户属于展会的专业采购商，签订协议意向很大。B 类客户属于潜力股，需要向其详细介绍公司及产品，表达合作诚意与合作意向。C 类客户为展会一般观众，可以向其简单介绍公司及产品。

2. 展前邀约方式

展前邀约一般采用电子邀请函、公开发布、电话邀请等方式。针对不同的客户，可以采取不同的邀约方式。

电子邀请函：比较广泛的客户邀约方式之一。需要选择恰当的时间，对有针对性的客户进行一对一发送，而不要群发邮件。

公开发布：在各大社交媒体软件如 LinkedIn、Facebook、Twitter 等，等待发布企业参展信息。恰当地使用社交软件，可以提升营销效果。通过社交软件发布内容时，一定要注意发布内容的独特性和时效性。

电话邀请：针对极其重要的客户，除了发送电子邀请函外，还可以通过电话邀请，直接加强沟通效果。

3. 展前电子邀请函

1）展前电子邀请函写作技巧

（1）简明扼要

最重要的是在电子邀请函中回答以下基本问题：谁、何时、何地、为什么。

（2）迅速

一般来说，建议提前6周左右与当地客户联系，并在活动前2个月内与国际客户联系，以便他们安排旅行和住宿。

2）展前电子邀请函模板

贸易展前电子邀请函样本是专门针对长期客户的。根据上面的要点，可以设计成适合任何类型的活动或客户的电子邀请函。也可以根据客户习惯和禁忌设计一下版面。例如，如果向俄罗斯客户发送邀请卡，应避免使用黄色，因为俄罗斯人比较忌讳黄色，认为黄色不吉利。

5.1.2　展中服务礼仪

1. 展台礼仪基本原则

首先，要有一个合适的展台设计，让展台的空间舒适而有"家"的感觉。一个舒适的空间，不仅可以让与会者看到产品和了解品牌，还可以放松、聊天，甚至可以连接到Wi-Fi并为手机充电。提供咖啡和饼干也可以吸引与会者。

其次，保持展位整洁。不要在展位上饮食，也不要把杯子、瓶子和用过的盘子放在展位周围。

2. 展台工作人员基本展位礼仪规则

1）展位工作人员职责及销售脚本

除销售脚本或"电梯游说"外，展台上的公司代表还应准备好回答基本问题或知道从哪里获取更多信息。展台还应始终由至少一名具有该专业知识或权限的人员管理，并且该人员应随时向展台人员和与会者提供专业知识解答。

📎 **知识链接**

电 梯 游 说

电梯游说（或电梯演讲）是对自己或与特定听众（通常是老板或面试官）分享想法的30～60秒的总结。之所以这样命名，是因为它应该足够短，足够吸引人，以至于你可以在乘坐电梯时自我介绍。电梯推销是一种快速与那些对你一无所知的人分享你的资历和专业知识的方式。

电梯游说主要回答三个问题："我是谁？""我该做什么？""我的要求是什么？"

2）着装要给人留下深刻印象

一些公司有公司服装（如马球衫、运动外套、正装衬衫等），而另一些公司则为员工提供关于颜色和服装风格的个人服装指导。以下是在展会期间着装的便捷提示：

根据所展示的市场和环境着装。

不要过分朴素，要注重形象。

如果你有公司制服，可优先选择制服。

利用个人魅力和个性单品从人群中脱颖而出。

选择舒适的衣服和鞋子。

3）接待与互动

顾客在最初被展台或品牌吸引后，展台人员是吸引客户的关键。以下肢体语言技巧有助于传达专业和平易近人的风度：

站起来，在展台前迎接与会者。

微笑并与来自四面八方的与会者进行眼神交流。

不要交叉双臂或双腿，双手不要放在口袋里。

避免坐立不安，倚靠展台墙壁和家具。

不要在展会上吃或嚼口香糖。

不要发短信、浏览手机或打电话。

5.1.3　展后跟进礼仪

1. 后续跟进礼仪基本原则

1）及时

在 24 小时内跟进。如果展览在周五，则在周一跟进。在你的竞争对手之前进入。你越早跟进潜在客户，将其转化为销售的机会就越大。

2）信息具体

（1）你是谁？不要用"亲爱的先生 / 女士"这种泛称，而要用客户的名字。

（2）我们在哪里见面？始终在主题标题和电子邮件文本中添加展览名称。

在后续电子邮件中，你可以添加展台照片。

3）通过各种方式联系你的潜在客户

活动结束后的几周内，通过 LinkedIn 致电或互动，或发送多封电子邮件——这是你的黄金机会窗口。

2. 后续跟进电子邮件模板

确保你的 B2B 电子邮件营销策略模板符合以下条件：及时（考虑一些邮件的自动跟进，但不要听起来像自动发送）；篇幅恰当（足以让你的潜在客户心心念念，但不足以惹恼他们）；定制的；不是销售——只是友好而不是纠缠不休。

1）"很高兴见到你"。

建议主题行：很高兴在 [展会名称] 见到您！

2）请求后续聊天

建议的主题行：让我们抓住 [痛点]！

发送后续聊天邮件后，就可以使用 HubSpot 远程会议工具进行沟通。

3）发送知识性资源

建议主题行：帮助解决 [痛点] 的资源。

在这个活动之后跟进的邮件模板中，你用的是内容营销，目的是提供信息，让对方感到心情愉快。这可以是一篇博客文章、常见问题解答页面或任何你认为相关的资源。

4）缓解他们的痛点

建议主题行：我如何帮助 [公司名称]？

5）更大、更紧急的报价

建议主题行：别忘了 [优惠促销]！

 同步测试

扫码做题。

同步测试：汉语版 –M5T1 判断正误

 案例分析

露西一周后要去参加莫斯科国际包装展览会。在展览会会前两天，她向潜在的客户群发送了展前邀请邮件（电子邮件略）。展览会当天，露西却发现客户很少，而且客户几乎没有成交意向。

讨论：露西为什么没能吸引潜在客户到她的展位？

 实训项目

国际会展礼仪

1. 实训目的

通过训练，掌握国际会展礼仪，并合理安排国际会展。

2. 实训内容

（1）背景资料：青岛贝来国际贸易有限公司要参加美国纽约国际办公文具展览会，以下是参会信息。

① 展览信息。

参展地：美国纽约。

展馆：贾维茨会议中心（美国纽约州纽约市西 34 街 655 号，邮编：10001-1188）。

时间：2023 年 02 月 05 日—08 日。

摊位号：B2 馆 101。

② 参会信息。

参展单位：青岛贝来国际贸易有限公司。

参加展览会人员：商务助理莉莉、销售经理肖恩、总经理汤姆。

本次展览亮点：公司推出了最新产品"绿色书写板"（俄罗斯进口樟子松木边框：环保、轻便、耐腐蚀、耐潮湿、美观），公司针对此次展览会推出"成交额 50 万美元以上，5% 折扣优惠活动"。

（2）以小组为单位，完成以下任务。

① 给公司潜在客户（迈克尔·汉福德）发一封电子邮件，邀请他参观你的展位。

② 编写销售脚本。

③ 角色扮演。练习在展台上向潜在客户介绍你的公司和产品。

④ 假设迈克尔·汉福德对你的产品表现出极大的兴趣，给他写一封后续邮件。

3. 实训要求

（1）采取"组内异质，组间同质"的原则，将学生分为若干小组，每组 4～6 人。

（2）每组提交一份展前电子邀请函、展中销售脚本、展后后续跟进邮件。

（3）每组展示本组的工作成果。

4. 实训考核

（1）评价方式：采取小组自评、小组互评、教师评价、企业导师评价四维评价方式，总评成绩 = 小组自评×20% + 小组互评×20% + 教师评价×30% + 企业导师评价×30%。

（2）评价指标：从素质目标、知识目标、能力目标 3 方面进行评价。

5.1 任务工作单	5.1 任务实施单	5.1 任务检查单	5.1 任务评价单

 思政课堂

绿色展会，中国在行动

2022 年 7 月 25 日，第二届中国国际消费品博览会暨全球消费论坛开幕式在海口举行。本届消博会推行"绿色办展、低碳办会"的理念，突出绿色低碳办展，专门出台了绿色办展指引，在运营、搭建、交通、餐饮方面全方位践行绿色低碳理念，努力打造环保节能型展会的标杆，突出履行社会责任。搭建环节，本次消博会展台施工单位、会展中心运营方、主场服务商签订《第二届消博会绿色低碳会展倡议书》，提出如下倡议：提高绿色低碳意识、鼓励绿色低碳设计、使用绿色低碳材料、奉行绿色低碳搭建、共创绿色低碳会展。服务环节，组委会使用能生物降解、易于回收材料制成的一次性餐饮具；餐厅的装饰采用环保无污染材料，服务员与食品进行直接接触时必须佩戴防护用品。在物流上，采用绿色运输方式，使用节俭燃料、清洁燃料，实现节能减排。在垃圾处理上，秘书处切实落实禁塑措施，同时对展会区域垃圾进行分类和无害化处理，并将严格督促展馆运营方执行垃圾分类处理，展馆内设置垃圾桶均为分类垃圾桶，为垃圾减量化、资源化、无害化处理奠定基础。

讨论：党的二十大报告指出"推动绿色发展，促进人与自然和谐共生"。中国倡导的绿色会展是如何体现推动绿色发展的？

中华礼仪

在中国，数字除计数的功能之外，还具有等级、秩序和自然象征等丰富的含义。中国

的古典道家思想提出：道生一，一生二，二生三，三生万物。这里一二三，象征着宇宙中的基本秩序。在中国古老的《易经》中，对于三、五、六、九等数字，有着更加神秘的解释。五行的理论，概括了自然界中五种基本能量的关系。在建筑等环境设计里，中国人也特别重视。中国人喜欢探讨数字的神奇作用。在数字技术特别发达的今天，人们对数字的探索永无止境。

任务 2

国际商务谈判礼仪

◎ 学习目标

■ **素养目标**
- 培养"尊重与自信"的处事态度。
- 培养弘扬文明、和谐、爱国、友善等价值观。
- 增强文化自信。

■ **知识目标**
- 了解商务谈判礼仪在商务活动中的重要性。
- 掌握国际商务活动中商务谈判的基本原则。
- 掌握不同国家商务谈判的风格。

■ **能力目标**
- 能够得体地完成商务谈判前、谈判中、谈判后的任务。

 情境导入

　　情境：李大卫毕业后进入一家大型出口公司，由于表现出色，他最近被提升为销售经理。上个月他的公司与一位重要的美国客户就开发新产品进行了谈判。大卫负责谈判。前几周，他一直在认真准备谈判。谈判进展顺利，双方最终达成了协议。两家公司决定签署合同，并于上周一举行了签约仪式。大卫负责布置签约大厅。当双方进入签约大厅时，客方谈判代表停下脚步，愤怒地离开了大厅。为什么会这样？大卫所在公司仔细检查了房间的布置情况，发现客人公司的国旗被放在签约台的左侧。

　　讨论：客方谈判代表为什么生气？

 知识储备

5.2.1　谈判前的准备工作

1. 商务谈判着装礼仪

谈判人员在商务会议上的着装、说话方式、所穿戴的配饰都会影响对方。虽然着装并不能代表个性，但如果想赢得对方的尊重，就必须穿着得体。

2. 安排会议室

1）桌子

许多房间的中央有桌子，周围有椅子。圆桌会议表示"公平"。长条桌有一个"主席"的位置。方桌有角落，谈判者可以坐在对面。

2）椅子

确保有足够的椅子，让每个人都能坐下，但要去掉很多额外的东西（除非你想营造一种特殊的效果）。

3）点心

在休息时可以提供饮料和食物，这样会让人们感到舒适。

3. 其他准备事项

1）收集谈判代表及公司的信息

信息可能包括谈判者的人数、职位、年龄、性别甚至爱好、特殊的饮食习惯等。

2）起草一份接待计划和谈判议程

在客人到达之前，通过电子邮件或传真将议程发送给谈判方。征求他们的意见，并做出可能的修改。如果不能满足客人要求，请向他们解释。

3）会见谈判代表并为他们送行

与谈判者核实他们到达的时间和地点。提前派工作人员到机场或火车站等待来访方。迎接和送别的级别和规模由 3 个因素决定：

（1）谈判代表的级别和目的；

（2）谈判者之间的关系；

（3）惯例。

基本规则是让同一行业中具有相同或相似职级、头衔和地位的人负责迎接和送别。

4）预订酒店并安排住宿

选择合适的酒店，确保有良好的会议设施和便利的交通。为谈判代表预订足够的房间，以防人数超出预期。明确客人是否有特殊的用餐习惯或要求。

5）安排观光和购物

如果时间允许，可以安排一些旅游观光和购物。当客人想游览城市时，询问他们是否需要帮助。

6）客人离开时送小礼物

在与外国商人做生意时，要了解送什么礼物最合适，以及什么时候可以交换礼物。

5.2.2 谈判中的商务礼仪

1. 问候

在商业界最常见的问候方式是握手。然而如果在法国或巴西等国家，亲吻脸颊是常态。如果在中东地区，在问候异性时最好点头致谢。

2. 寒暄

商务人士在谈判开始前进行寒暄，在谈判结束后进行简短交谈也是很常见的。这让每个人都有时间变得更加舒适，是建立持久商务关系的关键。然而在芬兰和德国等一些国家，闲聊并不是商业文化的一部分，会议会准时开始。谈判结束后，德国或芬兰的商务人士可能会举办晚宴进行非正式交谈。在墨西哥和沙特阿拉伯等国家，闲聊是意料之中的事，但最好知道哪些话题是禁区。例如，与墨西哥商人讨论该国的贫困状况是不恰当的，也不应该询问沙特阿拉伯女性家庭成员的情况。

3. 演讲汇报

确保你的汇报简明扼要，以事实为基础，易于理解。为演讲汇报做好充分准备，并准备好回答任何问题，这可能会让新客户在与你开展业务时更放心。

4. 决定谈判策略

当你决定使用哪种谈判策略时，考虑与你共事的商务人士的谈判礼仪是必不可少的。例如，在美国，在谈判过程中使用"硬推销"或说服手段让商人站在你这一边是合适的。然而，在澳大利亚，这是不合适的，可能会导致良好商业关系的结束。在中东和非洲部分国家或地区，讨价还价是常见的，也是意料之中的事——双方会就某一物品或服务进行价格磋商，直到达成令人满意的结果。

5. 等待决策

在许多公司，最终的谈判决定是自上而下做出的，这意味着高管们可能会举行额外的会议来决定谈判结果。在这段时间里保持耐心和包容，表明你尊重这个过程，而不是简单地专注于"按自己的方式"。以适当的方式跟进谈判过程，例如发送一封简短的电子邮件，表明你确实感兴趣，但不能显得太急躁。

📎 知识链接

不同文化的商务谈判非言语礼仪

非言语交际通过肢体语言传达意义。肢体语言包括眼神交流、姿势、面部表情和手势。由于在非语言交流中的文化差异，我们偶尔会无意识地冒犯他人。由于文化背景不同，人们对非语言交流的理解可能会存在很大差异。

眼神交流：眼神交流是非语言交流的一种主要形式，其差异最为显著。西方文化大多认为眼神交流是一种积极的姿态。它表现出尊重、专注、自信和诚实。亚洲、中东和西班牙等国家或地区则持相反的观点。眼神接触被认为是粗鲁甚至令人反感的，因此应尽最大可能避免。

头部运动：在中东国家或地区的文化中，表示"是"的头部运动与其他文化正好相反。你可以想象它是多么令人困惑。在这种情况下，以口头交流的方式表达"是"或"否"会容易得多。

手部和手臂手势：虽然在某些情况下，一个特定的手势对于另一种文化的代表来说毫无意义。但在其他情况下，竖起大拇指等手势可以有不同的解释。在许多文化中，它被视为"好"的标志，并不令人反感，但在伊朗和拉丁美洲等国家或地区中，则有粗俗的含义。

身体距离：来自不同文化背景的人对彼此之间的身体距离有不同的容忍度。在拉丁美洲和中东等国家或地区，可接受的距离比大多数欧洲人和美国人感到舒服的距离要短得多。人们都有特定的个人空间，他们不希望被侵犯。在某些文化中，即使是陌生人之间的密切身体接触，也是可以接受的。

身体接触：在许多文化中，握手被认为是可以接受的，即使是在陌生人之间也是如此。同样，亲吻、拍拍肩膀、搂抱、拥抱或触摸其他身体部位是不可接受的——亚洲和世界其他地区的许多人更加保守。这种行为被解释为冒犯甚至侵犯一个人的私人空间。这就是为什么你应该对触摸持谨慎的态度。在许多文化中，触摸被认为是粗鲁的。

5.2.3　不同国家的谈判风格

成功的跨文化谈判需要灵活性和对你正在接触的文化细微差别的理解。尽管在任何谈判中都希望达成最佳交易，但实现这一目标的途径因文化而异。扫码了解美国、加拿大、阿联酋和澳大利亚的谈判风格。

5.2.4　谈判后的签约仪式

1. 签约仪式的准备工作

1）布置签约大厅

签约大厅的安排和布置要根据签约仪式的类型和各国的风俗习惯。一般来讲，在签约大厅中要设置一个长方形的桌子作为签约桌。桌子上铺好桌布，桌子后面放着两把椅子作为双方签字的座位，面朝正门。各自的文本材料放在座位前面，签约的纸张放在文本的顶部。在国际商务谈判时，桌子中间要放置一个国旗架，并悬挂签署国的国旗。

2）安排座位

对于双边签字仪式，并排就座是最常见的。签约桌与门水平放置，有两把椅子。所有参与者都要在桌子后面。签字人坐在中间，其他工作人员站在他们后面。根据国际商业惯例，客人应坐在签约桌的右边。对于多边签字仪式，签字桌是一样的，但桌子后面通常只有一把椅子。每位签字人都会在轮到他的时候走到签约桌旁，签字完成后回到原来的座位上。

3）准备文本、文具、国旗和其他签字物品

摆放国旗的礼仪规则非常严格，正确遵守国旗礼仪和规则至关重要。在同一根旗杆上，一个国家的国旗永远不应该悬挂在另一个国家的国旗上方，因为这意味着一个国家比另一个国家更优越，或者相反。绝不允许国旗在地面上拖着。破损或褪色的国旗应取下，并更换为新旗。摆放国旗时，一定要谨慎地考虑，始终保持正确的方向和位置。为了表示尊敬，客人一方的国旗应放在签名桌的右侧。

 知识链接

文化的分类

在高语境文化中，人们更多地关注事件内部消息和周围发生的相关的环境信息，而不是事件本身。日本和中国是高语境文化的最佳示例，此外还有巴西、阿根廷、西班牙以及整个非洲和中东的许多国家或地区。

在低语境文化中，人们更关注事件本身，而不是围绕事件或信息的环境。源自西欧的文化更依赖低语境交流，包括澳大利亚、加拿大、新西兰和美国，以及欧洲大部分国家或地区，如图5-1所示。

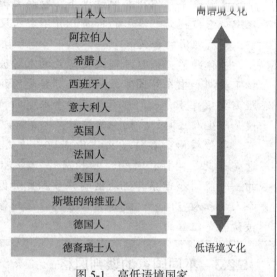

图 5-1　高低语境国家

2. 签约仪式的流程

（1）双方参会人员同时进入签约大厅。

（2）签署者就座，其他人站在签署者后面。

（3）签署者先在自己的副本上签名。

（4）双方的助手将签字的副本交给另一方的签署人签字。

（5）双方交换签名副本并握手。

（6）开香槟庆祝协议的签署。

（7）通常最后会合影留念。

在国际商务场合合影时，应遵守国际惯例，讲究"以右为尊"，即宜令主人居中，主宾居右，其他双方人员分主左宾右依次排开。简而言之，就是讲究"以右为上"。

 同步测试

扫码做题。

同步测试：汉语版 –M5T2 判断正误

 **案例分析**

● **案例 1**

日本松下电器公司创始人松下幸之助先生刚"出道"时，曾被对手以寒暄的形式探测了自己的底细，因而使自己产品的销售大受损失。当他第一次到东京，找批发商谈判时，刚一见面，批发商就友善地对他寒暄说："我们是第一次打交道吧？以前我好像没见过你。"批发商想用寒暄托词，来试探对手究竟是生意场上的老手还是新手。松下先生缺乏经验，恭敬地回答："我是第一次来东京，什么都不懂，请多关照。"正是这番极为平常的寒暄答复却使批发商获得了重要的信息：对方原来只是个新手。批发商问："你打算以什么价格卖出你的产品？"松下又如实地告知对方："我的产品每件成本是 20 元，我准备卖25 元。"批发商趁机杀价，"你首次来东京做生意，刚开张应该卖的更便宜些。每件 20 元，如何？"没有经验的松下先生在这次交易中吃了亏。

讨论：松下先生这次交易损失的原因是什么？

• **案例 2**

一名英国商人前往伊朗，与一家伊朗公司讨论合同细节。在逗留期间，他尊重伊斯兰教传统，在与伊朗商业伙伴的谈判中避免任何政治话题。一切都很顺利。在签署合同的当天，他非常高兴，在坐下时他对着伊朗合作伙伴竖起了大拇指。几乎就在同时，他的伊朗伙伴从座位上站起来，一言不发地离开了会议室。那个英国商人不知道发生了什么事。

讨论：为什么伊朗商人离开房间时看起来很生气？

 **实训项目**

掌握国际商务谈判礼仪

1. 实训目的

通过训练，掌握国际商务谈判礼仪。

2. 实训内容

（1）背景资料：天安进出口公司邀请阿联酋坎吉贸易公司进行商务谈判。天安进出口公司为电子产品出口商，客方阿联酋坎吉贸易公司为进口商。双方就一款最新手机产品进行商务谈判，主要围绕价格、包装、装运、付款方式等进行磋商。最终双方达成一致并进行签约仪式。

（2）以小组为单位，掌握国际商务谈判礼仪；列举谈判前的准备工作、模拟谈判中的商务礼仪和谈判后的签约。

3. 实训要求

（1）采取"组内异质，组间同质"的原则，将学生分为若干小组，每组 4～6 人。

（2）每组提交一份商务谈判礼仪实训报告，内容包括本案例展示以及跨文化交际中的商务谈判礼仪注意事项。

（3）每组讲解和展示本组的工作成果。

4. 实训考核

（1）评价方式：采取小组自评、小组互评、教师评价、企业导师评价四维评价方式，总评成绩 = 小组自评×20% + 小组互评×20% + 教师评价×30% + 企业导师评价×30%。

（2）评价指标：从素质目标、知识目标、能力目标 3 方面进行评价。

5.2 任务工作单

5.2 任务实施单

5.2 任务检查单

5.2 任务评价单

 **思政课堂**

深化文明交流互鉴　共建亚洲命运共同体

文明因多样而交流，因交流而互鉴，因互鉴而发展。我们要加强世界上不同国家、不同民族、不同文化的交流互鉴，夯实共建亚洲命运共同体、人类命运共同体的人文基础。

第一，坚持相互尊重、平等相待。每一种文明都扎根于自己的生存土壤，凝聚着一个国家、一个民族的非凡智慧和精神追求，都有自己存在的价值。人类只有肤色语言之别，文明只有姹紫嫣红之别，但绝无高低优劣之分。

第二，坚持美人之美、美美与共。每一种文明都是美的结晶，都彰显着创造之美。一切美好的事物都是相通的。人们对美好事物的向往，是任何力量都无法阻挡的！各种文明本没有冲突，只是要有欣赏所有文明之美的眼睛。我们既要让本国文明充满勃勃生机，又要为他国文明发展创造条件，让世界文明百花园群芳竞艳。

第三，坚持开放包容、互学互鉴。一切生命有机体都需要新陈代谢，否则生命就会停止。文明也是一样，如果长期自我封闭，必将走向衰落。交流互鉴是文明发展的本质要求。只有同其他文明交流互鉴、取长补短，才能保持旺盛生命活力。

第四，坚持与时俱进、创新发展。文明永续发展，既需要薪火相传、代代守护，更需要顺时应势、推陈出新。世界文明历史揭示了一个规律：任何一种文明都要与时偕行，不断吸纳时代精华。我们应该用创新增添文明发展动力、激活文明进步的源头活水，不断创造出跨越时空、富有永恒魅力的文明成果。

（资料来源：http://paper.ce.cn/jjrb/page/1/2019-05-16/01/2019051601_pdf.pdf）

讨论：党的二十大报告指出"全面推进中国特色大国外交，推动构建人类命运共同体"。如何理解文中的"美人之美、美美与共"？

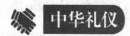 **中华礼仪**

四书五经

四书五经是中国古代封建社会儒家的经典书籍。四书是指《论语》《孟子》《大学》《中庸》，五经是指《诗经》《尚书》《礼记》《周易》《春秋》。汉武帝独尊儒术，置五经博士，专门研习五经。南宋时，大学者朱熹写成《四书章句集注》，简称《四书集注》，四书的名称就这样流传下来。四书五经的内容涉及文学、史学、哲学、政治、经济、教育、伦理、道德、天文、地理、艺术、科技等各个方面，是儒家施行儒学教化的重要教科书，是中国古代文人科举做官的必读书。对中国人的生存方式、心理素质、价值观念、审美观念等都产生了深远的影响。

Module 6

Banquet Etiquette

 Profile of the Module

In business, banquets have always been an important form of interpersonal communication. As early as in *The Book of Rites*, it is written that "the beginning of etiquette begins with food and drink", which indicates the close relationship between etiquette and diet. Since mankind entered civilisation, more attention has been paid to the etiquette of banquets, and the etiquette required for banquets has gradually become more standardised. In modern society, banqueting etiquette has developed and integrated even more, and the table has become a bridge to communicate feelings, exchange ideas and build careers. Banqueting activities take many forms and the etiquette is complicated. Mastering proper norms will help to promote the smooth development of business cooperation.

Task 1

Chinese Banquet Etiquette

 Learning Objectives

■ Moral Objectives
- To promote Chinese etiquette and establish cultural confidence.
- To cultivate students' global view and enhance their awareness of frugality.

■ Knowledge Objectives
- To master the basic procedures and etiquette requirements of Chinese banquet.
- To know the cultural differences between China and Western countries and get familiar with communication skills in Chinese business banquet.

- **Ability Objectives**
  - To be able to organize and participate in Chinese banquet following etiquette norms.

Lead-in: Case Study

Situation: On the evening of September 4, 2016, the G20 Summit Welcome Dinner was held at the Xizi Hotel in Hangzhou. It is a mammoth task catering to such illustrious guests, especially when the chefs have to consider various dietary restrictions but still need to display the best of Hangzhou haute cuisine.

The eventual inventive menu shows off the ingenuity and elegance of Chinese kitchen craft. The menu was completely pork-free but still managed to display the well-known fresh river fish in Hangzhou.

① Hors d'Oeuvres.

② Pine Mushroom Soup.

③ Sweet and Sour Mandarin Fish with Pine Nuts.

④ Stir-Fried Shrimps with Longjing Tea Leaves.

⑤ Orange-Flavored Crab Meat.

⑥ Hangzhou-Style Fillet Steak.

⑦ Braised Vegetables, Pastries, Fruits and Ice Cream, Coffee and Tea.

⑧ Red Wine Changyu 2012, Beijing China.

Food has always been a universal language cutting across boundaries and barriers. This dinner is considered as one of the best ways of international diplomacy. The organizers have chosen Hangzhou cuisine and showcased the perfect Chinese cuisine.

Chinese food is well loved all over the world and Brazilian President Michel Temer, for example, has admitted to being an ardent fan. The leaders attending the G20 Summit this time have tasted the historic Hangzhou cuisine cooked by a master chef in the beautiful scenery of Hangzhou.

（ Source: http://language.chinadaily.com.cn/2016-09/05/content_26705417.htm ）

Discussion:

（1）Food has always been a universal language. What information has the food of G20 conveyed?

（2）The menu was completely pork-free. Why is it arranged this way?

Basic Knowledge

As a state of ceremonies, China has always attached great importance to dieting etiquette. Banquet is not only about food, but also a way of business and cultural communication. Business banquets have traditionally been an essential part of doing business in China.

6.1.1   Categories of Chinese Banquet

Chinese banquets can be divided into formal banquets, casual banquets and family banquets.

微课：中餐宴请
种类

A formal banquet is grand and formal with three characteristics: designated attendees, designated time and a designated menu. Formal banquets have very strict requirements for the number of people present, the dress code and the seating arrangement.

Casual banquets are simple, with a preference for interpersonal interaction, and do not focus on scale and class. The venue for casual meals varies and there are fewer etiquette requirements. Generally speaking, only relevant people are invited to the banquet (spouses are usually not included), and there are no special requirements for dress and seating arrangements.

知识链接：国宴

A family banquet is held at home. The most important thing is to create an intimate, friendly and natural atmosphere. Generally, there are no special etiquette requirements for a family dinner. The male and female hosts act as chefs and waiters, jointly entertaining guests.

6.1.2   Etiquette for Attending Chinese Banquet

When attending a Chinese banquet, especially a formal banquet, people are supposed to follow strict and standardized procedures.

微课：中餐赴宴
礼仪

1. Prepare carefully

When you receive an invitation, you should reply as early as possible as to whether you will attend the banquet. If you are unable to attend it, you should explain and apologise to the host. Before attending a banquet, women should put on make-up and men should comb their hair and shave. If you are attending a family dinner, it is advised to prepare a gift for the hostess.

2. Be on time

Generally, it is better for guests to arrive 3-5 minutes earlier before the banquet starts. If for any reason you cannot make it on time, it is better to call the host in advance and explain the reason.

3. Be polite when taking a seat

Before entering the banquet hall, first make sure of your table and seating. When taking a seat, check whether you have sat with your name on the seat card and do not take a seat at random. If you are seated next to an elderly person or woman, offer to assist them to be seated first.

4. Pay attention to conversation

After the host and guest sit down, if you have tea, you can drink it gently. The guests may talk softly to those at the table and it is impolite to whisper to each other. What you talk about depends on who you are talking to.

5. Dine elegantly

When the host is making a toast, it is better to listen carefully and stop eating. Sit in a dignified manner and use Chinese tableware appropriately. Do not leave your seat and move around during the meal. Do not leave the table until the host has finished the meal and started to send the guests off.

6.1.3   Cuisine Order in Chinese Banquet

Traditionally, Chinese banqueting dishes consist of five parts: cold dishes, soups, hot dishes, desserts and fruits, and hot tea.

微课：中餐宴请
菜序

6.1.4   Ordering Dishes in Chinese Banquets

Business Banquets can tell how much the host has valued the guests. The following tips should be noted when we order food for a Chinese banquet.

Firstly, important business banquets must be ordered in advance in accordance with the budget for dishes and drinks. It is important to keep the number of dishes within the budget to avoid waste or lack of food. It is essential to ask your guests about diet taboos in advance. Avoid ordering food

微课：中餐点菜
技巧

that guests do not like, such as religious taboos or personal preferences. Consider your guests' cultural background and replace alcohol with beverages if alcohol is taboo in some countries. Secondly, if you need to order food in person, consider attendees' tastes. It is better to have both meat and vegetarian dishes at the table, with a mix of hot and cold diet. When ordering food, ask politely about people's taboos and preferences, and never ask for the price of a dish.

 Knowledge Related

Chinese Banqueting Menus

For high standard Chinese banquets, menus are often printed in advance and specially prepared for the occasion, marked in Chinese and in the language of the guest's country, showing great respect for the guest. When we are ordering dishes, in addition to considering the guests' food and cultural taboos, it is more acceptable to choose dishes that have obvious Chinese or local characteristics.

6.1.5   Dining Etiquette in China Banquet

Chinese are particular about food and the way they eat it. After you take a seat, the waiter will give you a towel to wipe the hands. If there are lobsters, chicken or fruit, a bowl of water may be served with some rose petals or lemon slices, which is not for drinking but for washing hands. At a standard Chinese banquet, the cold dish will be served first, then the soup, the hot dish, the main dish, the desserts and fruits at last. Here are some important tips for the table manners in China.

Be graceful and polite when taking food with chopsticks.

Don't make much noise when eating or drinking soup.

Don't talk with your mouth full.

Don't point at someone with chopsticks or play with chopsticks.

Don't pick teeth with toothpicks in front of guests.

When you fill the bowl with rice, it is better to have twice or more for one bowl. Don't insert chopsticks in the bowl with rice, as it indicates worshiping ancestors.

6.1.6　Use of Chinese Tableware

The biggest difference between Chinese and Western cuisine is the tableware used. Chinese tableware mainly consists of chopsticks, spoons, bowls and plates.

微课：中餐餐具
使用礼仪

1. Chopsticks

Chopsticks are used for picking up food. It is rude to use chopsticks to tickle or pick up anything other than food. When talking to someone, put your chopsticks down for a moment and do not tap your chopsticks against the bowl or plate to point at others with chopsticks. It is better to use serving chopsticks to pick up food when you eat with others.

2. Spoons

When using a spoon to take food, do not overfill it so that it will not spill over and stain the table. It is customary to use your right hand to take a spoon. If food is too hot, do not turn the spoon over and over or blow on it.

3. Plates

The function of a plate in Chinese banquet is to hold the food. Do not stack multiple plates on top of each other. Do not overload the plate with dishes. Food scraps, bones and fish spines should be placed gently at the front of the plate and removed by the waiter if necessary. Do not mix waste with dishes.

4. Bowls

知识链接：中餐
副餐具及筷子使
用禁忌

Bowls are used in Chinese cuisine to serve main courses and soups. Do not lift the bowl to eat. It is recommended to use chopsticks and spoons to assist in serving the food in the bowl. Do not pour any leftover food directly into your mouth.

6.1.7　Order of Tables and Seats in Chinese Banquet

In Chinese banquets, putting the right people in the right places is the highest treatment the host can give to his or her guests. Seating arrangements in Chinese cuisine vary with occasions and can be divided into two aspects: table arrangement and seating arrangement.

1. Table arrangement

The order of the tables is the order in which they are placed. Round tables are most commonly used in Chinese banquets. When we arrange the tables, basically the size and shape of the tables should be the same. In addition to the main table, which can be slightly larger, all other tables should be not too large or too small. Round tables can be arranged as follows:

微课：中餐桌次
庄次实册

Firstly, for the small banquet consisting of two tables, it can be arranged in a horizontal row or in a vertical row. When two tables are arranged horizontally, right-handed table is more honorable than left-handed one. The right and the left are determined by the position facing the main entrance. When the two tables are arranged vertically, the tables far from the door is more honorable than the table near the door. Arrangement for two tables in Chinese banquet is shown in the Figure 6-1 as follows.

For the banquet consisting of three or more tables, pay attention to the rules of "The position facing the door is more honorable", "The right position is more honorable" and "The position far away from the door is more honorable". Besides, other tables should also be taken into account in terms of their proximity to the main table. Usually, the closer to the main table, the more honorable the table is, and vice versa. Arrangement for three or more tables in Chinese banquet is shown in the Figure 6-2 as follows.

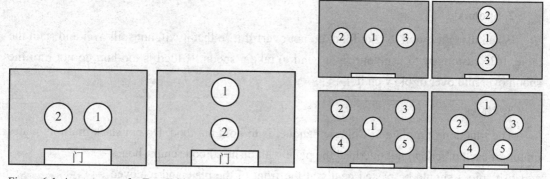

Figure 6-1 Arrangement for Two Tables in Chinese Banquet

Figure 6-2   Arrangement for Three or More Tables in Chinese Banquet

2. Seating arrangement

Three rules should be followed in Chinese Banquet seating arrangements.

The right position is more honorable than the left position: two people sit side by side, usually with the right as the more honorable seat and the left as the inferior seat. Chinese food is often served in a clockwise direction, so those seated on the right are given priority over those seated on the left.

The middle seat is more honorable: when three people are seated together, the person sitting in the middle takes precedence over the people on either side.

Facing the door is superior: when we are dining, it is customary that those seats facing the front door are considered to be more honorable and those seats with their backs to the front door are thought to be inferior position.

Besides, due to the different customs in different regions, it is recommended the guests obey the host's arrangement.

Seat arrangement in Chinese banquet is shown in the Figure 6-3 as follows.

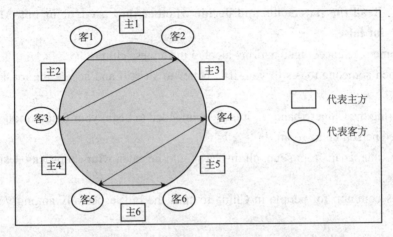

Figure 6-3　Seat Arrangement in Chinese Banquet

6.1.8　The Toast Etiquette in Chinese Banquet

In Chinese banquets, it is often said "No wine, no banquet". To some extent, Chinese wine culture is characteristic of Chinese banquets. Generally speaking, the order of toasting at a Chinese banquet is as follows.

微课：中餐敬酒礼仪

The host makes a brief speech and everyone drinks the first glass of wine together.

The host makes a toast to the guest of honour.

The accompanying guest makes a toast to the guest of honour.

The guest makes a toast to the host in return and the accompanying guests makes a toast to each other.

The host proposes a final toast to end the banquet by thanking the guests for coming.

Remember the following rules when making a toast.

It is advised to stand up and raise your glass with both hands when making a toast. More than one person can toast to the same person. Try not to toast to more than one person. When lifting your glass, keep your own glass slightly below the other person's glass. Do not urge others to over drink but to persuade them to drink moderately.

📖 Extended Reading

Scan the QR code, read the passage about "Chinese Dining Etiquette: 15 Rules for Eating in China" and finish the following tasks.

拓展阅读：中餐
就餐礼仪的 15
条规则

After-reading tasks

When you finish reading the text above, finish the following tasks.

Task 1　Read the statements and decide whether they are true or not. Mark "T" for true and "F" for false.

（1）Women are encouraged to drink alcohol in Chinese culture. （　　）

（2）When someone toasts to you, it is better to sit still and accept the toast in response.

（　　）

（3）During the Chinese banquet, it is recommended to begin your first introduction with the most respected person in the room. （　　）

（4）In China, apart from soup, all dishes should be eaten with chopsticks. Using fingers is not acceptable. （　　）

（5）It is common for people in China to split the bill, especially among young people.

（　　）

Task 2　Critical thinking

Do you agree with the author concerning dining etiquette in China? Can you think of other dining etiquette based on your own experience?

👥 Basic Knowledge Test

Fill in the blank

（1）When attending a Chinese banquet, especially a formal banquet, people are supposed to follow strict and standardized procedures, so how can you go to a Chinese banquet in an elegant and proper manner ?

同步测试：汉语
版 –M6T1
填空题

_____

_____ .

（2）Traditionally, Chinese banqueting dishes consist of five parts:

_____ .

（3）Traditionally, Chinese tableware mainly consists of _____

_____ .

（4）When arranging tables for a multi-table banquet, in addition to paying attention to the rules of _____,

other tables should also be considered in terms of their proximity to the main table.

（5）Three rules should be followed in Chinese banquet seating arrangement, and they are

_____ .

 **Case Study**

Zhang Ming, the sales manager, works in a foreign trade company Qingdao Brandland International Trade Co.. The company is mainly engaged in the export business of furniture and interior decoration. After contacting with foreign customers on AliExpress, Brandland company is planning to invite these potential clients to China for a short field tour and face to face communication. Zhang Ming is responsible to organize a formal welcome banquet.

Prior to the banquet, Zhang Ming learned about the other party's tastes and taboos by contacting the client's secretary, removing overly spicy dishes from the menu and choosing a list of Huaiyang dishes. Considering that there were ladies on the other side, white wine, red wine and drinks such as fruit juices were prepared for the banquet. In terms of seating arrangements, Zhang Ming also combined Chinese tradition with international common etiquette, arranging the guests of honor to face the door seat. In case the guests may not know the seating order, Zhang Ming also arranged for personnel to guide the guests to the proper seat in time. Besides, Zhang Ming got the clients the local specialty—green tea after the banquet.

Discussion:

（1）Supposeing you are the visiting guests from Britain, are you satisfied with Zhang Ming's organization of banquet? Please list your reasons.

（2）What do you learn from this case?

 Skills Training Tasks

Practice of Chinese Banquet Etiquette

Situation:

Suppose you are the sales manager Zhang Ming of Qingdao Brandland International Trade Co., and your team is going to organize a formal Chinese banquet to extend warm welcome to the Pakistan guests.

Basic information:

Persons present: 3 persons from Brandland companay, CEO Mr. Wang, sales manager Zhang Ming, Manager assistant Xu Feng. 3 persons from Goodgo company, Vice president Mr. Ahmad purchasing manager, Mr. Khan, assistant Mr. Sayyed.

Please work with group members to list out the items you may need pay special attention to and conduct role play to fulfill this banquet reception.

Scan the following QR codes to complete the tasks.

6.1 任务工作单　　　　　6.1 任务实施单　　　　　6.1 任务检查单　　　　　6.1 任务评价单

Curriculum Ideology and Politics

• Case 1

Respecting Food, Practising Frugality

On 22 May 2021, sad news came: Yuan Longping, the "father of hybrid rice", passed away! Thousands of people flocked to the streets in unison. Relevant information splashed across the Internet, triggering a network of memorials. Chinese and foreign circles — from the United Nations to governments, from senior party and government officials to ordinary people—have expressed their high respect and deep condolences.

The message is that a meal is not easy to come by, and half a thread and half a wisp is a constant reminder of the hardships of life. Why did Yuan Longping's death move people's hearts so much? Because he "pulled countless people out of hunger" and because he once again raised the world's awareness of food security. The "father of the world's hybrids" devoted his life to the study of rice, creating great wealth for his country, society and the world, and winning great fame for the benefit of humanity.

Food conservation and respect for food have always been excellent traditional virtues of the Chinese people. General Secretary Xi Jinping pointed out that "China is a large country with a large population, and solving the problem of eating well is always the top priority in the governance of the country". The Party and the government, while fighting corruption and promoting honesty, economizing and opposing waste, have never relaxed food production and have always focused on ensuring strategic food security.

Diligence has enabled the Chinese people to fill their granaries with food; thrift has enabled them to have a surplus of food. Today, although we no longer suffer from the food shortage, we cannot waste food freely even if we have a good harvest year after year. To cherish food is to show compassion for human beings and respect for labour.

(Source: https://www.mj.org.cn/hkxy/jpwz/202111/t20211108_245521.htm)

Discussion:

（1）Why do so many people express their high respect and deep condolences to Yuan Longping?

（2）What have you done to practice frugality of food?

• Case 2

Li Ming is the sales manager of Qingdao Brandland International Trade Co,. and he is about to meet a foreign customer from Malaysia, Mr. Feng. Li Ming cannot help feeling a little nervous. Beforehand, Li Ming made full arrangements: he learned about Mr. Feng's food preferences and taboos from his secretary, and finally chose a Southeast Asian-style restaurant. Li Ming reserved a private room and ordered the food in advance.

When Mr. Feng arrived, Li Ming greeted him warmly. He introduced himself to Mr. Feng and tried to be as clear and courteous as possible. The food was exquisite, mostly home-cooked

Malaysian food, and Mr. Feng seemed very pleased with it and they had a very pleasant exchange.

After the meal, most of the dishes on the plate had been eaten, but there were four small buns left on one plate, which Li Ming asked the waiter to pack. The waiter seemed puzzled, but Li Ming ignored him and carefully packed the buns into a handy box himself. At this point Mr. Feng cast an appreciative glance at him, "I didn't expect Mr. Li to be so thrifty, it is rare for young people nowadays." Li Ming smiled modestly, "It has become a habit to save food. My mother often instructs me that 'every single grain is the fruit of hard work' and the company all promotes frugality, so I've become a bit 'stingy' too." They looked at each other and laughed.

Three days later, Mr. Feng's company and Brandland signed the contract successfully, and Mr. Feng specifically asked Li Ming by person to participate in the cooperation.

Discussion:

（1）What do you think impressed Mr. Feng most?

（2）What have you learned from this case?

 Chinese Etiquette

When having dinner together, don't just focus on your own satiety; if you are eating with others, check the cleanliness of your hands. Don't rub rice balls with your hands; don't put extra rice into the pot; don't drink with your mouth full; don't eat with a squirting sound; don't gnaw on bones; don't put bitten fish back into your plate or bowl, and don't throw meat bones to the dog. Don't eat steamed rice with your hands instead of chopsticks; don't gulp down soup, and don't mix vegetable soup in front of your master. Do not pick your teeth in public, or drink from a stained meat sauce.

Task 2

Western Banquet Etiquette

 Learning Objectives

■ Moral Objectives

- To prepare students the awareness of intercultural communication and establish cultural confidence.
- To develop students' dignified and elegant behaviour to create a good professional image.

■ Knowledge Objectives

• To master the basic procedures and etiquette requirements of Western banquet.

• To know the cultural differences between China and Western countries and get familiar with communication skills in Western business banquet.

■ Ability Objectives

• To be able to organize and participate in Western banquet following etiquette norms.

 Lead-in: Case Study

Situation: Xiao Chen works for a multinational company. Once, Chen's American boss asked him to take some clients to a Western-style restaurant in a five-star hotel. But Xiao Chen had never dined in Western-style restaurant, so he had to wing it.

When Xiao Chen sat down, he first wiped his knife and fork with a delicately folded cloth on the table. During the meal, Chen struggled to cut the food with his knife and fork which clattered so loudly that he had no choice but to cut into large pieces and then put them in his mouth. Xiao Chen also spat the chicken bones and fish spines on the white tablecloth. In the middle of the meal, Chen casually put his knife and fork side by side and put his napkin on the table, then got up to go to the washroom and came back to find that the unfinished dishes had been taken away and the table had been cleaned up. He was so angry that he argued with the waiter.

Discussion:

（1）Do you think Xiao Chen has adopted proper table manners?

（2）Please point out Xiao Chen's improper behavior and share your suggestion.

 Basic Knowledge

In many Western countries, everything to do with eating is highly valued because it offers two of the most appreciated aesthetic pleasures at the same time — good food and good conversation.

6.2.1 Dressing Codes in Western Banquets

Western cuisine is very popular in international business banquets. Before the banquet, you should choose the right dress according to the theme of the banquet. The "4Ms" is the principle we must follow: menu, mood, music and manners. Before a Western dinner, choose the appropriate dress for the theme and occasion. It is advisable to read the dress code on the invitation letter before going to the dinner.

微课：西餐着装
规范

1. Ladies' dressing code

It is customary for ladies to wear an evening gown or a small dress to a party. Accessories are an essential part of the dress code, such as shawls, handbags and jewellery. Jewellery can be of high quality such as pearls, sapphires and diamonds. Once seated, ladies usually place their handbags on the floor at their feet, in addition to their small clutches.

2. Men's dress code

Men should wear a full suit with a formal shirt, tie or bow tie, and black shoes with dark socks. Upon entering the ballroom, you should be escorted to your seat by a waiter and should not be seated unannounced. When seated, take your seat from the left side of the chair. If a lady is present, you should help pull out the chair and help her to take her seat first.

知识链接：西餐晚宴着装规范

6.2.2   Sequence of Dishes in Banquets

Sequence of dishes in western cuisine is quite different from that in Chinese cuisine. For example, in the Chinese banquet, cold dishes are first served, then hot dishes, with soup the last one. In Western cuisine, soup is often the prelude to the start of the main meal. A formal Western meal usually consists of seven courses, as shown in Figure 6-4.

微课：西餐宴请菜序

1. Appetizers

Appetizers are in small portion and have a distinctive flavour. Caviar, smoked salmon, baked snails, etc. are common appetizers. Do not eat too many appetizers.

2. Soups

Soups are broadly divided into four categories: clear, creamy, vegetable and cold soups. Do not make any noise when drinking soup and do not blow through your mouth. Use a spoon to ladle it from the inside out.

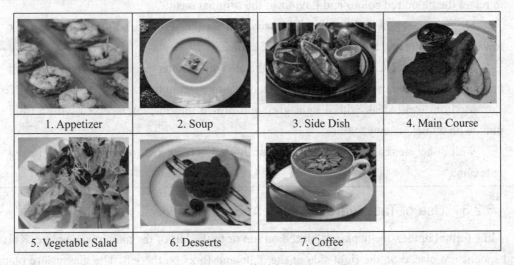

| 1. Appetizer | 2. Soup | 3. Side Dish | 4. Main Course |
| 5. Vegetable Salad | 6. Desserts | 7. Coffee | |

Figure 6-4   Sequence of Dishs in Western Banquet

3. Side dishes

Usually aquatic dishes are served with eggs, bread and pastry boxes. Fish dishes are usually served with lemon. Squeeze the lemon juice with your hand to shield it. The bread is torn into small pieces by hand, buttered and served in the mouth.

4. Main courses

Meat and poultry dishes are the mainstay of Western cuisine. Steak is a classic main course. When you order the steak, it is important to know the doneness of the steak. To eat steak, use a fork to take the meat from the left side and then cut the meat with a knife along the right side of the fork.

5. Vegetable salad

Vegetable salads are arranged after meat dishes and are usually prepared with lettuce, tomatoes, cucumbers and asparagus. At dinner parties, people eat vegetable salads with a fork.

6. Desserts

The main desserts are puddings, ice creams, fruit and cakes. Granular fruits such as grapes, spat out seeds of which, are first placed in the palm of your hand and then put in a plate.

7. Coffee

When drinking coffee, you should hold the cup by the ear with your right hand and gently hold the saucer with your left hand. It is not advisable to swallow it in large gulps and make a noise.

 Knowledge Related

Steak Ripeness

Near rare/blue: steaks are heated front and back on a hot iron plate for 30-60 seconds to retain the blood red colour and flavour of the original meat.

Medium rare: steak cut open and browned on the top and bottom, turning pink towards the centre and then fresh meat in the centre.

Medium rare: The steak is pink inside the area and is interspersed with light grey and brown of the cooked meat, with a balanced temperature throughout.

Medium well: steak with a light grey and brown interior, interspersed with a little pink, with a thick, chewy texture.

Well done: steak that is brown in colour throughout, cooked to perfection and heavy in texture.

6.2.3　Use of Tableware in Western Banquets

In a formal dinner, the napkin is placed on top or to the left of the main course plate. Knives and spoons are placed on the right side of the plate and forks on the left. The glasses are placed

微课：西餐餐具
使用礼仪

in the upper right-hand corner, the largest goblet for water, the second largest for red wine and the slender glass for white wine. The smaller glasses are used for champagne. The bread plate and butter knife are placed on the left hand side and the small spoons and knives and forks for coffee or snacks are placed opposite the main course plate.

　　To help memorize the arrangement of tableware, we can refer it as "left solid, right liquid", while others use "left B, right D", with Bread on the left and Drinks on the right. You can also use "BMW" to remember, with B for Bread on the left, M for Meat in the middle and W for Water on the right, as shown in Figure 6-5.

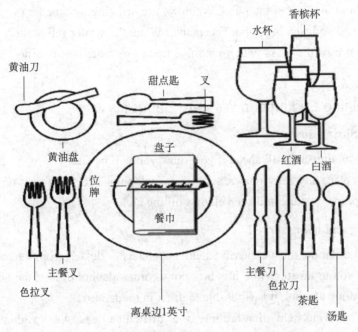

Figure 6-5　Placement of Tableware in Western Banquet

　　After we get to know the cutlery in Western cuisine, the party is about to begin. How can these table wares be used correctly?

1. Napkins

　　After ordering food, open the napkin, fold it inwards by a third and lay it flat on your lap. If you are going out during the meal, the napkin should be placed on the seat surface. At the end of the meal, the napkin should be folded and placed to the right of the plate. Napkins should only be used for wiping the mouth but not for wiping anything else.

2. Knives and forks

　　The knife is held in the right hand and the fork in the left. Use the knife and fork in order from the outside in. When putting down the knife and fork during the meal, place them in a figure of "八" on the side of the plate. At the end of the meal, the knife is placed on the right and the fork on the left, side by side or at a slight angle to the right on the plate. At no time should one end of the knife and fork be placed on the plate and the other end on the table.

3. Spoons

There are three types of spoons: soup spoons, dessert spoons and coffee spoons. These three types of cutlery are not interchangeable. When using a spoon, we are not supposed to stir the food. It is better to take the proper amount of food at a time and keep the spoon as clean as possible.

4. Wine glasses

知识链接：欧式
与美式餐具摆放

The correct way to hold a glass is to use the thumb, middle finger and index finger to hold the foot of the glass. When we are drinking, it is better to hold the glass tilted and sucking is not acceptable. When the waiter refills the glass, touch the rim of the glass with your fingertips to indicate that it is not needed.

6.2.4 Dining Etiquette in Western Banquets

1. Arrival/Sitting down

（1）Arrive on time and call ahead if you know you will be late.

（2）Do not place any bags, purses, sunglasses, cell phones, or briefcases on the table.

（3）Have proper posture and keep elbows off the table.

2. Ordering and being served

（1）Do not order the most expensive item, appetizers or dessert from the menu, unless your host encourages you to do so. While it is best not to order alcohol even if the host does. In case we may need to drink alcohol, it is advisable to drink in moderation.

（2）Avoid ordering items that are messy or difficult to eat（i.e. spaghetti, French onion soup）.

（3）Wait for everyone to be served before beginning to eat, unless the individual who has not been served encourages you to begin eating.

3. During the meal

（1）Eat slowly and cut only a few small bites of your meal at a time.

（2）Chew with your mouth closed and do not talk with food in your mouth.

（3）Pass food items to the right（i.e. bread, salad dressings）. If you are the individual starting the passing of the bread basket, first offer some to the person on your left, then take some for yourself, then pass to the right.

（4）Pass salt and pepper together, one in each hand. If someone has asked you to pass these items, pass them on to others first and don't keep occupying them yourself.

（5）Do not use excessive amounts of sweeteners - no more than two packets per meal is the rule of thumb.

（6）Bread should be eaten by tearing it into small pieces, and only apply a few bites of butter at a time. Do not cut bread with a knife or eat whole.

（7）Gently stir your soup to cool it instead of blowing on it. Use a spoon to scoop out the soup from the side close to the body.

4. After dinner

（1）When you are finished, leave your plates in the same position. Do not push your plates aside or stack them.

（2）Lay you fork and knife diagonally across the plate, side by side, pointing at 10:00 and 4:00 on a clock face. This signifies to the waiter that you have finished eating your meal.

（3）The person who initiates the meal generally pays and tips appropriately（15% for moderate service, 20% for excellent service）.

（4）Always remember to thank your host.

 Knowledge Related

In Western dining etiquette, food cannot be processed with teeth. Generally, bread is torn into small pieces and then eaten. Don't bite a whole piece of bread. When smearing butter and jam, break the bread into small pieces, and then spread the jam.

6.2.5　Seating Arrangements in Western Banquets

At Western banquets, the most commonly used table is the long one. In a formal banquet, the man (first host) sits at the main table, following the principle of right-handedness being more honorable, with the lady guest of honour on his right. The hostess sits opposite the man, with the male guest of honour on her right. The rest of the guests are seated with men and women cross arranged. Specifically, this includes the following principles.

微课：西餐座次
安排

1. The right side being more honorable

In the row of seating, that the right side is more honorable is still the basic principle. In terms of a particular position, the right side of the position is more honourable. For example, the male guest of honour sits to the right of the hostess, as shown in Figure 6-6.

2. Cross-arrangement

Formal Western dining is considered to be a sociable occasion, and generally men and women are cross-arranged, and strangers and acquaintances are cross-arranged. Therefore, a guest is often opposite and flanked by people of the opposite sex, and possibly less familiar.

3. Seats facing the door being superior

Seats facing the front door of the restaurant are reserved for honoured guests; those with their backs to the door are reserved for the host.

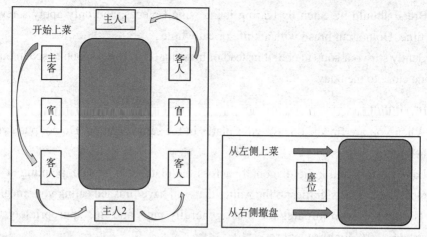

Figure 6-6   Seating Arrangements in Western Banquets-the Right Position is More Honorable

4. Ladies first

In Western dining etiquette, women are given priority. When people are taking seat, the hostess tends to have the main seat, with the male host sitting in the second main seat.

5. Distance positioning

As a rule, the order of seating at the Western table is the same as that of Chinese food, with seats closer to the main table being better than those further away, as shown in Figure 6-7.

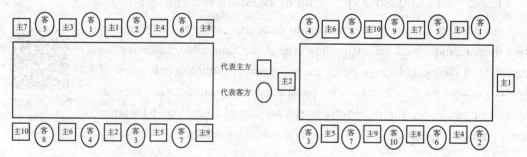

Figure 6-7   Seating Arrangements in Western Banquets

 Knowledge Related

Table Manners for Eating a Whole Fish

Trout is often presented whole. When the head of the trout is not detached in the kitchen, remove it behind the gills.

To fillet and debone the body, hold the trout with a fork and slit from the head to the tail with a knife, then open the fish and lay it flat on the plate.

To remove the skeleton from the body, place the tip of the knife under the backbone, lift with the fork, and place it on the side of the plate.

Table Manners for Handling Bones

If you inadvertently ingest any fish bones, remove them with your fingers and place them on the side of the plate.

6.2.6　Drinking Etiquette in Western Banquets

In Western cuisine, red wine is served with red meat and white wine with white meat.

微课：西餐饮酒礼仪

When the main course is red meat such as lamb or beef, it is usually paired with dry red wine. When eating various seafood, scallops, crabs, prawns, and various fish, people usually paired them with dry white wine. Desserts are served with sparkling wine, usually champagne.

Before a Western dinner party begins, the host pours the wine for the guests. One third of a glass is preferred for red wines, one half of a glass for white wines and three quarters of a glass for sparkling wines. The order in which the wine is poured is usually first for the guest of honour, then for the second guest, and first for the female guest, then for the male guest. When we are raising a glass, it is better to hold the foot with fingers instead of the palm of our hand. Quiet dining without persuading others to drink is the feature of Western cuisine.

 Knowledge Related

The Origin of the Clinking of Glasses

It is said that around the time of ancient Rome, warriors would drink a glass of wine before they dueled. Before drinking, each side would give a little of the wine in the glass to the other to prove that there was no poison in it, and then drink it all. This custom has been passed down and has evolved into the clinking of glasses at banquets today.

Extended Reading

Scan the QR code, read the passage about "How to Have Table Manners in Western Dinner Party" and finish the following tasks.

拓展阅读：西餐晚宴中的餐桌礼仪

After-reading tasks

When you finish reading the text above, finish the following tasks.

Task 1　Read the statements and decide whether they are true or not. Mark "T" for true and "F" for false.

(1) If you are not familiar with other guests, you don't need to talk to them or join in the topic of conversation. (　　　)

(2) If you need to leave the table, put your napkin on the table. (　　　)

(3) If there isn't assigned seating in the banquet, it is better to give the guest of honor or the host the best seat at the table. （　　　）

（4）Some fancier restaurants will even bring guests a dish of water to dip their hands in. （　　　）

（5）If you get an important phone call during the dinner, you may excuse yourself from the table to take it so you don't disturb any other guests. （　　　）

Task 2　Critical thinking

（1）Among the 10 rules, which one impresses you most and why?

（2）Could you list the similarities and differences between Chinese table manners and Western table manners?

 Basic Knowledge Test

Fill in the blank

（1）Dress codes in attending Western banquets:

Woman: _____

_____.

Man: _____

_____.

同步测试：汉语版 –M6T2 填空题

（2）Traditionally, Western banqueting dishes consist of five parts:

_____

_____.

（3）Traditionally, Western tableware mainly consists of _____

_____.

（4）Please list out the principles of seating arrangements in Western banquets _____

_____.

（5）In Western banquet, how would you indicate you have finished the dinner?

_____

_____.

 Case Study

The trials and tribulations of the aristocratic Crawley Family captivated audiences around the world for six seasons before culminating in a record-breaking finale on at the end of the year 2015.

Although many dining etiquette rules of Downton Abbey still apply today, other customs, such as wearing hats and gloves for all meals before 6 p.m., no longer apply. The tradition of women retiring to the parlour for coffees and liquor to allow the men to talk about politics has also been dispensed with.

If you were invited to a formal dinner at Downton Abbey, you would be well advised to bear the following etiquette rules in mind:

Do not sit down until the hostess takes her seat. Remain standing behind your chair and then move to the right of the chair and sit from the left.

When the hostess places her napkin on her lap, that's your signal to do the same. A napkin should never be tucked into your shirt; it belongs on your lap.

Your back should never touch the chair and you must not bring your mouth towards the table to eat.

You should not pass comment on the food (because it was cooked by the chef, not the Lady of the house).

Only married women were allowed to wear tiaras to formal dinners. These tiaras had often been gifted to them on their wedding day and helped to distinguish the married women from the single women.

Even though it's not our custom to wear a pair of gloves as we "dress for dinner" these days—and your host and hostess may not be Lord Grantham and Lady Cora—you'll be an impressive dinner guest if you follow these Downtown Abbey dining etiquette tips for your next formal social event.

（Source:https://thebritishschoolofexcellence.com/british-culture/a-guide-to-downton-abbey-etiquette/）

Discussion:

（1）Which rules of dining etiquette in Downtown Abbey impress you most?

（2）What other dining etiquette of Western banquet do you know?

Skills Training Tasks

Task: Practicing Western banquet etiquettes

Basic information:

Suppose you are Li Ming, the sales manager of Qingdao Brandland company. The company will host a Chinese Banquet to welcome Pakistan clients.

① Objects: table and chair; related tableware.

② Place: etiquette training room.

③ Persons present: 3 persons from Brandland company, CEO Mr. Wang, Vice president Mr. Qin, sales manager Li Ming. 3 persons from Goodgo company, Vice president Mr. Ahmad, purchasing manager Mr. Khan, assistant Mr. Sayyed.

Practice requirement:

Students work in small groups to practise seating, serving, tableware use and conversation etiquette for a Western dinner under the guidance of the teacher.

Scan the following QR codes to complete the tasks.

6.2 任务工作单　　　　6.2 任务实施单　　　　6.2 任务检查单　　　　6.2 任务评价单

Curriculum Ideology and Politics

Respect Cultural Differences to Reduce Cultural Misunderstandings

The differences in beliefs, historical backgrounds, geographical locations, living environments and habits between China and the West have led to different food cultures. It is because of these differences that food culture is so diverse. Respecting the differences between Chinese and Western food cultures not only can make the table dishes in new age rich and colorful, but also reduce the barriers to cross-cultural communication and promote the development of both sides.

A case in point is the D&G, the Italian luxury brand's video fiasco in late November 2018. By calling chopsticks "stick-shaped cutlery" and "pliers," D&G has openly shown to be disrespectful toward Chinese and Asian cultures, which use chopsticks in their daily lives.

Their arrogant approach does not reflect Sino-Italian cultural openness and respect for each other, which dates back to centuries ago. In fact, it is curious to note that the Italian Jesuit Matteo Ricci, besides being a cultural symbol for Sino-Italian friendship, was also the first Westerner to bring the knowledge of chopsticks to Europe more than 400 years ago.

D&G's use of clichés and misrepresenting Chinese culture is their biggest mistake. This story teaches us that it is vital to understand more cultures to become more sensitive toward cultural differences. This is especially true for D&G, which has made a huge amount of money through selling in China in past years. The two designers' recent apology is a small step toward reconciliation, however more will be needed to rebuild trust with China and with its people.

D&G's controversial promotional videos are very insensitive and offensive, however such attitudes do not at all represent Italian perceptions of Chinese culture, and should in no way affect the strong historical respect and cultural appreciation between the peoples and the societies of China and Italy.

（Source: https://www.chinadaily.com.cn/a/201811/26/WS5bfbabcba310eff30328b193.html）

Discussion:

（1）What mistakes did D&G make in this case?

（2）Share your suggestions of redesigning this video.

Chinese Etiquette

The Book of Rites says: "The beginning of rites began with food and drink". The ritual of food is the basis of all rituals and is used to distinguish the differences and the ranks of the noble and the inferior. Since the Spring and Autumn and Warring States period, people have been paying special attention to food etiquette. According to historical records, "daily eating should reflect filial piety and respect for teachers", and Confucius pointed out in *The Analects of Confucius—The Country Party* that one should "eat without speaking and sleep without speaking". The diet emphasizes both order and standardization, including the direction of the seats, the arrangement of chopsticks and spoons, and the order of serving. How to use cutlery and how to eat meat in diet are reflected in the etiquette of a banquet. It is required that "try to move your body forward as much as possible to avoid contaminating the seat due to diet" when attending the banquet. At the beginning of the banquet, it is required that "when the food is served, the guest needs to stand up". When the banquet is almost over and the host is not full, "the guests are not supposed to rinse their mouths and stop eating." The details of these ancient civilizations all reflect "etiquette". But here "etiquette" is not simply a form of ritual, but an inherent ethical spirit.

（Sources：https://www.jianshu.com/p/5f2821e58b43）

Tea and Coffee Etiquette

 Learning Objectives

■ Moral Objectives

• To promote Chinese etiquette and establish cultural confidence.

• To cultivate students' global view and enhance their awareness of intercultural communication.

■ Knowledge Objectives

• To master the basic procedures and etiquette requirements of drinking tea and coffee.

• To know the cultural differences between China and Western countries and respect customs and traditions of other countries.

■ Ability Objectives

• To be able to drink tea and coffee by following etiquette norms.

 Lead-in: Case Study

Situation: China is the homeland of tea, and the *Tea Book* has it that "tea is the drink of the Shennong clan". Tea has gone beyond history and borders and is loved by people all over the world. General Secretary Xi Jinping has always attached great importance to the heritage of tea culture, vigorously promoting the development of the tea industry. On numerous foreign occasions, he has used tea to introduce topics and discussions, enhancing exchanges and mutual trust, deepening friendship and cooperation, which shows the elegance of a great leader in the aroma and charm of tea.

On 16th July 2014, in Brazil, General Secretary Xi Jinping spoke about the "friendship of tea" between China and Brazil. The first Chinese tea farmers came to Brazil 200 years ago to grow tea and teach the art of tea across thousands of miles of land. At the 1873 World Exhibition in Vienna, Brazilian tea won widespread acclaim. The genuine friendship between the Chinese and Brazilian people over the long years is just like the hard work of the Chinese tea farmers, where hope is planted, joy is harvested, and friendship is nurtured.

On 21st May 2020, General Secretary Xi Jinping sent a letter to the International Tea Day series to express his warm congratulations. He pointed out that tea is originated in China and becomes prevalent in the world. The establishment of the "International Tea Day" by the United Nations reflects the international community's recognition and importance of the value of tea, which is very meaningful for revitalising the tea industry and promoting tea culture. As a major tea producing and consuming country, China is willing to work with all parties to promote the sustainable and healthy development of the global tea industry, deepen the cross-fertilization and mutual appreciation of tea culture, so that more people will know and love tea, share the fragrance and charm of tea, and enjoy a better life.

(Source: http://www.qstheory.cn/laigao/ycjx/2021-03/26/c_1127258942.htm)

Discussion:
（1）What kind of role does tea play in China's diplomatic interaction?
（2）What qualities of the Chinese people are reflected in the tea culture?

6.3.1 Etiquette for Drinking Tea

Tea originates in China. The Chinese are accustomed to treating guests with tea and have had tea drinking etiquette.

微课：饮茶礼仪

1. Categories of Chinese tea

Until now, six major types of tea have been developed: green tea, black tea, yellow tea, oolong tea, white tea, and black tea.

Green tea: Green tea belongs to the non-fermented tea. The production of green tea stands first in the list of several major tea types in China.

Black tea: It is a fully fermented tea. The raw materials are suitable new leaves of tea trees.

知识链接：中国古代饮茶的历史

Yellow tea: Yellow tea belongs to the lightly fermented tea. The most distinctive feature of yellow tea is its "yellow soup and yellow leaves".

Oolong tea: Oolong tea is a semi-fermented tea, with both the light fragrance of green tea, and the dense taste of black tea.

Dark tea: Dark tea is a post-fermented tea, which is unique to China.

White tea: It is a slightly fermented tea and is a traditional famous tea created by Han Chinese tea farmers.

2. Use of tea ware

Traditionally, Chinese tea utensils consist of the following categories, as shown in Figure 6-8.

| 茶壶 | 盖碗 | 公道杯 | 品茗杯 |
| 煮水器 | 茶道六君子 | 茶巾 | 杯托 |

Figure 6-8　Traditional Chinese Tea Ware

1）Teapot

The teapot is an important part of the tea set and is the main brewer of tea, consisting of five main parts: handle, lid, base, body and spout.

2）Covered bowl

The covered bowl has the same status as the teapot in the tea set. It is made up of three parts: the cup holder, the cup body and the lid. The main material of the lidded bowl is white porcelain, but there are also ceramic lidded bowls and glass lidded bowls.

3）Fairness cup

Also known as the "sea of tea", it is used to receive the tea broth from the main brewer and then distribute it to the guests.

4）Tasting cups

Tasting cups are commonly known as "tea cups". Each person has one to receive the tea soup. They come in a variety of sizes and shapes, and are made of glass, porcelain, ceramic, etc..

5）Boilers

Also known as a "handy brewer", it has the advantage of boiling water quickly and controlling the water temperature precisely. Boilers are available in aluminium, iron and glass.

6）The six gentlemen of the tea ceremony

These are "tea buckets, tea needles, tea pins, tea clips, tea funnels and teaspoons", each of which has its own use when making tea, making the process more aesthetically pleasing.

7）Tea towel

It can be used when the tea tray and tea utensils need to be wiped.

8）Cup holder

As the name implies, it is used to hold the tea cup and prevent burning table surface.

3. Tea servers' etiquette

1）Tea preparation

The host will generally not pick a tea to brew directly, but will first ask the guest what tea they like. Before brewing, the host will also introduce the name and characteristics of the tea, so that the guest has a basic understanding of the tea they are going to drink.

2）Taking the tea

To put the tea leaves into the pot or cup, it is common for the host to use a bamboo or wooden spoon to pick the tea leaves, rather than grabbing them with hands. If there is no spoon, you can tilt the tea cone to the pot or cup and shake it gently so that the right amount of tea leaves fall into the pot or cup.

3）The etiquette of pouring tea

When pouring tea, don't fill the cup too full, because the water is easy to overflow and scald people. 7/10 of water in the cup is the most appropriate. When serving tea, we should first give it to the elderly and then to the young. In addition to ranking according to seniority, we should pour tea to the guests first and then our families.

4）The etiquette of bringing tea to guests

When bringing the tea to the guests, it is best to use the tray. When serving tea, we should always remember to use both hands to serve it to the other party in a balanced manner. For teacups with lugs, you should use your right hand to hold the lugs and your left hand to hold the bottom of the cup and bring the tea to the guest. A tea cup without lugs should be held at one third of the cup, with the right hand holding the cup and the left hand holding the bottom, to present the tea to the guest.

Bringing the tea to the guest, you should bow slightly and say "please drink the tea". You can also reach out hand and say "please" at the same time. After all the people present have drunk the tea, the person in charge of the tea can drink the tea himself, otherwise it is disrespectful to the guests.

5）Tea refilling etiquette

As the host, we should be enthusiastic and proactive in adding tea. The host cannot brew the tea into colorless tea. After brewing for two or three times, the tea needs to be changed. In addition, if a new guest arrives while drinking tea, it is important to show welcome and change the tea immediately.

4. Tea drinkers' etiquette

1) Sit upright

When the host is making tea for guests, the guest should sit upright, with feet side by side and palms resting easily on the knees. Do not lean back on the seat.

2) Express gratitude

When the host offers you tea, you should accept it with both hands and slightly bow in your seat to express your gratitude. If there are many people and the environment is noisy, it is also acceptable to show appreciation by knocking on the finger — that is, using the second knuckle of the index finger and middle finger gently to click on the desktop of the tea table three times.

3) Tea tasting etiquette

When beginning to drink tea, we should hold the middle of the cup with our right hand. It is not acceptable to hold the cup with both hands or touch the rim of cup. It is recommended to drink tea in small sips and taste it slowly.

4) Timely compliments

After drinking tea, you should express your appreciation for the host's tea, tea making skills and fine tea ware. When it is time to say goodbye, you should once again express your gratitude for the host's hospitality.

5. Taboos for drinking tea

（1）Don't touch the rim of the cup when serving or drinking tea. This is a matter of hygiene. Accidental touching rim of tea cup while handing it to a guest may leave others a bad impression.

知识链接：中国茶道

（2）Don't "chug" or "bottom up". Tea drinking is not the same as wine drinking. Do not drink it quickly without stop.

（3）Don't make strange noises. The ancients had the saying "Do not speak at the feeding or sleeping time ". When drinking tea, you should taste gently without making any noises.

（4）Do not hand out cigarettes or smoke at will. It is rude to smoke without the host's consent when drinking tea, and it is also rude to start handing out cigarettes as soon as you sit down.

6.3.2　Etiquette for Drinking Coffee

Coffee, a common drink in Western countries, is a beverage made from roasted and ground coffee beans. Drinking coffee requires particular attention to behavior and etiquette.

微课：喝咖啡礼仪

1. Categories of coffee

Depending on the ingredients added to the coffee, coffee can be divided into several varieties.

Black coffee: Black coffee is pure coffee with neither sugar nor milk added. It helps to neutralise the sweetness of food.

White coffee: White coffee is also known as French coffee. It is coffee that is served with milk, cream or a special plant powder. The drinker may add sugar if preferred. It is suitable for all situations, especially in informal settings.

Strong black coffee: Produced by a special steam-pressured method, it is extremely strong and should not be drunk in large quantities, nor with milk or cream.

Irish style coffee: It is served without milk but with a certain amount of whiskey.

Turkish style coffee: Turkish style coffee has a large cup and is slightly cloudy. This is because the coffee grounds are not removed and are served in the cup with the coffee.

2. Coffee drinking etiquette

1）Manners

After the conversation is on track, you can sit fully in the chair, lean lightly against the back of the chair, or place your hands on the armrests of the chair to show appropriate relaxation rather than laziness.

2）Etiquette of adding sweets

When adding sugar to your coffee, if it is white sugar, use the spoon in the sugar jar to scoop some sugar into the coffee, and be careful not to touch the coffee. If it is a sugar cube, you need to pick it up with a clip and place it on the bottom of your coffee cushion before putting the spoon into the coffee and stirring gently.

3）Use the saucer and coffee spoon properly

For formal occasions, coffee is served in a cup, then placed on a saucer and served with a coffee spoon. The proper way to hold a coffee cup is to hold it out with your right hand. Hold the lug with your thumb and forefinger, and then gently lift the saucer with your left hand as you enjoy your coffee.

The coffee spoon is used to stir the coffee. Do not use the coffee spoon to mash the sugar cube in the cup and do not let it stand in the coffee cup. When not in use, it can be placed in a coffee dish.

🎣 Knowledge Related

Words Used to Describe the Taste of Coffee

Flavor	Acidity	Body
Aroma	Bitter	Bland
Briny	Earthy	Exotic
Mellow	Mild	Soft
Sour	Spicy	Strong
Winy		

Extended Reading

Scan the QR code, read the passage about "All You Should Know About Chinese Tea" and finish the following tasks.

拓展阅读：你该
知道的关于中国
茶的一切

After-reading tasks

When you finish reading the text above, finish the following tasks.

Task 1　Read the statements and decide whether they are true or not. Mark "T" for true and "F" for false.

（1）The difference of types of Chinese tea lies in the processing of the tea leaves. （　　）

（2）According to legend, tea was discovered in 2737 BC by Chinese Emperor Huang Di. （　　）

（3）Tea was regarded as one of the seven daily necessities, along with firewood, rice, salt, soy sauce, vinegar, and oil. （　　）

（4）The Gongfu tea ceremony is a less meditative experience. It is an elaborate ceremony without strict ritual. （　　）

（5）Due to the cultural importance of tea and the prominence of tea ceremonies, the Chinese tea ware evolved independently. （　　）

Task 2　Critical thinking

What is the Chinese tea ceremony, according to the author? How would you introduce Chinese tea to Western guests?

Basic Knowledge Test

Read the statements and decide whether they are true or not. Mark "T" for true and "F" for false.

同步测试：汉语
版 –M6T3 判断
正误

（1）As a host, before brewing the tea, it is better to introduce the name and characteristics of the tea, so that the guest has a basic understanding of the tea they are going to drink. （　　）

（2）When bringing the tea to the guests, you can just use one hand to hold the rim of the teacup. （　　）

（3）It is not advisable to remain quiet when tasting tea. The noise "ah" is recommended to compliment the refined taste of tea. （　　）

（4）The coffee spoon is used to stir the coffee. After adding the milk or sugar to the coffee, the spoon is used to vigorously stir them into the coffee. （　　）

（5）The most elegant way to hold a coffee is to hold it by the ears with the index finger going through the ears. （　　）

 **Case Study**

Wang Li is a new employee of Hengxin Foreign Trade Company, working as an assistant manager. One day, the sales manager received a customer from the UK and instructed Wang Li to prepare coffee for the guest. Wang Li quickly went to the pantry, but she found that the company has prepared different brands of hand ground coffee as well as instant coffee. Wang Li was in a bit of a quandary as to which one to brew. As time was running out, she chose the most convenient-instant coffee.

Wang Li served the coffee to the client without a cup and saucer, nor did she prepare milk or sugar. She placed the cup in front of the client with one hand. The British customer showed a look of obvious disbelief. The manager was embarrassed and immediately asked about the customer's preferred taste and brand, and personally went to prepare a new coffee for the customer. The whole reception was thus disrupted and no purchase was made.

Discussion:

（1）What mistakes did Wang Li make during reception?

（2）What would you do in this situation?

 Skills Training Tasks

Situation:

Suppose you are the manger assistant of Qingdao Brandland International Trade Co. and your manager asks you to prepare Chinese tea for the American guests. What would you do?

Basic information:

① Objects: table and chair; three types of Chinese tea, green tea, red tea and white tea; tea ware; hot water.

② Place: etiquette training room.

③ Persons present.

3 persons from Brandland company, CEO Mr. Wang, Vice president Mr. Qin, sales manager Li Ming.

3 persons from Goodgo company, Vice president Mr. Smith, purchasing manager, Mr. Flan, assistant Mr. Brown.

Practice requirement:

Students work in groups to practice making and serving tea to guests during business reception.

Scan the following QR codes to complete the tasks.

6.3 任务工作单　　　　6.3 任务实施单　　　　6.3 任务检查单　　　　6.3 任务评价单

Curriculum Ideology and Politics

● Case 1

Chinese Traditional Etiquette: The Principle of Serving Tea

One important Chinese custom is to serve tea to guests. Qi Shizhu, the emperor of the Southern Dynasties, and Liu Na, etc., advocated the substitution of tea for wine. In the Tang Dynasty, Liu Zhenliang created the "ten virtuous of tea," claiming the tea can not only keep fit, but also "express one's regard to others," "sublime one's personality" and "cultivate one's conducts." In the Tang and Song Dynasties, many scholars were fond of drinking tea and described tea in their pieces.

The basic principle of serving tea is to present the guest with a cup of hot tea as soon as they step into the house. You are also supposed to ask the guest's preference before the tea is served. As the old proverb goes, "wine should be served full while tea half." People should pay attention not to fill the cup with 80% water as advised. The temperature of the tea is generally mild to prevent scalding. The color of tea is even and matches with the tray. The host serving tea holds the bottom of tray with left hand and the edge of cup with right hand.

(Source: https://www.chinaculturetour.com/culture/etiquette-customs.htm)

Discussion:

(1) How do you understand "wine should be served full while tea half"?

(2) What spirits are conveyed in the principle of serving tea?

● Case 2

The World's Prime Coffee Growing Zone

Since the first coffee tree was planted in 1892 in Binchuan County, Dali Bai Autonomous Prefecture, Yunnan coffee has been cultivated for more than 100 years. The natural conditions have made the coffee produced here renowned for its excellent quality, both at home and abroad.

In 2022, 1.3 million mu of coffee will be planted in Yun'nan Province, of which 650,000 mu (50%) will be planted in the Pu'er region. Pu'er has become the main coffee producing region in China with the largest coffee growing area, the highest production and the best quality. Pu'er coffee is an alpine small grain coffee grown in the most suitable latitude and altitude zone, and is praised as one of the "best quality coffees" in the world, attracting first-class coffee companies at home and abroad such as Nestle, Starbucks, Ruixing and Three and a Half Ton to purchase.

In recent years, the National Coffee Key Laboratory, the Yunnan Small Grain Coffee Breeding Base of the Ministry of Agriculture and Rural Development, and the Southwest Yunnan Coffee Meteorological Service Centre have been established in Pu'er one after another. Pu'er has become the most concentrated place in the country for coffee research, teaching and service guarantee institutions, and a system for the development of the whole coffee industry chain has been constructed.

Today, Pu'er is focusing on building "one base and four centres" which are "the world's high-quality coffee planting base, the country's important coffee deep processing centre, coffee technology innovation centre, international coffee trading centre, coffee research and training and cultural exchange centre", to promote Pu'er coffee to the whole country and the world.

（Source: https://new.qq.com/rain/a/20221124A065HH00）

Discussion:

（1）Have you ever tasted the coffee produced in Yun'nan?

（2）What method would you think of to promote Yun'nan coffee to the world?

 Chinese Etiquette

The nature of tea is calm and peaceful. Traditional tea drinking etiquette also includes the following.

Salute with extended palm: This is the most frequently used etiquette during the tea tasting process, indicating "please" and "thank you". When two people are facing each other, they both extend their right palm in response. When two people are sitting side by side, the one on the right extends the right palm in salute and the one on the left extends the left palm in salute.

Finger-knocking: This salute evolved from the ancient Chinese head-knocking ceremony. The previous finger tapping ceremony was quite meticulous, requiring bending the wrist and holding an empty fist, and tapping the knuckles of the fingers. Over time, it gradually evolved into bending one's hand and tapping a few fingers on the table to show gratitude.

模块 6
商务宴请礼仪

 模块导读

在商务活动中，宴请一直是人际交往的一种重要形式。早在《礼记·礼运篇》中就记载有"夫礼之初，始诸饮食"，意思是所有的礼仪开端于饮食。人类自进入文明社会后，更加注重宴请礼仪，宴请中需要讲究的礼仪也逐渐规范。在现代社会，宴请礼仪有了更大的发展和融合，餐桌成为沟通感情、交流思想和搭建事业的桥梁。宴请活动形式多样，礼仪繁杂，掌握其规范将有利于促进商务合作的顺利开展。

任务 1

中餐宴请礼仪

◎ 学习目标

■ **素养目标**
- 弘扬中华礼仪，树立文化自信。
- 具备国际视野，提升节约意识。

■ **知识目标**
- 掌握中餐宴请的基本流程和礼仪规范。
- 认识中西方差异，熟悉中餐商务宴请沟通技巧。

■ **能力目标**
- 能够按照礼仪规范组织、参与中餐宴请活动。

情境导入

情境： 2016 年 9 月 4 日晚上，G20 峰会欢迎晚宴在杭州西子宾馆举行。要迎合这些当代杰出人物的口味是一项艰巨的任务，尤其是厨师们需要考虑不同的饮食限制，同时还要展现出杭州高级烹饪的精髓。

最后呈现出来的是一份别出心裁的菜单，同时展现了中式餐具的精巧雅致。全部菜肴都不含猪肉，但是很好地展现了杭州当地知名的鱼和河鲜。

① 冷盘。

② 清汤松茸。

③ 松子鳜鱼。

④ 龙井虾仁。

⑤ 膏蟹酿香橙。

⑥ 东坡牛扒。

⑦ 四季蔬果、点心、水果冰激凌、咖啡和茶。

⑧ 张裕干红。

食物是全世界通用的语言，可以跨越界限和障碍。这次晚宴称得上是最好的国际外交，组织方选择杭帮菜，展现了最完美的中国美食。

中国美食一直被世界各地的人们钟爱。例如，巴西总统米歇尔·特梅尔（Michel Temer）就曾说他是中国食物的忠实粉丝。而这次参加 G20 峰会的领导人在风景优美的杭州品尝到了由宗师级大厨掌勺、历史悠久的杭帮菜。

（Source: http://language.chinadaily.com.cn/2016-09/05/content_26705417.htm）

讨论：

（1）食物是一种通用语言，G20 峰会的菜品传达了哪些信息？

（2）G20 峰会的菜品里没有用猪肉，组织方为何会做此安排？

知识储备

作为一个礼仪之邦，中国自古以来非常重视饮食礼节。宴会不仅是食物，也是一种商业和文化交流的方式。商务宴请一直是在中国开展商务活动的一个重要组成部分。

6.1.1 中餐宴请种类

中餐宴请可以分为正式宴请、便宴和家宴。

正式宴请是一种隆重而正规的宴请，具备三个特点：确定的人员、确定的时间和确定的菜单。正式宴请对于到场人数、穿着打扮、席位排列等都有十分严谨的要求和讲究。

便宴形式从简，偏重于人际交往，不注重规模和档次。用便宴的地点不尽相同，礼仪要求较少。一般来说，便宴只安排相关人员参加，不邀请配偶，对穿着打扮、席位排列没有特别要求。

家宴，也就是在家里举行的宴会。家宴最重要的是制造亲切、友好和自然的气氛。通常，家宴在礼仪上往往不做特殊要求。男女主人充当厨师和服务员，共同招待客人。

6.1.2　中餐赴宴礼仪

参加中式宴请时，尤其是比较隆重的正式宴请，仪式和程序都应该是严谨规范的。

1. 认真准备

收到邀请，应尽早答复是否出席。如不能出席，应向主人解释、道歉。出席宴会前，女士应化妆，男士应梳理头发并剃须。衣着要整洁、美观。若参加家庭宴会，应给女主人准备一定的礼品。

2. 按时赴宴

一般情况下，宾客最好在中餐宴会开始前 3～5 分钟到达。如因故不能准时赴宴，应提前打电话通知主人，说明原因。

3. 礼貌入座

在进入宴会厅之前，首先了解自己的桌次和座次。入座时，核对座位卡是否是自己的名字，不可随意入座。如邻座是长者或女士，应主动协助他们先入座。

4. 注意交谈

主客坐定后，如有茶，可轻轻饮用。与同桌人轻声交谈，不可交头接耳。谈话内容要看交谈对象而定。

5. 文雅进餐

主人致辞祝酒时，应注意倾听，不可吃东西。坐姿端庄，熟练使用中餐餐具。用餐时不要离开座位四处走动。用餐完毕，主人开始送客之后才能离席。

6.1.3　中餐宴请菜序

传统上，中式宴席菜品包含五部分：冷菜、汤、热菜、甜品和水果、热茶。

6.1.4　中餐点菜技巧

商务宴请重在体现主人对此宴请的用心程度。中餐宴请点菜时要注意以下技巧。

首先，重要的商务宴一定要提前依照预算将菜品和酒水点好。在预算范围内，菜品数量合理，避免铺张浪费或不够吃。提前询问客人饮食禁忌，如宗教禁忌或个人喜好，避开客人不喜欢的食物。酒水要考虑客人的文化背景，有些国家忌酒，则换成饮料。其次，如需要当面点菜，要兼顾出席人的口味。一桌菜最好是有荤有素，冷热搭配。当面点菜时，要礼貌地询问大家的忌口和喜好。点菜时，切忌询问菜品价格。

🔗 **知识链接**

中餐宴请菜单

对于规格较高的中餐宴请，往往会提前印制好为本次宴请特制的菜单，用中文及来宾国家语言标注，体现出对来宾的极大尊重。在讲定节目时，除考虑来宾的食文化禁忌之外，可以选择一些明显有中国特色或地方特色的菜品。

6.1.5　中餐就餐礼仪

中国人对食物很讲究，也讲究吃东西时的礼仪。入座后，服务员会给你一条毛巾用来擦手。当有龙虾、鸡肉或水果的菜肴时，可能会有一碗水，里面有一些玫瑰花瓣或柠檬片，这不是饮料，而是用来洗手的。在一个标准的中餐宴会上，先上冷盘，然后是汤、热菜、主菜，最后是点心和水果。下面是一些关于中国餐桌礼仪的重要提示：

用筷子夹菜时要优雅、有礼貌。

吃饭或喝汤时不要发出太大的声音。

嘴里有食物时不要说话。

不要用筷子指着别人或玩弄筷子。

不要用牙签剔牙。

往碗里盛米饭时，最好是分两次或两次以上来添加。不要把筷子插在盛米饭的碗里，因为这表示拜祖先。

6.1.6　中餐餐具使用礼仪

中餐和西餐相比最大的不同就是所用的餐具。中餐餐具主要包含筷子、汤匙、盘子、碗等。

1. 筷子

筷子是用来夹取食物的。用筷子挠痒或夹取食物之外的东西都是失礼的。与人交谈时，要暂时放下筷子，不要用筷子敲击碗盘，指点对方。众人吃饭最好使用公筷夹菜。

2. 汤匙

用勺子取食物时，不要过满，以免溢出弄脏餐桌。使用汤匙时要用右手。若食物太烫，不可用汤匙翻来翻去，也不要对着它吹气。

3. 盘子

盘子在中餐中的作用是盛放食物。盘中盛放的菜肴不要过多。食物残渣、骨头、鱼刺应轻轻放在食碟的前端，必要时让侍者端走。不要让厨余与菜肴混淆。

4. 碗

碗在中餐中用于盛放主食和羹汤。不要端起碗来进食；食用碗内盛放的食物时，应以筷子、汤匙辅助。碗内剩余的食物，不可直接倒入口中。

6.1.7　中餐桌次座次礼仪

在中式宴请中，把合适的人安排在合适的位置，这是主人能够给宾客的最高待遇。中餐席位的排列，在不同的情况下，有一定的差异，可以分为桌次排列和座次排列两方面。

1. 桌次排列

桌次即桌子的摆放次序。中式宴请多采用圆桌形式布置菜肴。在安排桌次时，所用餐桌的大小、形状要基本一致。除主桌可以略大外，其他餐桌都不要过大或过小。圆桌排列的次序有以下两种情况。

一是由两桌组成的小型宴请。这种情况又可以分为两桌横排和两桌竖排的形式。当两桌横排时，桌次是以右为主、以左为次。这里所说的右和左，是由面对正门的位置来确定的。当两桌竖排时，桌次讲究距离门口以远为上、以近为下。中餐两桌桌次安排如图6-1所示。

二是由三桌或三桌以上的桌数所组成的宴请。在安排多桌宴请的桌次时，除要注意"面门定位""以右为主""以远为上"等规则外，还应兼顾其他各桌距离主桌的远近。通常，距离主桌越近，桌次越高；距离主桌越远，桌次越低。中餐三桌及以上桌次安排如图6-2所示。

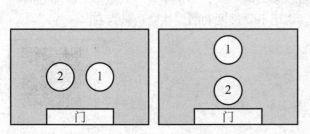

图6-1　中餐两桌桌次安排

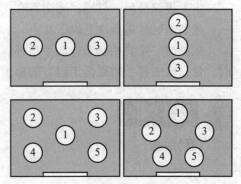

图6-2　中餐三桌以上桌次安排

2. 座次排列

中餐座次的排列，可以遵循三个原则。

右高左低原则：两人一同并排就座，通常以右为上座，以左为下座。这是因为中餐上菜时多以顺时针方向为上菜方向，居右坐的要比居左坐的优先受到照顾。

中座为尊原则：三人一同就座用餐，坐在中间的人在位次上高于两侧的人。

面门为上原则：就餐时，按照礼仪惯例，面对正门者是上座，背对正门者是下座。

此外，由于各地习俗不同，座次位置还应遵循主人安排。

中餐座次安排如图6-3所示。

6.1.8　中餐敬酒礼仪

在中式的宴席上，人们常说无酒不成席。酒桌文化在一定程度上也代表了中餐文化。一般而言，中式宴席上敬酒的顺序如下。

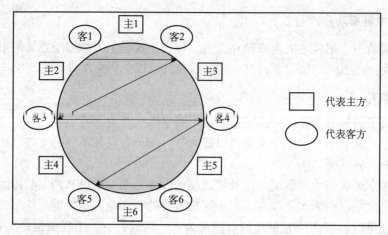

图 6-3　中餐座次安排

主人简单致辞，大家一起饮第一杯酒。

主人向主宾敬酒。

陪客向主宾敬酒。

主宾回敬主人，陪客互敬。

主人提议最后一杯酒，感谢宾客光临，结束宴会。

敬酒的时候需要注意以下几点。

敬酒时一定要站起来，双手举杯。可以多人敬一人，尽量不要一人敬多人。端起酒杯时，让自己的杯子略微低于对方的杯子。切记不要过度劝酒，饮酒适量为宜。

 同步测试

扫码做题。

同步测试：汉语版 –M6T1 填空题

 案例分析

张明就职于青岛贝来国际贸易有限公司，工作岗位为销售经理，主要从事家具和室内装饰的出口业务。在与阿里速卖通网站上的英国客户取得联系后，该公司计划邀请这些潜在客户到中国进行一次简短的实地考察和面对面的交流。张明负责组织一个正式的中式欢迎宴会。

在宴会前，张明通过联系客户秘书，了解到对方的口味和禁忌，去除了菜单中过辣的菜品，选择了清淡的淮扬菜。考虑到对方有女士，在宴请中准备了白酒、红酒及果汁等饮料。在座次安排上，张明也将中国传统和国际通用礼仪相结合，将贵宾安排到面门位次，同时为防止来宾不了解座次安排，张明还安排了人员及时引导贵客入席。此外，张明还准备了具有地方特色的小礼品——绿茶，在宴请结束后送给来访客户。

讨论：

（1）假设你是来自英国的客人，你对张明安排的宴会满意吗？请列出理由。

（2）你从这个案例中学到了什么？

实训项目

中餐宴请礼仪实训练习

1. 实训目的

通过训练，掌握中餐宴请的礼仪要求。

2. 实训内容

（1）情境：假设你是青岛贝来国际贸易有限公司的销售经理张明，你的团队准备组织一次正式的中式宴会，对巴基斯坦客人表示热烈欢迎。

（2）到场人员：青岛贝来国际贸易有限公司 3 人，总裁王先生，销售经理张明，经理助理徐峰。古德购公司 3 人，副总裁阿玛德先生，采购经理可汗先生，助理赛义德先生。

3. 实训要求

（1）采取"组内异质，组间同质"的原则，将学生分为若干小组，每组 4～6 人。

（2）每组提交一份中餐宴请注意项目列表，内容包括宴请前、宴请中和宴请后礼仪规范。

（3）每小组在礼仪实训室分角色扮演，完成中餐宴请接待流程。

4. 实训考核

（1）评价方式：采取小组自评、小组互评、教师评价、企业导师评价四维评价方式，总评成绩 = 小组自评 × 20% + 小组互评 × 20% + 教师评价 × 30% + 企业导师评价 × 30%。

（2）评价指标：从素质目标、知识目标、能力目标 3 方面进行评价。

宴请前	1. 2. 3. 4.
宴请中	1. 2. 3. 4.
宴请后	1. 2. 3. 4.
其他事项	1. 2. 3. 4.

6.1 任务工作单

6.1 任务实施单

6.1 任务检查单

6.1 任务评价单

思政课堂

● 案例 1

敬畏粮食，厉行节俭

2021年5月22日，一则令人悲痛的消息传来——"杂交水稻之父"袁隆平院士逝世了！成千上万的人们不约而同涌上街头，相关信息在网络刷屏，引发全网追悼；中外各界——从联合国到各国政府，从党政高层到普通民众，纷纷表示崇高敬意和深切哀悼。

一粥一饭当思来之不易，半丝半缕恒念物力维艰。袁隆平的逝世为什么如此牵动人心？因为他"把无数人从饥饿中挽救出来"，因为他又一次唤起了世人对粮食安全的警惕。这位"世界杂交水稻之父"一生都致力于"米"的研究，他为国家和社会乃至世界创造了巨大的财富，赢得了巨大的声誉，造福整个人类。

节约粮食、敬畏粮食一直以来都是中华民族优秀的传统美德。习近平总书记指出，"我国是一个人口众多的大国，解决好吃饭问题始终是治国理政的头等大事"。党和政府，在雷厉风行反腐倡廉、厉行节约、反对浪费的同时，始终没有放松粮食生产，始终着力保障粮食的战略安全。

勤劳，让中国人"粮满仓"；节俭，让中国人"食有余"。今天，我们虽然告别了粮食短缺的历史，但即便粮食连年丰收，也不能随意糟蹋粮食。珍惜粮食，就是体恤人力、尊重劳动。

讨论： 党的二十大报告指出"在全社会弘扬勤俭节约精神"。本案例中为什么人们自发怀念袁隆平院士？在日常生活中，你又是怎样践行节约粮食的？

● 案例 2

李明是贝来外贸公司的销售经理，他马上要接待来自马来西亚的外商客户冯先生，李明不免有些紧张。事先，李明做了周密的安排：他通过对方秘书了解了冯先生的饮食喜好和禁忌，最终选择了一家东南亚风格的餐厅预订了包间，点好了菜。

冯先生到来后，李明热情迎接。他向冯先生做了自我介绍，尽量使自己谈吐清晰，彬彬有礼。开始上菜了，菜品十分精致，大多是马来西亚家常菜，冯先生看起来很满意，两人交流也非常愉快。

用餐过后，盘里的菜大都已经吃完了，就一个盘子里还剩下四个小包子，李明吩咐服务员打包。服务员似乎不解，李明不加理会，自己动手认真地把包子装入方便盒内。

这时冯先生向他投来了赞赏的目光："没想到李总这么节俭，对于现在的年轻人来说，难能可贵。"李明谦虚地笑了："养成习惯了，家母经常嘱咐我'粒粒皆辛苦'，公司也都提倡节俭，所以我也变得有些'小抠'了。"说罢，两人相视，哈哈大笑。

三天后，冯先生的公司和贝来外贸公司顺利签下合同，冯先生特地点名要求李明参与合作。

讨论： 党的二十大报告指出"实施全面节约战略"。在本案例中，李明身上的什么特质打动了冯先生？从本案例中，你学习到了什么？

中华礼仪

《礼记·曲礼上》记载：共食不饱，共饭不泽手。毋抟饭，毋放饭，毋流歠，毋咤食，毋啮骨，毋反鱼肉，毋投与狗骨。毋固获，毋扬饭。饭黍毋以箸。毋嚃羹，毋絮羹，毋刺齿，毋歠醢。

译文：大家一起吃饭时，就要注意手的卫生。不要用手把饭搓成团，不要把多取的饭放回锅中，不要大口喝，以免满嘴汁液外流，不要吃得啧啧作响，不要啃骨头，以免弄出声响，不要把咬过的鱼肉又放回锅里，不要把肉骨头扔给狗。不要争抢着吃好吃的食物，也不要为了贪快而吹饭中的热气，吃黍米蒸的饭时不要用筷子，羹汤中的菜要经过咀嚼，不可以大口囫囵地喝下，不要当着主人的面拌菜汤。不要当众剔牙齿，也不要喝油腻的肉酱。

任务 2

西餐宴请礼仪

学习目标

■ **素养目标**
- 具备跨文化交际意识，树立文化自信。
- 培养庄重优雅的行为举止，塑造良好的职业形象。

■ **知识目标**
- 掌握西餐宴请的基本流程和礼仪规范。
- 认识中西方差异，熟悉西餐商务宴请沟通技巧。

■ **能力目标**
- 能够按照礼仪规范组织、参与西餐宴请活动。

情境导入

情境：小陈在一家跨国公司工作。一次偶然的机会，小陈的美国老板让他带一些客户去吃西餐，地点是在一家五星级酒店。可小陈此前没有吃西餐的经验，只好临场发挥。

他坐下后，首先拿桌子上一块叠得很精致的布擦了自己的刀叉。用餐时，小陈使用刀叉努力地切开食物，刀盘摩擦发出阵阵刺耳的响声，没办法他只得切成一大块儿后就放进嘴里狼吞虎咽起来，并将鸡骨头、鱼刺吐在洁白的台布上。中途，小陈随意将刀叉并排放，并将餐巾往桌上一放，就起身去了趟洗手间，回来后发现盘子已经被端走了，餐桌已经收拾干净。他非常生气，就与服务员争吵起来。

讨论：

（1）小陈在餐桌上的举止得体吗?

（2）请指出小陈的不当行为并分享你的建议。

知识储备

在许多西方国家，所有跟吃饭有关的事都备受重视，因为它同时提供了两种备受赞扬的美学享受——美食与交谈。

6.2.1　西餐着装规范

在国际商务宴请中，西餐非常流行。西餐宴会前，应根据宴会的主题选择合适的穿着。吃西餐讲究"4M"原则：menu（精美的菜单）、mood（迷人的气氛）、music（动听的音乐）和 manners（优雅的进餐礼仪）。西餐宴会前，应根据主题、场合选择合适的穿着。赴宴前，最好仔细阅读邀请函上的着装要求。

1. 女士着装规范

通常，女士要穿晚礼服或小礼服出席宴会。配饰是着装中必不可少的部分，如披肩、手袋、首饰等。首饰可选择珍珠、蓝宝石、钻石等高品质材料。女士入座后，除小手包外，通常会把手提包放在脚边的地板上。

2. 男士着装规范

男士应穿全套西服搭配正式衬衫，领带或者领结，以及黑色皮鞋与深色袜子。进入宴会厅后，需由侍者带领入座，不可贸然入座。坐下时，从椅子左侧入座。如有女士在场，应帮忙拉开椅子，先帮助女士入座。

6.2.2　西餐宴请菜序

与中餐相比，西餐的菜序具有明显的不同。例如，中餐上菜的顺序是先冷后热，以汤收尾。而西餐，汤往往是正餐开始的前奏。正式的西餐一般有七道菜。西餐宴请菜序如图 6-4 所示。

1. 开胃菜

开胃菜数量较少，具有特色风味。常见品种有鱼子酱、燻鲑鱼、焗蜗牛等。开胃菜不要吃太多。

2. 汤

西餐的汤大致分为清汤、奶油汤、蔬菜汤和冷汤 4 类。喝汤时不要发出任何声音，也不要用嘴吹。要用汤匙从里向外舀。

1. 开胃菜	2. 汤	3. 副菜	4. 主菜
5. 水果沙拉	6. 甜品	7. 咖啡	

图 6-4　西餐宴请菜序

3. 副菜

通常水产品类菜肴与蛋类、面包类、酥盒类菜肴均称副菜。鱼类菜肴一般会搭配柠檬。挤柠檬汁时应用手遮挡一下。面包用手撕成小块儿，涂上黄油，送入口中。

4. 主菜

肉禽类菜肴是西餐的主菜。牛排是经典的主菜，点菜时，要了解牛排的熟度。吃牛排时，用叉子从左侧将肉叉住，再用刀沿着叉子的右侧将肉切开。

5. 蔬菜沙拉

蔬菜类沙拉安排在肉类菜肴之后，一般用生菜、西红柿、黄瓜、芦笋等制作。在晚宴中，人们会用叉子来吃蔬菜沙拉。

6. 甜品

甜品主要有布丁、冰激凌、水果和蛋糕等。粒状水果如葡萄，吐出籽后，先放在手掌中，然后放在碟子里。

7. 咖啡

喝咖啡时，应右手拿着杯耳，左手轻轻托着咖啡碟。不宜大口吞咽，不可发出声响。

🔗 **知识链接**

牛排的熟度

近生牛排（near rare/blue）：牛排正反面在高温铁板上加热 30～60 秒，保留原肉的血红色和味道。

三分熟牛排（medium rare）：牛排切开后上下两侧呈熟肉棕色，向中心处转为粉色，然后中心为鲜肉色。

五分熟牛排（medium）：牛排内部为区域粉红可见且夹杂着熟肉的浅灰和棕褐色，整个牛排温度口感均衡。

七分熟牛排（medium well）：牛排内部主要为浅灰和棕褐色，夹杂着少量粉红色，质感偏厚重，有咀嚼感。

全熟牛排（well done）：牛排通体为棕褐色，整体已经享熟，口感厚重。

6.2.3 西餐餐具使用礼仪

在正式的晚宴中，餐巾置于主菜盘的上面或左侧。盘子右边摆放刀子、汤匙，左边摆放叉子。玻璃杯放在右上角，最大的高脚杯用来装水，次大的用来装红葡萄酒，而细长的玻璃杯用来装白葡萄酒。小的酒杯用来装香槟。面包盘和奶油刀置于左手边，主菜盘对面放咖啡或者吃点心所用的小汤匙和刀叉。

为了方便记忆，可以用"左固体，右液体"来帮助记忆，也有人用"左 B 右 D"来记忆，左边放 Bread（面包），右边放 Drinks（饮品）。还可以用"BMW"来记忆，B 指左边放 Bread（面包），M 指中间放 Meat（主菜为肉类），W 指右边放 Water（水）。西餐餐具摆放如图 6-5 所示。

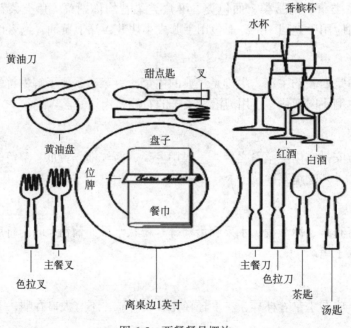

图 6-5 西餐餐具摆放

认识了西餐中的餐具后，宴会就要开始了。怎么才能正确地使用这些餐具呢？

1. 餐巾

点完菜后，把餐巾打开，往内折 1/3，然后平铺在腿上。用餐中暂时离开的话，餐巾应放在座椅的椅面上。就餐完毕时，应该把餐巾叠好放在盘子右边。餐巾只可以擦嘴，不能擦其他东西。

2. 刀叉

右手持刀，左手持叉。从外向内依次使用刀叉。进餐中放下刀叉时，应摆成"八"字形状，分别放在餐盘边上。用餐结束，刀在右边，叉在左边，并列纵放或向右稍微倾斜放在餐盘里。任何时候，都不可将刀叉的一端放在盘上，另一端放在桌上。

3. 餐匙

餐匙分汤匙、甜品匙和咖啡匙三种。这三种餐具不可相互代替。使用餐匙时，不要在所取食物中乱搅，每次取食应数量适中，尽量保持餐匙干净。

4. 酒杯

正确的握杯姿势是使用大拇指、中指和食指握住杯脚。喝酒时，应倾斜酒杯，不能吸着喝。侍者添酒时，用指尖碰一下杯沿，表示不用了。

6.2.4 西餐用餐礼仪

1. 到达 / 坐下

（1）准时到达，如果你知道自己会迟到，请提前打电话。

（2）不要将任何包、钱包、太阳镜、手机或公文包放在桌子上。

（3）就餐时，要保持正确姿势，肘部不要放在桌子上。

2. 点菜和上菜

（1）不要点菜单上最贵的食物、开胃菜或甜点，除非主人鼓励你这样做。即使主人点了酒，最好也不要点。如果饮酒，也应适可而止。

（2）避免点琐碎或难以夹起来的食物（如意大利面条、法国洋葱汤）。

（3）等到每个人的菜都上了才开始吃，除非没有上菜的人鼓励你开始吃。

3. 用餐期间

（1）缓慢进食，每次只吃一小口饭。

（2）闭嘴咀嚼，不要含着食物说话。

（3）将食物递给右边的人（如面包、沙拉酱）。如果你是开始传递面包篮的人，先给你左边的人一些，然后自己拿一些，再传递到右边。

（4）将盐和胡椒粉一起递给对方，两手各拿一份。如果有人要求你传递这些物品，那就先传给别人，自己不要一直拿着它们。

（5）不要使用过量的甜味剂，每餐不超过两包，这是经验法则。

（6）吃面包时应将其撕成小块，每次只涂抹几口黄油。不要用刀切面包或整块吃。

（7）轻轻搅拌你的汤来冷却它，而不是吹气。喝汤时，用勺子舀。

4. 吃完后

（1）把盘子放在原来的位置，不要把盘子推到一边或叠起来。

（2）把你的刀叉斜放在盘子上，并排放在一起，指向钟面上的 10 点和 4 点。这向服务员表示你已经吃完了。

（3）发起用餐的人一般会买单并给予适当的小费（一般服务为 15%，优秀服务为 20%）。

（4）一定要记得感谢主人。

知识链接

　　西方就餐礼仪中，不能用牙齿咬开食物，一般都是用手把面包撕成小块再入口，不要拿一整块面包去咬。涂抹黄油和果酱时，应先将面包掰成小块，然后抹上酱。

6.2.5　西餐座次安排

　　在西餐宴会上，最常见的桌子是长桌。正规的宴请是男主人（第一主人）坐主位，遵照以右为尊的原则，其右侧为第一贵宾夫人，女主人坐在男主人的对面，右侧为第一贵宾，其余客人男女插开坐。具体来说包括以下几个原则。

1. 以右为尊

　　在排定座位时，以右为尊仍然是基本原则。就某一特定位置而言，右侧之位更尊贵。如男主宾坐在女主人右侧。西餐座次安排（以右为尊）如图6-6所示。

2. 交叉排列

　　正式西餐被认为是交际场合，一般男女交叉排列，陌生人和熟人交叉排列。因此，一个客人的对面和两侧往往是异性，而且有可能是不太熟悉的人。

3. 面门为上

　　面对餐厅正门的座位留给尊贵的客人，背对门的座位留给主人。

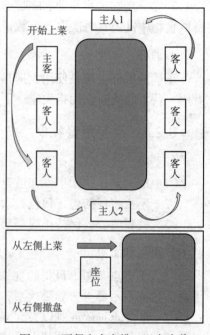

图6-6　西餐座次安排　以右为尊

4. 女士优先

　　在西餐礼仪中，女士为尊。在排定座位时，主位一般是女主人，男主人坐第二主位。

5. 距离定位

　　通常情况下，西餐桌上位次的主次也跟中餐一样，距离主位近的座位要好于距离主位远的座位。西餐座次安排如图6-7所示。

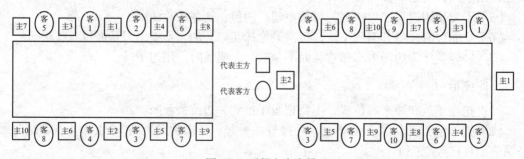

图6-7　西餐座次安排

知识链接

吃整条鱼的餐桌礼仪

鳟鱼通常是整条端上餐桌。鳟鱼的头在厨房里没有被拆开时，要把它从鱼鳃后面取出来。

将鱼身切片和去骨，用叉子夹住鳟鱼，用刀从头到尾切开，然后打开鱼身，平放在盘子上。

把骨架从鱼的身体上取下来，把刀尖放在背脊下，用叉子提起，然后放在盘子的一侧。

处理鱼骨头的餐桌礼仪

如果你不小心食入了任何鱼骨，请用手指将其取出并放在盘子的一侧。

6.2.6　西餐饮酒礼仪

一般来说，在西餐中，红酒配红肉，白酒配白肉。

在主菜为羊肉、牛肉等红肉时，一般要搭配干红葡萄酒。在吃各种海鲜、鲜贝、螃蟹、大虾和各种鱼类的时候，一般搭配干白葡萄酒。甜点搭配起泡酒，一般是香槟酒。

西餐宴会开始前，主人先给客人斟酒。红葡萄酒以三分之一杯为好，白葡萄酒以二分之一杯为好，起泡酒倒满四分之三杯。斟酒的顺序一般是先主宾，后次宾；先女宾，后男宾。举杯时，手指握住杯脚，而不是手掌。安静用餐、不劝酒是西餐显著的标志。

知识链接

碰杯的由来

据传，在古罗马时，勇士们在决斗之前，双方要先喝一杯酒，而喝酒之前，双方要把酒杯中的酒给对方一点，证明里面没有毒药，然后一饮而尽。这个习俗流传下来，逐渐演变成今天宴席上的碰杯了。

 同步测试

扫码做题。

同步测试：汉语版 –M6T2 填空题

 **案例分析**

电视剧《唐顿庄园》中贵族克劳利家族的考验和磨难吸引了全世界的观众。在持续了六季后，《唐顿庄园》于2015年迎来大结局。

虽然唐顿庄园的许多用餐礼仪规则今天仍然适用，但其他习俗，如在下午6点之前的所有用餐者都要戴帽子和手套，已经不再适用了。女性退到客厅喝咖啡和酒，让男性谈论政治的传统也已经被免除了。

如果你被邀请参加唐顿庄园的正式晚宴，最好牢记以下礼仪规则。

在女主人入座之前，不要坐下来。继续站在你的椅子后面，然后移到椅子的右边，从左边坐下。

当女主人把她的餐巾放在腿上时，这是你做同样动作的信号。餐巾绝不应该塞进衣服里，它应该放在你的腿上。

坐下时，后背不应该接触椅子，吃饭时不要探头去寻找食物。

不要对食物发表评论（因为它是由厨师烹饪的，不是女主人做的，无须恭维）。

只有已婚妇女才被允许佩戴头饰参加正式晚宴。这些头饰往往是她们在婚礼当天收到的礼物，用来区分已婚和单身。

尽管我们现在的习惯不是在"穿衣吃饭"时戴上一副手套，你的主人和女主人可能不是格兰瑟姆勋爵和科拉夫人，但如果你在下一次正式的社交活动中遵循这些《唐顿庄园》的用餐礼仪技巧，你会成为一个令人印象深刻的晚宴客人。

讨论：

（1）《唐顿庄园》中的哪些用餐礼仪规则最让你印象深刻？

（2）你还知道西方宴会的其他用餐礼仪吗？

西餐宴请礼仪实训练习

1. 实训目的

通过训练，掌握西餐宴请的礼仪要求。

2. 实训内容

（1）情境：假设你是青岛贝来国际贸易有限公司的销售经理李明，你的公司准备组织一次正式的中式宴会，对巴基斯坦客人表示热烈欢迎。

（2）到场人员：青岛贝来国际贸易有限公司3人，王总、秦副总、销售经理李明。古德购公司3人，副总裁阿玛德先生，采购经理可汗先生，助理赛义德先生。

3. 实训要求

（1）采取"组内异质，组间同质"的原则，将学生分为若干小组，每组4～6人。

（2）每组提交一份中餐宴请注意项目列表，内容包括宴请前、宴请中和宴请后礼仪规范。

（3）每小组在礼仪实训室分角色扮演，在教师的指导下练习西餐的入座、上菜、餐具使用和谈话礼仪。

4. 实训考核

（1）评价方式：采取小组自评、小组互评、教师评价、企业导师评价四维评价方式，总评成绩＝小组自评×20%＋小组互评×20%＋教师评价×30%＋企业导师评价×30%。

（2）评价指标：从素质目标、知识目标、能力目标3方面进行评价。

宴请前	1. 2. 3. 4.

宴请中	1. 2. 3. 4.
宴请后	1. 2. 3. 4.
其他事项	1. 2. 3. 4.

6.2 任务工作单　　6.2 任务实施单　　6.2 任务检查单　　6.2 任务评价单

尊重文化差异　减少文化误读

中西方的历史背景、地理位置、生活环境、宗教信仰、生活习惯不同，导致中西方饮食文化不同。也正因为这些不同，使得饮食文化多种多样。尊重饮食文化差异，不仅会使新时代的餐桌内容变得丰富多彩，而且可以减少跨文化交际的障碍，促进双方的发展。

2018 年 11 月末，意大利奢侈品牌 D&G 视频风波就是一个失败的案例。D&G 将筷子称为"棒形餐具"和"钳子"，对经常使用筷子的中国文化和亚洲文化公开表示出了不尊重。

D&G 的傲慢做法未能反映中意文化始于几个世纪前的开放和相互尊重。历史上，意大利耶稣会传教士利玛窦不仅是中意友谊的文化象征，也是 400 多年前第一位将筷子知识带到欧洲的西方人。

D&G 最大的错误是使用陈词滥调歪曲中国文化。了解更多文化并尊重文化差异非常重要，对于 D&G 来说尤其如此。过去几年 D&G 在中国获利丰厚，两位设计师的道歉只是朝着和解迈出的一小步，但要重建中国人民的信任，还需更多的努力。

D&G 有争议的宣传视频欠缺考虑，具有冒犯性，但这本质上不代表意大利人民对中国文化的看法，也不应影响中意两国人民相互的历史尊重和文化欣赏。

（资料来源：https://www.chinadaily.com.cn/a/201811/26/WS5bfbabcba310eff30328b193.html）

讨论：党的二十大报告指出"尊重世界文明多样性，以文明交流超越文明隔阂、文明互鉴超越文明冲突、文明共存超越文明优越"。在本案例中 D&G 品牌推广犯了哪些错误？如果由你来重新设计视频，你会怎么做？

中华礼仪

《礼记·礼运》曰："夫礼之初，始诸饮食。"礼仪产生于饮食，食之礼是一切礼仪的基础，用以区分贵贱的差别和等级。自春秋战国时期，人们便开始分外注重饮食礼仪，据史书记载，"日常进食应体现出孝亲敬师"。孔子在《论语·乡党》中指出应"食不言，寝不语"，饮食同时讲究秩序和规范，座席的方向、箸匙的排列、上菜的次序等。在进食时，对于如何使用餐具、如何吃饭食肉都有讲究。例如宴席之礼，赴宴时入座要求"虚坐尽后，食坐尽前"；宴席开始时要求"食至起，上客起"；宴席将近结束，主人未辩，"客不虚口"。这些古代文明的细枝末节，都体现着"礼"。但这里的"礼"，并不是简单的一种礼仪，而是一种内在的伦理精神。

任务 3

茶与咖啡礼仪

学习目标

■ **素养目标**
- 弘扬中华礼仪，树立文化自信。
- 具备国际视野，提升跨文化交际意识。

■ **知识目标**
- 掌握饮茶及喝咖啡的基本流程和礼仪规范。
- 了解中西方差异，尊重他国传统习俗。

■ **能力目标**
- 能够按照礼仪规范饮茶、喝咖啡。

 情境导入

情境：中国是茶的故乡，《茶经》有云："茶之为饮，发乎神农氏。"茶穿越历史、跨越国界，深受世界各国人民喜爱。习近平总书记一直非常重视茶文化的传承，大力推动茶产业发展，并且在众多外事场合以茶引题、以茶论道，增进交流互信，深化友好合作，在茶香茶韵中展现大国领袖的风采。

2014 年 7 月 16 日，在巴西，习近平总书记讲述中巴的"茶之友谊"。他在巴西国会发表演讲时指出：中国和巴西远隔重洋，但浩瀚的太平洋没能阻止两国人民友好交往的进程。200年前，首批中国茶农就跨越千山万水来到巴西种茶授艺。在1873年维也纳世界博览会上，巴西出产的茶叶赢得了广泛赞誉。中巴人民在漫长岁月中结下的真挚情谊，恰似中国茶农的辛勤劳作一样，种下的是希望，收获的是喜悦，品味的是友情。

　　2020年5月21日，习近平总书记向"国际茶日"系列活动致信表示热烈祝贺。他指出，茶起源于中国，盛行于世界。联合国设立"国际茶日"，体现了国际社会对茶叶价值的认可与重视，对振兴茶产业、弘扬茶文化很有意义。作为茶叶生产和消费大国，中国愿同各方一道，推动全球茶产业持续健康发展，深化茶文化交融互鉴，让更多的人知茶、爱茶，共品茶香茶韵，共享美好生活。

（资料来源：https://www.gov.cn/govweb/xinwen/2014-07/17/content_2719171.htm，http://www.xinhuanet.com/politics/leaders/2020-05/21/c_1126013834.htm）

> **讨论：**
> （1）茶在中国的对外交流中扮演了什么样的角色？
> （2）茶文化体现了中国人身上什么样的品质？

知识储备

6.3.1　饮茶礼仪

茶叶的原产地在中国。中国人习惯以茶待客，并形成了相应的饮茶礼仪。

1. 茶的种类

目前，中国茶已经形成了六大种类：绿茶、红茶、黄茶、乌龙茶、黑茶和白茶。

绿茶：绿茶属于不发酵茶。绿茶产量居我国六大茶类之首。

红茶：红茶属于全发酵茶，是以适宜的茶树新芽为原料制成的茶。

黄茶：黄茶属于轻微发酵茶，其最大的特点就是"黄汤黄叶"。

乌龙茶：乌龙茶属于半发酵茶，既有绿茶的清香，又有红茶的浓郁。

黑茶：黑茶属于后发酵茶，是我国特有的一种茶。

白茶：白茶属于微发酵茶，是汉族茶农创制的传统名茶。

2. 茶具使用礼仪

传统意义上，中国茶具主要包含如下几类，如图6-8所示。

1）茶壶

茶壶是茶具中的重要组成部分，是泡茶时的主泡器，由把、盖、底、身、壶嘴五个主要部分组成。

2）盖碗

盖碗在茶具中具有与茶壶同样的地位，由杯托、杯身和盖子三个部分组成。盖碗的主要材质为白瓷，也有陶制盖碗、玻璃盖碗等。

茶壶	盖碗	公道杯	品茗杯
煮水器	茶道六君子	茶巾	杯托

图 6-8　中国传统茶具

3）公道杯

公道杯也称"茶海"，主要作用是接受主泡器泡好的茶汤，再分给客人。

4）品茗杯

品茗杯俗称"茶杯"，每人一只，接收公道杯分杯的茶汤。其大小、外形多样，有玻璃、瓷、陶等材质。

5）煮水器

煮水器也称"随手泡"，具有快速煮水，精确控制水温的功能。煮水器有铝、铁、玻璃等材质。

6）茶道六君子

茶道六君子分别是"茶筒、茶针、茶则、茶夹、茶漏、茶匙"，六种道具在泡茶时分别有自己的用处，使泡茶的流程在利于操作的同时更加美观。

7）茶巾

茶巾可以在茶盘、茶具需要擦拭时使用。

8）杯托

顾名思义，杯托用于放置茶杯，防止烫伤桌面。

3. 奉茶者礼仪

1）备茶

作为主人一般不会直接挑选一款茶来泡，而是会先询问客人喜欢什么茶。在冲泡之前，还要介绍茶叶的名称和特点，让客人对准备喝的茶有基本的了解。

2）取茶

取茶时，不能徒手去抓，应使用竹或木制的茶匙摄取。若没有茶匙，可将茶筒倾斜对准壶或杯轻轻抖动，使适量的茶叶落入壶或杯中。

3）倒茶礼仪

倒茶不能倒满，容易溢出烫伤人，七分满最为合适。斟茶时，要遵循先尊老人、后卑幼的顺序，还应先敬宾客、再敬自家人。

4）敬茶礼仪

将泡好的茶端给客人时，最好使用托盘。端茶时，一定要用双手，保持平衡地递给对方。有杯耳的茶杯，通常要用右手抓住杯耳，左手托住杯底，把茶端给客人。如果是没有杯耳的茶杯，要手持杯子的三分之一处，右手拿杯，左手托底，把茶呈给客人。

将茶端至客人面前，应略躬身，说"请用茶"。也可伸手示意，同时说"请"。在场的人全都喝过茶之后，掌茶人才可以自己饮茶，否则就是对客人的不尊重。

5）续茶礼仪

作为主人，应该热情主动地添加茶水。主人泡茶不能将茶冲泡成无色茶，冲泡两三次后需要换茶叶。此外，如果喝茶途中来了新客人，要表示欢迎，立即换茶。

4. 饮茶者礼仪

1）端正坐姿

当主人泡茶招待客人时，作为客人应端正坐姿，双脚并列、手掌轻松搁在膝盖上。不可斜靠在座椅上。

2）表示感谢

当主人请自己喝茶时，应双手接过，并在座位上略欠身，表示感谢。如果人多，环境嘈杂，也可行叩指礼表示感谢——用食指和中指的第二个指关节在茶桌的桌面上轻轻敲三下。

3）品茶礼仪

端茶时要用右手握茶杯的中部，不要双手拿杯，也不要握住杯口处。在饮茶时，要小口喝，慢慢品尝。

4）及时赞美

喝完茶后，应对主人的茶叶、泡茶技艺和精美的茶具表示赞赏，并在告辞时再一次对主人的热情款待表示感谢。

5. 饮茶禁忌

（1）奉茶或饮茶时不要触碰杯沿。这是一个关乎卫生的问题，如果在给客人递杯子的时候，不小心触碰了杯沿，会给人留下不好的印象。

（2）不可"一口闷"或"亮杯底"。喝茶与喝酒不一样，切忌"一口闷"或"亮杯底"。

（3）喝茶时不要发出怪声。古人有"食不言，寝不语"的说法。在饮茶时应细细品味，不要发出声音。

（4）不可随意递烟、吸烟。喝茶的时候，未经主人同意就随意吸烟是不礼貌的行为，一坐下就开始派烟，也会显得很失礼。

6.3.2 喝咖啡礼仪

咖啡作为西方国家常用的饮品，是用经过烘焙磨粉的咖啡豆制作出来的饮料。饮用咖啡特别需要注意举止适度，遵守礼仪。

1. 咖啡的种类

根据饮咖啡时添加的配料不同，咖啡可被分为多个品种。

黑咖啡：既不加糖，也不加牛奶的纯咖啡。它有助于化解食物的甜腻。

白咖啡：也称法式咖啡。这是一种加牛奶、奶油或特制植物粉末的咖啡。饮用者可根据喜好加糖。它适合在各种情况下，尤其是在非正式场合饮用。

浓黑咖啡：以特殊的蒸汽加压的方法制成，极浓，不宜多饮，也不宜加入牛奶或奶油。

爱尔兰式咖啡：饮用时不加牛奶而是加入一定量的威士忌酒。

土耳其式咖啡：土耳其式咖啡杯大量大，稍显浑浊，因为咖啡渣并未被去除，而是被装入杯中与咖啡一起饮用。

2. 咖啡饮用礼仪

1）仪态

在交谈进入正轨后，你可以坐满椅子，身体可轻靠椅背，或者手搭放在椅子扶手上，展现适当的放松而非懒散。

2）加糖礼仪

给咖啡加糖时，如果是白砂糖，用糖罐里的公匙舀适量糖放进咖啡里就可以了，注意公匙不要接触到咖啡；如果是方糖，你需要用夹子把它夹起来，放在咖啡垫的底部，然后把勺子放进咖啡里，轻轻搅拌。

3）正确使用咖啡杯碟和咖啡匙

在正式场合，咖啡是盛入杯中，然后放在碟子上，和咖啡匙一起端上桌的。持握咖啡杯的得体方法是伸出右手，用拇指和食指握住杯耳后，左手轻托咖啡碟，慢慢享用。

咖啡匙是专门用来搅拌咖啡的。不要用咖啡匙来捣碎杯中的方糖，也不可让方糖立于咖啡杯中。不使用咖啡匙时，可将其放在咖啡碟里。

📎 **知识链接**

用来描述咖啡味道的词语

风味	酸度	醇度
气味	苦味	清淡
咸味	泥土的芳香	独特性
芳醇	温和	柔润
发酸	辛香	浓烈
葡萄酒味		

 **同步测试**

扫码做题。

同步测试：汉语版–M6T3判断正误

 **案例分析**

王丽是恒信外贸公司的一名新员工，工作岗位为经理助理。一天，

销售经理接待了来自英国的客户，嘱咐王丽去给客人准备咖啡。王丽快速来到茶水间，但她发现公司配备了不同品牌的手磨咖啡以及速溶咖啡。王丽一时有些为难，不知冲泡哪一种。因时间紧迫，她只好选择了最为方便的速溶咖啡。

王丽将咖啡端给客户时并没有使用杯碟，也没有准备奶和方糖，她单手持杯放到客户面前。英国客户露出了明显不解的神情。经理颇为尴尬，立马询问了客户喜欢的口味及品牌，又亲自去给客户重新准备了咖啡。整个接待过程也因此打乱了节奏，双方未达成任何购买意向。

讨论：

（1）王丽在接待过程中犯了哪些错误？

（2）在这种情况下你会怎么做？

 **实训项目**

饮茶礼仪实训练习

1. 实训目的

通过训练，掌握饮茶礼仪的规范和要求。

2. 实训内容

（1）情境：假设你是青岛贝来国际贸易有限公司的经理助理，你们公司正接待来访的美国客户。你的经理要求你为美国客人准备中国茶。你会怎么做？

（2）到场人员：青岛贝来国际贸易有限公司3人，王总经理、秦副总经理、销售经理李明。美国Goodgo公司3人，副总裁Smith先生，采购经理Flan先生，助理Brown先生。

3. 实训要求

（1）采取"组内异质，组间同质"的原则，将学生分为若干小组，每组4~6人。

（2）学生以小组为单位，使用中国传统茶具，练习在商务接待中为客人泡茶和敬茶。

4. 实训考核

（1）评价方式：采取小组自评、小组互评、教师评价、企业导师评价四维评价方式，总评成绩＝小组自评×20%＋小组互评×20%＋教师评价×30%＋企业导师评价×30%。

（2）评价指标：从素质目标、知识目标、能力目标3方面进行评价。

6.3 任务工作单　　　6.3 任务实施单　　　6.3 任务检查单　　　6.3 任务评价单

 **思政课堂**

● **案例1**

中国传统礼仪：上茶原则

中国的一个重要习俗是为客人提供茶。南朝皇帝齐世祖、陆纳等人都主张用茶代替酒。唐代，刘贞亮创造了"茶之十德"，声称茶不仅能健身，还能"表敬意""可雅致"和"恪行道"。在唐宋时期，许多学者都喜欢喝茶，并在他们的作品中描写茶。

上茶的基本原则是让客人一进门就给他们一杯热茶。你还应该在上茶前询问客人的喜好。正如古谚语所说："酒满敬人，茶满欺客。"倒茶时，最好倒八分满，茶的温度要适宜，不要过热，防止烫伤。茶的颜色均匀，与茶盘相匹配，端茶者左手托茶盘底部，右手托边缘。

讨论： 党的二十大报告指出"中华优秀传统文化源远流长、博大精深，是中华文明的智慧结晶"。弘扬传统文化是当代大学生义不容辞的使命。在本案例中，你怎么理解中国传统茶文化中"酒满敬人，茶满欺客"的说法？敬茶的原则体现了什么精神？

● **案例 2**

世界咖啡黄金种植带

自 1892 年在大理白族自治州宾川县种下第一株咖啡树起，云南咖啡已走过百余年。得天独厚的自然条件让这里产出的咖啡品质优异，享誉国内外。

2022 年，云南省咖啡种植面积达 130 万亩，其中普洱产区 65 万亩（占 50%）。普洱已成为中国咖啡种植面积最大、产量最高、品质最优的咖啡主产地区。普洱咖啡是在最适宜的纬度和海拔带种植的高山小粒咖啡，被赞誉为全球"质量比较好的咖啡"之一，吸引了雀巢、星巴克、瑞幸、三顿半等国内外一流咖啡企业前来采购。

近年来，国家咖啡重点实验室、农业农村部云南小粒种咖啡良种繁育基地、滇西南咖啡气象服务中心等相继落户普洱。普洱成为全国咖啡科研、教学、服务保障机构最集中的地方，构建了咖啡全产业链发展体系。

如今，普洱正着力建设"一基地四中心"，即世界优质咖啡种植基地、全国重要的咖啡精深加工中心、咖啡技术创新中心、国际咖啡交易中心、咖啡研学培训和文化交流中心，推动普洱咖啡走向全国、走向世界。

讨论： 党的二十大报告指出"全面推进乡村振兴。深入实施种业振兴行动，强化农业科技和装备支撑"。云南咖啡黄金种植带发展前景广阔。你曾喝过云南种植咖啡吗？作为新时代的大学生，如果由你来推广云南咖啡，你会采用什么样的方式？

中华礼仪

茶的本性是恬淡平和。传统饮茶礼仪包括以下内容。

伸掌礼： 品茗过程中使用频率最高的礼节，表示"请"和"谢谢"，主客双方都可采用。两人面对面时，均伸右掌行礼对答。两人并坐时，右侧一方伸右掌行礼，左侧一方伸左掌行礼。

叩指礼： 从古时中国的叩头礼演化而来的。早先的叩指礼是比较讲究的，必须屈腕握空拳，叩指关节。随着时间的推移，逐渐演化为将手弯曲，用几根指头轻叩桌面，以示谢忱。

Module 7
Intercultural Business Etiquette

 Profile of the Module

Increased globalization has been one of the most important developments in the past decade. Business across borders has grown significantly. In the twenty-first century, the ability to conduct business effectively with trading partners around the world relies on cross cultural knowledge and cultural intelligence. Savvy companies who view the development of international business etiquette and communication skills as a strategy will have the business advantage and will distinguish their company from competing firms.

Cultural diversity will be revealed at daily practices and business situation such as: Greeting, Gift Giving, Taboos, Handshakes, Table Manners (Business Meals), Body Language, the Spoken Words, the Written Words (e-mail, text messages) and other face-to-face interactions. Being attuned and aware to cultural diversity is essential in business interaction. Companies who fail to understand the importance of cultural differences will result in embarrassing and unprofessional encounters with business partners, which may harm the business relationship. Intercultural communication will present one's personal character reflected in his or her behavior, projecting personal values, habits and etiquette.

Task 1

Business Etiquette in Major "Belt and Road" Countries

Learning Objectives

■ Moral Objectives
  • To cultivate students' values of equality, justice, civility, harmony.

- To have a sense of China as a responsible great power, neither humble nor arrogant, and maintain China's national image.

■ Knowledge Objectives

- To get familiar with the profile, customs and etiquette of major "Belt and Road" countries.
- To grasp the business etiquette rules and taboos of major "Belt and Road" countries.

■ Ability Objectives

- To be able to conduct business exchanges and communications effectively by understanding the importance of cultural differences and respecting others.
- To be able to avoid cultural conflicts, respect exotic cultures, and conduct business activities successfully under cross-cultural communication.

 Lead-in: Case Study

Situation: A Malaysian is talking to his American colleague.

Malaysian: May I ask you a question?

American: (Looking up) sure.

Malaysian: What time is it now?

American: (Looking puzzled) It is half past five.

Malaysian: Might you have a little soup left in the pot?

American: (Looking more puzzled) Sorry? I can't get your point.

Malaysian: (Becoming more explicit since the colleague is not getting the point）I will be off to the urban to in a staff training program until eight o'clock tonight. I will be dog-tired and starving then.

American: (Finally getting the point) Would you like me to drive you to a restaurant to have dinner?

Malaysian: That'll be great!

Discussion: Why can't the American get the point at first?

 Basic Knowledge

7.1.1 Malaysia

1. Profile

Malaysia is a federal constitutional monarchy located in Southeast Asia, within the equatorial region, where a tropical rainforest climate is apparent all year round.

微课：马来西亚
国家概况

Malaysia, the 18th largest trading country in the world, is the world's second largest producer of palm oil and related products, the third largest natural rubber producer and exporter, and the third largest LNG (liquefied natural gas) exporter.

The Malaysian constitution says it guarantees freedom of religion while making Islam the state religion. Approximately 61.3% of the population practice Islam, 19.8% practice Buddhism, 9.2% Christianity, 6.3% Hinduism and 1.3% practice Confucianism, Taoism and other traditional Chinese religions.

2. Business taboos

1）Dining taboos

Due to the large Muslim population, drinking alcohol, eating pork and dog meat, and taking food with the left hand are not accepted.

Do not drink alcohol in dinner but drink tea or soft drinks instead.

微课：马来西亚
商务禁忌

2）Dressing taboos

Due to the large Muslim population, business dress should not be too revealing. Therefore, the sleeve-less or short-sleeved shirt is not accepted despite the gender. Women should dress modestly, covering shoulders, upper arms and knees.

微课：马来西亚
商务着装

3）Gesture taboos

Don't point to people with your index finger.

Don't greet, shake hands or deliver information with your left hand because "left hand" is considered to be dirty and filthy in Islamic culture.

Don't touch other people's heads or backs because their heads and backs are considered sacred and can't be touched.

Don't sit with your legs apart and cross your legs.

Don't show the soles of your feet in front of others. It's insulting to show the soles of your feet to others.

4）Talk taboos

Don't talk about personal life like family.

Don't talk about taboo animals, that is, horse, pig, dog and tortoise. Dogs are believed to be filthy and dirty, bringing plague. Tortoises are believed to be inauspicious and erotic.

Don't talk about taboo numbers, that is, 0, 4, 13.

5）Gift-giving taboos

Don't take gifts with your left hand.

Don't open the gift box in the giver's presence. It is customary to accept the gift with both hands and open it after your Malaysian colleagues have left.

Don't send gifts made from pig leather, like pig leather glove, pig leather belt, etc.

6）Business visit taboos

Don't initiate the handshaking unless the Malaysian businesswoman initiate the gesture. In business activities, men often shake hands. Men and women rarely shake hands. A nod or a single bow is OK.

7.1.2　Russia

1. Profile

The Russian Federation has one hundred and forty seven million people. Moscow is the capital. Russian is the official language, with other co-official languages in various regions.

微课：俄罗斯
国家概况

Here are some fun facts about Russia. Russia is so large that it covers nine time zones. Russia is the first country to launch a man into space. Moscow is officially the biggest city in Europe. Red is a prominent color in Russian culture and history. Russia covers half the northern hemisphere and has 12 seas.

2. Business greeting

Shake hands firmly and maintain direct eye contact. Russians show great respect to women. "Lady first" is a popular exercise in Russia. Avoid shaking hands and giving things across a threshold of a house or room. It is best to cross the threshold completely before shaking a host's hand when arriving and leaving.

Never use first names unless invited to do so. You can use "Gospodin"（Mr.）or "Gospozha"（Mrs.）plus their surname. Using their professional or academic titles is appreciated. If you know the person's full name and you know him very well, it would be more appreciated if you use a combination of his name and his patronymic.

3. Business negotiation

Patience is an extremely important virtue among Russians. Russians are known as great "sitters" during negotiations, because this demonstrates their tremendous patience. Don't expect your Russian counterpart to be on time; this may be just an attempt to test your patience. Don't expect an apology from a late Russian, and do not demonstrate any kind of attitude if your business appointments begin one or two hours late.

When shaking hands with someone, be sure to take off your gloves, as it is considered rude not to do so. Be sure to have plenty of business cards. One side should be printed in English, the other in Russian.

Be free to express your views; do not remain just a listener. Good topics of conversation include peace, culture, history, the current changes taking place in Russia, and etc. Russians are very affectionate towards children, so don't hesitate to show photographs of your children. Avoid topics such as complaints about Russia, conflicts with ethnic minorities and comparing Russia to other developed countries.

4. Business dress code

Businessmen in Russia usually wear well-tailored dark suits with fine shoes. Men often do not take off their jackets in negotiations. When attending dinner at a friend's home, casual dress and a nice shirt without a tie are appropriate.

Business women dress rather conservatively. Don't wear too flashy outfits. Women should always cover their heads with a scarf when visiting an Orthodox church. Skirts should be worn rather than pants.

5. Business dining

Do not begin eating until all the guests have received food on their plates and your host invites you to begin. Be open to taking a drink or having a toast, as refusing to do so is a serious breach of etiquette.

Going out for a drink when invited is highly recommended as it shows interest in strengthening the relationship and promoting good will.

微课：俄罗斯
商务礼仪

6. Business gift giving

It is extremely difficult to do business in Russia without help from a local. To help with this, giving gifts is a good idea when doing business in Russia.

If attending dinner at a family residence, it is appropriate to bring a gift, such as a bottle of wine, dessert, or a bouquet of flowers. Make sure the number of flowers is odd. An even number of flowers is often associated with funerals in Russia.

知识准备："一
带一路"其他主
要国家礼仪风俗

 Extended Reading

Scan the QR code, read the passage about "Business Etiquette in Vietnam – Customs and Tips" and finish the following tasks.

拓展阅读：越南
商务礼仪

After-reading tasks

When you finish reading the text above, finish the following tasks.

Task 1   Read the statements and decide whether they are true or not. Mark "T" for true and "F" for false.

（1）Paying tips are customary in Vietnam. （   ）

（2）Direct disagreement or raising of questions in public can be seen as a person to "lose face" in Vietnam. （   ）

（3）Bright colors attire is preferred in Vietnam. （   ）

（4）Discussing one's family and personal life is normal and is seen as a sign of friendliness and interest in Vietnam. （   ）

（5）For first-time meetings, it's best to meet at your potential partner's home. （   ）

Task 2   Critical thinking

Supposing you are going to visit your Vietnamese customer, what should you pay attention to?

Basic Knowledge Test

Read the statements and decide whether they are true or not. Mark "T" for true and "F" for false.

（1）No gifts made from pig leather, like pig leather glove, pig leather belt, etc. for Muslims. （   ）

同步测试：汉语
版 –M7T1 判断
正误

（2）In Malaysia and Indonesia, don't sit with your legs apart or cross your legs. And it's insulting to show the soles of your feet to others. （   ）

（3）Due to the large Muslim population in Malaysia and Indonesia, alcohol, pork and dog meat, and taking food with the left hand are not accepted. （   ）

（4）Cows are sacred to Hindus, and thus beef is not acceptable for Indian Indonesians who believe in Hinduism. （   ）

（5）In Malaysia, you should avoid talking about taboo animals, including horse, pig, dog and tortoise. （   ）

 **Case Study**

• **Case 1**

Xijie Logistics International invited Malaysia Kuala Lumpur Import and Export Trading company for business negotiations. Xijie Logistics International arranged the negotiation conference on Friday but was told that Friday was not the appropriate date. Then they decided on 9 am, Saturday. But the next day, Malaysian business partners did not show up until 10 am. This really annoyed representatives from Xijie Logistics International, who thought Malaysia Kuala Lumpur Import and Export Trading company didn't mean to cooperate. During the negotiation, Malaysian business partners have been bargaining with the price and Xijie Logistics International was unwilling to make any concessions on price. Xijie Logistics International gave a banquet, entertaining the distinguished guests with Moutai, the famous Chinese Baijiu. They tried to persuade their Malaysian business partners to drink alcohol but only to annoy them. What was worse, Xijie Logistics International forgot to tell the chef not to cook with lard oil. Malaysian business partners left the banquet angrily and the negotiations were deadlocked.

Discussion: What accounts for the negotiation deadlock?

• **Case 2**

Michael, an English employee from Trade Promotions Services, went to PT. Laxam International to attend the conference. He gave his Indonesian business partners gifts but only to annoy them. Mr. Zhang, Chinese Indonesian, sales manager, received a fine Big Ben clock; Sari, Indonesian, secretary, received adorable toys dogs; Budi, Malay, Indonesian, salesman, received a pig leather bag; Sinta, Indian Indonesian received a Parker pen with a cow leather bag.

Discussion: Why were Michael's business partners annoyed?

Skills Training Tasks

Skills Training Task 1

Business Gift Giving in Malaysia

Xiaoliu, a Chinese employee from Xijie Logistics International, went to Malaysia Kuala Lumpur Import and Export Trading company, to attend the conference. He gave his Malaysian business partners gifts but only to annoy them. Mr. Zhang, Chinese Malaysian, sales manager, received Moutai, a famous Chinese wine; Mr. Foo, Malay, salesman, received a Galloping Horses decoration; Mrs. Min, Malay, secretary, received a pair of pig leather gloves; Mr. Gandhi, Indian Malaysian received a cow leather belt.

Tasks:

（1）List the business gift-giving taboos Xiaoliu has violated.

（2）Share your ideas with your partners the rules of business gift giving in Malaysia.

（3）Suggest the appropriate gifts for Xiaoliu's Malaysian business partners.

Scan the following QR codes to complete the tasks.

7.1.1 任务工作单　　　7.1.1 任务实施单　　　7.1.1 任务检查单　　　7.1.1 任务评价单

Skills Training Task 2

Business Negotiation with Indonesians

Xijie Logistics International invited PT. Laxam International for business negotiations. Xijie Logistics International arranged the negotiation conference on Friday but was told that Friday was not the appropriate date. Then they decided on 9 a.m., Saturday. But the next day, Indonesian business partners did not show up until 10 a.m.. This really annoyed representatives from Xijie Logistics International, who thought PT. Laxam International didn't mean to cooperate. During the negotiation, Indonesian business partners have been beating around the bush, which annoyed the Chinese who would like to get down to business directly. Besides, Indonesian business partners had been bargaining with the price and Xijie Logistics International was unwilling to make any concessions on price. The negotiation took three more days than expected and finally reached an agreement. After the negotiation the Chinese felt relieved after the negotiation and relaxed themselves with their legs crossed. This made Indonesian business partners annoyed. What was worse, when the two parties were signing the contract, the left-handed Chinese manager signed the paper with his left hand. Indonesian business partners felt humiliated and left angrily without signing the contract.

Tasks:

（1）List the business negotiation taboos the two sides have violated.

（2）Share your ideas with your partners about the rules of business negotiation in Indonesia. Scan the following QR codes to complete the tasks.

7.1.2 任务工作单   7.1.2 任务实施单   7.1.2 任务检查单   7.1.2 任务评价单

 Curriculum Ideology and Politics

National road 58 in Cambodia, was open to the public. The 174-kilometer road plays a crucial role in the economic and tourist development for Cambodia's western development. Not only was it built by a Shanghai-based construction company, it was also partly funded by a concessional loan from China under the country's prominent Belt and Road Initiative. To date, China has built more than 3,000 km of roads and eight river bridges in Cambodia. The projects in Cambodia are only a snapshot of the BRI. In 2013, President Xi Jinping proposed the initiative during his visit to Southeast and Central Asia. Inspired by historical Silk Road, the BRI is a global infrastructure development program, seeking common development and prosperity. As of 2020, over 2,000 projects with 138 countries and 31 international organizations have taken under the BRI, including construction of ports, roads and bridges. During the COVID-19 pandemic, the China-Europe freight trains, a signature project of the BRI became lifeline for the transportation of PPE and others goods between the Eurasia continents. As of May 2021, the freight trains delivered over 3.4 million TEU of goods to 22 European countries, contributing a new reliable link in the global supply chain. The proposal of building a community with a shared community for mankind reflects China's responsibility as a great power. China has always had this sense of responsibility. The CPC sees the world as a shared space among all mankind and strives to resolve global affairs through cooperation rather than dominance.

（Source: China Daily）

Discussion: What is BRI? How has China been taking its responsibility as a great power?

 Chinese Etiquette

In Chinese culture, the word "face" does not signify simply the front part of the head. To offer a person a handsome present is to "give him face." But if the gift be from an individual it should be accepted only in part, but should seldom or never be altogether refused.

（Source: Arthur H. Smith，Chinese Characteristics）

Task 2

Business Etiquette in Major European Countries

 Learning Objectives

■ Moral Objectives

- To cultivate students' values of equality, justice, civility, harmony.
- To have a sense of China as a responsible great power, neither humble nor arrogant, and maintain China's national image.

■ Knowledge Objectives

- To get familiar with the profiles, customs and etiquettes of major European countries.
- To grasp the business etiquette rules and taboos of major European countries.

■ Ability Objectives

- To be able to conduct business exchanges and communications effectively by understanding the importance of cultural differences and respecting others.
- To be able to avoid cultural conflicts, respect exotic cultures, and conduct business activities successfully under cross-cultural communication.

 Lead-in: Case Study

Situation: An American businessman meets his German client for the first time to negotiate the price of a batch of new products.

German: Hello, it's 10:10 now. If I remember correctly, our meeting time is arranged at 10:00, right?

American: (laughing) Yes. I got stuck in a traffic jam on my way here, so I got here late.

German: Let's get started. Here's my business card. (handing it out with both hands)

American: (taking the card with one hand) Ah, your name is very special. Is it a very rare name in Germany?

German: Here is our product quotation and please have a look.

American: (looking impatient) I heard there's a great restaurant nearby. It's getting late. Shall we dine there and talk over lunch?

> **German:** Sorry, I've already wasted all morning. I'm going back to the office. Please make it another time. (He's so angry that he leaves the conference room)
>
> **Discussion:** Why did the negotiation come to a deadlock?

 **Basic Knowledge**

7.2.1 The United Kingdom

1. Profile

The United Kingdom of Great Britain and Northern Ireland, commonly known as the United Kingdom (UK) or Britain, is a sovereign country in western Europe. Lying off the north-western coast of the European mainland, the United Kingdom includes the island of Great Britain, the north-eastern part of the island of Ireland and many smaller islands. The United Kingdom has a temperate climate, with plentiful rainfall all year round.

微课：英国
国家概况

The United Kingdom is a constitutional monarchy within a parliamentary democracy, which consists of four parts——England, Scotland, Wales and Northern Ireland. The capital of the United Kingdom and its largest city is London, a global city and financial centre.

Forms of Christianity have dominated religious life in what is now the United Kingdom for over 1400 years. 59.5% are Christians, with the next largest faiths being Islam (4.4%), Hinduism (1.3%), Judaism (0.4%). 25.7% are irreligious.

The UK's official language is English. French and German are the two most commonly taught second languages in England and Scotland.

2. Business dining

If you invite Britons out to dinner, it's better to include people with the same background and similar professional level in the list. The following points can be useful when you are dining with your British clients:

Smoking at meals is considered rude. No cigarettes in dinner.

Having food made from animal blood is the taboo for Christians. Due to the large Christian population in the UK, Briton don't eat food made from animal blood.

British people always put their hands on the table, but they will not put their elbows on the table, nor lift their chin or cheeks.

3. Business dress code

In formal business occasions (reception, visit, banquet, etc.), men usually wear a three-piece suit and tie. Women wear evening dresses or suits and shoes with heels.

Britons don't like striped ties which are usually associated with uniform ties in the army or school of old days. So striped ties are not recommended in formal occasions.

In summer, a man can wear a short sleeve shirt instead of a suit, but also a tie. If you are invited to have afternoon tea, unless there is a special regulation, men do not have to wear suits and ties. They can wear casual business clothes, but they cannot wear sportswear or sports shoes. In formal occasions, suits can't go with sports shoes.

4. Business body language

Don't make gestures of V-shape with your back of hand outward. In Britain, Australia and New Zealand, this gesture means "Up yours", which is quite insulting.

When talking with British people, don't stand too close to each other or put your hands on the other's shoulder, which will make British people feel very uncomfortable.

Don't cross your legs.

5. Business negotiation

When chatting with the British, you can talk about the weather and sports. Use more polite expressions and sentence patterns, such as "please", "thank you", "Excuse me", "May I have the honor..." Don't talk about personal life like family, salary, religion, marriage or the British monarchy or politics.

6. Business gift giving

British people usually don't exchange gifts in business situations. When you are invited to an English home, bring a small gift to the hostess. You can send flowers, chocolate, wine, champagne or books. When the host or the hostess receives the gift, he or she will open it immediately. There are some taboos you need to draw your attention to:

Don't send the British white lilies and chrysanthemums because they are used for the funeral. Don't give souvenirs with the company logo of the giver.

Don't choose clothes, soap and other items related to private life. Don't use dark green wrapping paper to wrap gifts, because British people don't like dark green which they will associate with Nazi. Blue, red and white are Britons' favorite colors.

Don't send gifts with patterns of elephants, peacocks or owls or these animals' decorations or the toys.

7. Business greeting

Here are some taboos in business greeting with Britons:

Don't shake hands with one foot inside the door and the other outside. Don't shake hands for the four cross-cutting.

In business activities, men often shake hands.

Men and women rarely shake hands. A nod or a single bow is OK.

微课：英国商务
问候禁忌

7.2.2 France

1. Profile

France is the largest country in Western Europe. It lies on the western edge of the continent of Europe and shares its borders with six neighbouring countries: Belgium and Luxembourg to the north, Germany and Switzerland to the east; Italy to the south-east and Spain to the south-west.

微课：法国
国家概况

France has one of the highest populations in the European Union. About 84% of the French population are Roman Catholic. In addition, 8% are Muslim (mainly North African immigrants), 2% are Protestant, and 1% are Jewish, while 4% are unaffiliated with any religion or church.

French is the national language of France and is highly regarded as a symbol of the culture. The people of France generally prefer to speak and be spoken to in French. In addition, the large immigrant population brings numerous other languages, adding to the ethnic diversity of France.

2. Business greeting

At a business or social meeting, shake hands with everyone present when arriving and leaving. A handshake may be quick with a light grip.

Men may initiate handshakes with women.

When family and close friends greet one another, they often kiss both cheeks.

微课：法国
商务问候

Use last names and appropriate titles until specifically invited by your French host or colleagues to use their first names. First names are used only for close friends and family.

Colleagues on the same level generally use first names in private but always last names in public.

Address people as Monsieur, Madame or Mademoiselle without adding the surname.

Madame is used for all adult women, married or single, over 18 years of age (except for waitresses, which are addressed as Mademoiselle.)

Academic titles and degrees are very important. You are expected to know them and use them properly.

3. Business negotiation

The French use many idioms and metaphors (like "raining cats and dogs") that would be difficult for non-native speakers to understand without additional context or explanation from the speaker himself/herself.

微课：法国
商务谈判

The French may be reluctant to share information freely with someone they don't know well enough or who isn't from France. Asking personal questions can make them feel uncomfortable and offend them, so it's best to wait until you have built some trust before asking personal questions about their work, lives or families.

4. Business dining

The French do not like to discuss business during dinner. Dinner is more of a social occasion and a time to enjoy good food, wine and discussion. The following points can be useful when you are dining with your French clients:

微课：法国
商务宴请

Do not ask for a martini or scotch before dinner — they are viewed as palate numbing.

Before dinner, pernod, kir, champagne, vermouth may be offered. Wine is always served with meals. After dinner, liqueurs are served.

Senior managers socialize only with those of equivalent status.

Spouses are not included in business lunches but may be included in business dinners.

A female guest of honor is seated to the right of the host. A male guest of honor is seated to the left of the hostess.

Never start eating until your host and hostess have begun. Wait until toast has been proposed before you drink wine.

Almost all food is cut with a fork and a knife.

Send a thank-you note or telephone the next day to thank the hostess.

5. Business gift giving

In France, when business people meet for the first time, they usually don't give each other gifts. The best way to express gratitude is to hold a special event or dinner rather than give a gift.

微课：法国
商务馈赠

When invited to someone's home, always bring a small gift for the hostess. If possible, send flowers the morning of the party (popular in Paris). Otherwise, present a gift to the hostess upon arrival. Never send a gift for a French colleague to his/her home. A gift to the hostess will probably not be unwrapped immediately (unless no other guests are present or expected).

A gift should be of high quality and wrapped beautifully. Give candy, cookies, cakes and flowers. Do not give gifts with your company logo stamped on them (the French consider this garish). Do not give gifts of 6 or 12 (for lovers). Do not give gifts of odd numbers, especially 13. Do not give chrysanthemums or red roses. Do not give wine unless it is of exceptional quality.

7.2.3　Spain

1. Profile

Spain is at the crossroads of the Atlantic and Mediterranean, Europe and Africa. It is the second largest country in Western Europe and the European Union.

微课：西班牙国
家概况

Spain is a multi-ethnic country, composed of more than 20 ethnicities. Spain has a population of 48 million, 96% of which are Catholic. The official language is Spanish. There are also three regional official languages: Catalan, Basque and Galician.

Spaniards are known for their passion for entertainment. Sports play an important role in Spanish life. Spaniards like to play and watch football. Almost every town has some football fields. Bullfighting is quite popular in Spain. It is regarded as a spectacle of the country, a symbol of courage, wisdom, grace and will.

Spain is regarded as one of the most attractive countries in Europe for its friendly residents, relaxed lifestyle, attractive food, energetic nightlife and world-famous folklore.

2. Business dress code

Appearance is extremely important to Spaniards. They dress elegantly, even for casual occasions. Here are the tips:

Dress conservatively. Avoid bright or flashy colors.

Shoes are the most important element of dress. Shabby-looking shoes can ruin a very nice outfit.

For business, men should wear jackets and ties, even in warm weather. If the senior person takes his/her jacket off during a meeting, you may do so, too.

Women should wear dresses, blouses and skirts.

3. Business negotiation

For Spaniards, interpersonal relationship is the focus of business negotiation. Spaniards prefer to get to know each other before they start a business relationship. Meetings usually start with a discussion of general topics to connect with each other at a personal level to build a strong working relationship. In many cases, social relations can play a role of guarantee, or even replace the written contract.

微课：西班牙
商务谈判

Spaniards are afraid of losing face, so they don't admit that they have difficulty in understanding. Therefore, it is better for each person to have a manuscript written in Spanish during the negotiation, which will be very helpful for them to understand.

In Spain, the decision-making process can be very slow. The opinions of all management levels have to be asked. Only the person with the highest position can make the final decision.

4. Business dining

In Spain, a lot of business agreements are reached at lunch, and dinner is often for entertainment or celebration. Topics can involve personal issues, families and so on. Here are the tips:

微课：西班牙
商务宴请

Attempt to give a toast in Spanish. Be brief when toasting. It is acceptable for women to give toasts.

Tip everyone for everything.

Spaniards don't waste food. It is better to decline food rather than leave it on your plate.

5. Business gift giving

For Spaniards, gifts are a way of showing respect, not bribery. When invited to someone's home, always bring a small, wrapped gift for the hostess. You can choose gifts from your own country or region, such as wine, tie and scarf.

微课：西班牙商务馈赠

If you receive a wrapped gift, you should open it immediately and express gratitude. You can also write a thank-you letter afterwards.

Gifts are normally not exchanged at business meetings, but small gifts may be appropriate at the successful conclusion of negotiations.

知识储备：欧洲其他主要国家礼仪风俗

Extended Reading

Scan the QR code, read the passage about "Business Etiquette of Netherlands" and finish the following tasks.

拓展阅读：荷兰商务礼仪

After-reading tasks

When you finish reading the text above, finish the following tasks.

Task 1   Read the statements and decide whether they are true or not. Mark "T" for true and "F" for false.

（1）Since an apology for a late arrival can be accepted, being on time is not regarded as important in the Netherlands. (   )

（2）Gift giving is not frequently seen in business situation in the Netherlands. (   )

（3）If you are luckily invited into a Dutch home, you must take a gift for the hostess. (   )

（4）When you are not sure what to wear for a business event, you'd better be well-dressed. (   )

（5）Dutch are known as quite competitive in international trade business. (   )

Task 2   Critical thinking

Supposing you are going to receive a Dutch client, what should you pay attention to?

Basic Knowledge Test

Read the statements and decide whether they are true or not. Mark "T" for true and "F" for false.

（1）British people usually shake hands when they meet each other, and embracing is only between close friends. (   )

（2）Germans tend to do everything in a perfect way in business and private life. (   )

同步测试：汉语版 –M7T2 判断正误

（3）People in small towns of Italy spend little on buying clothes or makeups. （　　）

（4）In Spain, if you receive a gift, you should open it in front of the giver and express gratitude. （　　）

（5）Portuguese are good at accepting changes and innovations. （　　）

Qingdao Brandland International Co., Ltd. is going to send Xiaoli, the company's sales manager, to attend this year's Canton Fair where he will meet and talk with customers from European countries, including Germany, France, Italy, Spain, and Portugal and so on. To make full preparation, Xiaoli has listed the important points for attention. Here are the outlines:

When meeting with Germans, I will lay out the detailed procedures of the meeting and send them to the customers in advance. I think we can communicate in English.

When talking with French, I will try to have them reach the agreement with us during the meeting, and I think English will also be useful.

When talking with Italians, I will directly give them our offer, and hope they can accept them at once and reach an verbal agreement.

When talking with Spaniards, I will begin the meeting with some casual topics, so that we can better know each other.

When talking with Portuguese, I will show my honesty to cooperate and guarantee the quality of our products.

Discussion: What do you think of each point? Can you give some suggestions to improve the plan?

 Skills Training Tasks

A Plan for a Business Banquet

Qingdao Brandland International Co. Ltd. has some European customers coming to China to pay a visit. After the negotiations, the company would like to provide them with a fancy banquet. Since they are from the UK, Germany, France, Italy, Spain and Portugal, the manager needs to summarize the key points, so that the chef can make good preparations. These are the outlines of the plan.

（1）Quality beer and sausages will be provided at the banquet.

（2）French people are very concerned about food qualities and tastes, so we need to choose the finest ingredients for cooking.

（3）Wine is indispensable and Chinese liquor is a good choice. We can have conversations on the topics of economy and politics when we are proposing a toast, so that we can build a good relationship with the European customers.

（4）We should arrange some entertainment activities, so that they can better enjoy the banquet.

（5）An adequate amount of tableware should be prepared, especially spoons and chopsticks.

Tasks:

（1）List the business taboos that have been violated in this plan.

（2）Try to revise the plan to avoid the taboos and give more advise to improve the plan.

Scan the following QR codes to complete the tasks.

7.2 任务工作单　　　7.2 任务实施单　　　7.2 任务检查单　　　7.2 任务评价单

 Curriculum Ideology and Politics

China remains a key market for European companies as its economic resilience and large domestic market are vital for them to stay globally competitive, according to a survey released on August 29, 2022 by the China Council for the Promotion of International Trade. For instance, European aircraft manufacturer Airbus SE launched a new research center in Suzhou, Jiangsu province, in June, to focus on research for its futuristic hydrogen-powered aircraft. German chemical group BASF SE gave the green light for the construction of its planned Verbund site chemical production project in Zhanjiang, Guangdong province, in July.

China's advantages, including a complete industrial system, a lucrative market, social stability, and positive long-term economic fundamentals, as well as the smooth operation of China-Europe freight train services, have created a solid foundation for the growth of European companies, said Sang Baichuan, dean of the Institute of International Economy at the University of International Business and Economics in Beijing.

（Source: China Daily）

Discussion: Why is the Chinese market so attractive for EU countries? What does the EU market mean for China's economic development?

 Chinese Etiquette

If you are not sure what to give to your friends or relatives during China's Spring Festival, a "red envelope" can be a universal gift. Red envelopes are red paper packets packed with money. You can give your friends or relatives' children red envelopes as a way to express your greetings. As in Chinese custom, during the Chinese New Year, seniors will give children red envelopes with lucky money inside to express their love.

Task 3

Business Etiquette in Major Asian Countries

◎ Learning Objectives

■ Moral Objectives

• To cultivate students' values of equality, justice, civility, harmony.

• To have a sense of China as a responsible great power, neither humble nor arrogant, and maintain China's national image.

■ Knowledge Objectives

• To get familiar with the profile, customs and etiquette of major Asian countries.

• To grasp the business etiquette rules and taboos of major Asian countries.

■ Ability Objectives

• To be able to conduct business exchanges and communications effectively by understanding the importance of cultural differences and respecting others.

• To be able to avoid cultural conflicts, respect exotic cultures, and conduct business activities successfully under cross-cultural communication.

 Lead-in: Case Study

Situation: In September 1972, Japanese Prime Minister Kakuei Tanaka, visited China. He was greeted by Zhou Enlai, Ye Jianying and other Chinese leaders. When his private plane landed in Beijing, Tanaka, dressed in a gray suit, walked down the boarding ladder quickly, reached out his hand to offer a handshake with Premier Zhou, and said something rather elegant: "My name is Kakuei Tanaka, Prime Minister of Japan. I am 54 years old. Please feel free to advise me in the future." During his visit in China, he was warmly welcomed and accommodated by the Chinese government.

Discussion:

（1）Why did Kakuei Tanaka introduce himself in such a way?

（2）What Japan's business etiquette can we know from Kakuei Tanaka's words and behavior?

Basic Knowledge

7.3.1　Japan

1. Profile

Japan is a sovereign island nation in East Asia. Located in the Pacific Ocean, it lies off the eastern coast of the Asian mainland and stretches from the Sea of Okhotsk in the north to the East China Sea in the southwest.

微课：日本国家概况

Japanese is the official language of Japan. Most Japanese sentences can be expressed in at least eight honorific forms. Japanese communication usually focuses on a lot of details.

There is no national religion in Japan. Shintoism is a native religion in this country. Other than that, Japanese also believe in other religions, such as Buddhism, Christianity and so on.

2. Business greeting

Being familiar with the western customs, Japanese usually express their greetings via a gentle handshake. Bowing is a traditional Japanese greeting. When bowing, you need to bend the same degree to indicate equity with the counterpart. Since peering is impolite, you have to look down to avoid direct eye contact, keep our palms upward and rest them flat on your laps while bowing.

Never frown if a Japanese happens to ask you questions about privacy because it is their attempt to select the best conversational appellation that matches your occupation or title. The Japanese are never expecting to see their business cards being kept in your pockets, especially in the rear ones of the pant.

3. Business negotiation

Business negotiation generally starts between the directors and then expands to the middle managements. Senior members in the Japanese delegation should always be respected as age is as important as position in Japanese culture.

Japanese is always serious about their jobs, so do not make jokes about work. Never flatter blindly just for the fear of being alienated.

In Japan, "I'm sorry." is frequently used. Do not criticize or refuse directly but express it euphemistically and indirectly.

Be patient when speaking with a Japanese interpreter in English. Speak slowly, pause for a long time in the middle, and avoid colloquial usage. The interpreter's output may take longer than your statement, because it uses long honorific expressions.

4. Business dining

If you are invited to a Japanese family, bear in mind that it is a great honor which deserves your gratitude. Allow the host to order dishes for you. You should be in high spirits and thank the host after dinner.

When dining at home, the family sit around a low table. You can either cross or side your legs. If you are not picking up dishes, put the chopsticks on the holder to make sure they are not pointing at people. When refilling, avoid holding the cup with one hand.

5. Business gift giving

Gift giving is very common in Japan. For the Japanese, the act of gift giving is more significant than the gift itself.

微课：日本商务
禁忌

Imported Scottish whisky, French brandy or electronic toys for children are all considered as exquisite gifts. Avoid giving even items. "4" is an unlucky number. Do not wrap the gift with black or white paper and do not give white flowers, because white is associated with death.

7.3.2   South Korea

1. Profile

South Korea, officially known as the Republic of Korea, is a sovereign state in East Asia, located in southern Korean Peninsula. Korean is the official language of South Korea. English is popularized in Korean schools, so businessmen are usually able to use English fluently.

微课：韩国国家
概况

Although there are many religions coexisting in South Korea, Confucianism has the strongest influence on the whole society, which forms the ethical and moral system that controls all social relations.

2. Business greeting

When the Korean meet, they bow slightly to greet each other. But western males should not shake hands with Korean females; western women should take the initiative to shake hands with Korean men.

In South Korea, if you are particularly interested to know someone in a party, invite another person to introduce you. Don't introduce by yourself. You can address others by professional title or surname. Married females retain their maiden names. The elderly are highly respected by people, so you should take the initiative to greet them to show your politeness.

3. Business negotiation

In Korea, the foundation of successful business relationship is to build a harmonious relationship based on mutual respect among individuals. Therefore, prepare plenty of business cards. Business card is very important because it shows your status and is the key to winning due respect in Korean culture.

It is important and delicate to preserve people's face, that is, to maintain the dignity of others. Therefore, do not make people embarrassed in public.

Compared with North America and European countries, the pace of Korean companies is much slower. Before reaching an agreement, you should be patient and never mention your deadline.

4. Business dining

The most abundant meal of the day is held in the evening. Most Korean people treat their guests in restaurants or cafes. Therefore, it's a great honor for you to be invited to a Korean family dinner. Don't refuse this kind of invitation, and try to invite them in return before leaving Korea.

South Koreans believe that putting chopsticks in parallel will bring bad luck. And it is rude to stick rice on chopsticks. The food picked up from the plate should not be eaten before it is put into individual's plate.

5. Business gift giving

Gifts are usually given on business occasions. The appropriate gifts include items with company logos (do not give gifts made in Japan or South Korea).When the giver is at present, do not open the gift in front of him or her.

微课：韩国商务禁忌

It is often customary to give the other a gift of equal value. Therefore, the recipients' financial ability should be taken into account when a choice is made. If you receive a gift that is too expensive, you can express your gratitude and then refuse to accept.

知识储备：印度

 Extended Reading

Scan the QR code, read the passage about "Singapore Business Etiquette" and finish the following tasks.

拓展阅读：新加坡商务礼仪

After-reading tasks

When you finish reading the text above, finish the following tasks.

Task 1　Read the statements and decide whether they are true or not. Mark "T" for true and "F" for false.

（1）Government are important in Singapore's business as they can help a lot in setting up a company. （　　）

（2）People in Singapore will show friendliness and trust at once when they negotiate with business partners. （　　）

（3）You can shake everyone's hand when you meet people or leave, and you may also be expected to bow. （　　）

（4）In Singapore, you can talk about business over dinner and drinks just like in other Asian countries. （　　）

（5）When invited to a Singapore family, if you're not good at chopsticks, you can choose to use knife and fork. （　　）

Task 2　Critical thinking

Supposing you are going to Singapore for a business trip next month, what should you prepare in advance?

Basic Knowledge Test

Read the statements and decide whether they are true or not. Mark "T" for true and "F" for false.

（1）In Japan, when bowing, you should bow to larger degree than the other one as a way of showing your respect and modesty. （　　）

（2）Japanese would ask lots of personal questions in order to choose the most appropriate way of addressing people. （　　）

（3）In South Korea, a married women usually change her original name into her husband's. （　　）

（4）Compared with that of western companies, the pace of Korean companies tends to be slower. （　　）

（5）A foreigner can greet an Indian woman by shaking her hand.（　　）

同步测试：汉语
版–M7T3 判断
正误

Case Study

Qingdao Brandland International Co., Ltd. received a group of customers from India to negotiate business. At the meeting, the two sides should negotiate about the price of the products and so on. Before the meeting began, the Chinese company prepared tea and desserts for the Indian customers. At the beginning of the meeting, the Chinese representative Xiaowang chatted with the Indian side for a while, mainly introducing the local customs of Qingdao to them, and asking whether the other side had adapted to the life in China, instead of talking about the business directly. Afterwards, he then slowly came to the point. When it came to the price of supply, the Indian side asked for a 20 percent discount. Instead of rejecting it immediately, Xiaowang said he would think over it again before making a final decision. The Indian side also proposed to shorten the current logistics time from one month to half a month. Xiaowang did not say no, but nodded and said, "We will try our best to shorten the logistics time for you." After learning about the client's religious background, the Chinese company invited the Indian clients to dine at an authentic halal restaurant after the meeting. Eventually, the Indian customer placed a substantial order with Qingdao Brandland before leaving China.

Discussion: Why was the negotiation finally so successful?

Skills Training Tasks

A Visit to a Korean Family

Jack, a salesman from an international trading company in the U.S., was invited to visit a Korean customer's home and have dinner there. He did not prepare a gift in advance, so he bought a set of luxurious cosmetics at a local department store in Korea as a gift to his hostess. When Jack arrived at the client's house, he warmly shook his hand with the client and the hostess, and immediately took out the gift. However, the hostess looked very embarrassed after the greeting, and even more displeased when she saw the gift. Jack, however, didn't seem to be aware of these subtle signs. At the table, the client treated him warmly. When Jack had finished, he placed the chopsticks parallel on the table, with some residue left on the plate. Back home, Jack's customers didn't buy his company's products.

Tasks:

（1）List the mistakes Jack has made in visiting the client's home.

（2）Suggest appropriate gifts and dinning manners for Jack when he dines in a Korean family.

Scan the following QR codes to complete the tasks.

7.3 任务工作单　　　7.3 任务实施单　　　7.3 任务检查单　　　7.3 任务评价单

 ## Curriculum Ideology and Politics

Trilateral Cooperation Vision for the Next Decade（Excerpt）

We recalled that two decades ago, visionary leaders of China, the ROK and Japan launched the trilateral cooperation in the wake of the Asian financial crisis. Over the past 20 years, the three countries have constantly enhanced mutual trust, deepened cooperation, and pursued common development.

We shared the view that the next decade will witness profound changes in the international community, the emergence of new global growth drivers and rapid advance of the scientific and technological revolution and industrial transformation. The interests and future of all countries are more intertwined than ever before. It is increasingly important for us, as important countries responsible for peace and stability in Asia, to enhance trilateral cooperation and work together with other countries to make active and due contributions to a wide range of issues facing the region and the international community. Stronger trilateral cooperation serves the common interests of our countries and peoples, and will contribute significantly to the peace and development of the region and world.

Discussion: What does the trilateral cooperation mean for China's economic development?

 **Chinese Etiquette**

Chopsticks, kuai zi, are the most important eating utensils in China. Chinese use them during each meal. They're made of single material with two sticks. They're made of wood or bamboo and use the theory of leverage to pick up various kinds of food easily. Manners are important when using chopsticks just like using forks and knives in the West. Chinese have used kuai zi for at least 3,000 years. They have been spreaded to Asian countries like Japan and South Korea. The materials come from nature. They represent the wisdom of the Chinese.

Task 4

Business Etiquette in Major American Countries

 Learning Objectives

■ Moral Objectives

• To cultivate students' values of equality, justice, civility, harmony.

• To have a sense of China as a responsible great power, neither humble nor arrogant, and maintain China's national image.

■ Knowledge Objectives

• To get familiar with the profile, custom and etiquette of major American countries.

• To grasp the business etiquette rules and taboos of major American countries.

■ Ability Objectives

• To be able to conduct business exchanges and communications effectively by understanding the importance of cultural differences and respecting others.

• To be able to avoid cultural conflicts, respect exotic cultures, and conduct business activities successfully under cross-cultural communication.

 Lead-in: Case Study

Situation: An American International Trading Company invited a Chinese Import and Export Company for business negotiations. They arranged the negotiation conference on 9 a.m., Tuesday. But on that day, Chinese businessmen were stuck in the traffic jam, didn't inform their American partners and arrived thirty minutes late. This really annoyed American representatives. Besides, perceiving Americans are open and enthusiastic people, Chinese partners stood and sat very close to them, which made American businessmen feel uncomfortable. What's more, during negotiation, American counterparts sometimes interrupted mid-sentence, openly challenged and stated their disagreements, which really annoyed Chinese businessmen, who thought their American counterparts were really rude and aggressive. The negotiations were deadlocked.

Discussion: What accounts for the negotiation deadlock?

 Basic Knowledge

7.4.1　The United States

1. Profile

United States, officially known as the United States of America, abbreviated U.S. or U.S.A., by name America, the country in North America, is a federal republic of 50 states. The United States is a federal constitutional republic.

微课：美国国家概况

The U.S. dollar is the currency most used in international transactions and is the world's foremost reserve currency. The United States has one of the world's largest and most influential financial markets. The New York Stock Exchange is by far the world's largest stock exchange by market capitalization.

Christianity is by far the most common religion practiced in the U.S.: Protestant denominations account for 52%, Roman Catholic 24% and Mormon 2%. Other religions include Judaism (1.9%), Islam (0.9%), Buddhism (0.7%), Hinduism (0.7%).

2. Business taboos

1）Dining taboos

When you are invited to a business dinner, it is very important to respond either yes or no. Saying no is fine, but do not say you will attend and then not show up.

微课：美国商务禁忌

Never begin eating until everyone is served and the host has started eating.

It's considered impolite to burp, slurp, eat with your mouth open, chew loudly, or blow your nose at the table.

Americans do not eat domesticated animals such as cats or dogs. Consuming organ meats in the U.S. is not very common and exists usually as part of a regional dish. Eating horse meat is very taboo for Americans.

2）Dressing taboos

It is advisable to dress conservatively in business meetings.

For men, light colored suit, such as pink suit is not suitable for business occasions. Suits of dark color like black, navy blue, gray or brown are most common, and are conventionally considered as perfect business formals.

Women are discouraged to wear flashy shoes or open-toe shoes in business occasions. And limited accessories are fine and it is best to avoid overly revealing clothing.

3）Gesture taboos

It's acceptable to use your finger to point to something, but it's considered rude to point at a person.

It's also considered very rude to gesture with your middle finger raised as it is a symbol of disrespect.

4）Talk taboos

Keep the conversation light and avoid any personal topics like finances, political or religious opinions.

Race is a sensitive subject throughout the country. To avoid offending anyone, refer to Americans of different ethnicities as such: African American, Italian American, Asian American, etc.

5）Gift-giving taboos

It is not common to bring gifts to an initial business meeting, although they will be welcome.

Avoid anything too expensive as it may be be seen as a potential bribe.

6）Business greeting taboos

A handshake is the customary greeting for both men and women socially or for business. Apart from greeting close family members or friends, Americans tend to refrain from greetings that involve hugging and close physical contact.

Most conversations start with a greeting such as "How are you?" or "How's your day going?" It would be considered taboo if you answered the question literally. An expected response is "Fine" or "Good."

7.4.2　Canada

1. Profile

Canada is a country in the northern part of North America. Canada is a parliamentary democracy and a constitutional monarchy in the Westminster tradition, with a monarch as head of state and a prime minister who serves as the chair of the Cabinet and head of government.

微课：加拿大
国家概况

The economic growth in Canada has been so effective and consistent that today it is the 10th largest economy in the world based on GDP. Like many other developed countries, the Canadian economy is dominated by the service industry, which employs about three-quarters of the country's workforce.

The 2011 Canadian census reported that 67.3% of Canadians identify as being Christians; of this number, Catholics make up the largest group, accounting for 38.7 percent of the population. About 23.9% of Canadians declare no religious affiliation. The remaining are affiliated with non-Christian religions, the largest of which is Islam (3.2%), followed by Hinduism (1.5%), Sikhism (1.4%), Buddhism (1.1%), and Judaism (1.0%).

2. Business taboos

1）Dining taboos

Do not drink in public. Drinking alcohol in public is prohibited by law in all of Canada.

微课：加拿大
商务禁忌

Do not smoke in British Columbia. Smoking is banned on all public transport, in public buildings, including restaurants and bars, and workplaces.

Do not begin eating until the host starts.

Do not rest your elbows on the table.

You are seldom expected to eat with your hands. If the type of food is easier to eat in that way, be guided by what your host does.

In many French-speaking areas it is considered to be rude to eat while walking on the street.

2）Business dress taboos

Appropriate business attire usually depends on region and industry. The dress code for business is usually formal, with suits and ties commonly expected.

Accessories should be minimal for both genders and women should stay away from wearing overly revealing clothing.

Don't wear too much scent. It can be a threat to people with asthma or allergies, which are common with Canadians.

3）Business gesture taboos

Middle finger raised is an extremely obscene gesture of anger/frustration towards someone else.

Yawning is considered rude if the yawn isn't covered by a hand.

Don't point or stare at strangers. It is considered rude.

Avoid using the "V" sign. It represents a serious offence. Express your joy for victory otherwise!

4）Business talk taboos

Politics is generally considered a mostly private matter in Canada. Voting is done in secret and Canadians have a legal right to keep their political preferences hidden. As a result, "who did you vote for?" can be an uncomfortable question.

People don't like to be judged, so religious views are rarely discussed openly in public.

Beyond that, attempting to explain or promote one's religious beliefs in any sort of uninvited setting is almost always regarded as preachy, irritating and self-righteous.

It is very important that the topic of conversation does not involve the relationship between the French and English-speaking populations of Canada.

Mentioning America or Americans can often provoke intense argument or discussion. Don't make comparisons that emphasizes any inferiority or similarity to the U.S..

5）Gift-giving taboos

Giving gifts to strangers is generally rare in Canada, unless the person in question has done some favour or is otherwise considered to be "owed" one as thanks.

Gifts for "no occasion" can be sweet, but also hold a high potential to create lingering feelings of awkwardness for the recipient, especially with expensive gifts.

Do not give white lilies as they are used at funerals.

Do not give cash or money as a present. It is generally only done within families.

6）Business greeting taboos

It is considered extremely rude and offensive not to shake hands with someone after they extend their hand to you.

A foreign man shouldn't kiss the hand of a French Canadian woman.

Eye contact during conversations is viewed as a sign of respect, but staring is considered rude and to be avoided, especially in the larger cities.

Extended Reading

Scan the QR code, read the passage about "The Etiquette of Business in Latin America" and finish the following tasks.

拓展阅读：拉丁
美洲国家商务
礼仪

After-reading tasks

When you finish reading the text above, finish the following tasks.

Task 1　Read the statements and decide whether they are true or not. Mark "T" for true and "F" for false.

（1）Gift giving is more acceptable with the first visit and can help build stronger business relationships and friendships. （　　）

（2）The main language spoken in Latin America is Spanish, where people are proud of their language and aren't particularly eager to use English. （　　）

（3）The sign for "okay" formed by your forefinger and thumb is offensive in Brazil and Colombia. （　　）

（4）In Latin America, your conversational partner may stand close to you with casual arm touching or shoulder patting. Don't move back. （　　）

（5）In business meetings, you're expected to arrive on time, but your host isn't, and the more important he is, the earlier he'll be. （　　）

Task 2　Critical thinking

Supposing you are going to visit your Latin American customer, what should you pay attention to?

 Basic Knowledge Test

Read the statements and decide whether they are true or not. Mark "T" for true and "F" for false.

（1）The U.S. dollar is the currency most used in international transactions and is the world's foremost reserve currency. （　　）

（2）In the U.S.A., it's acceptable to use your finger to point to something or a person. （　　）

（3）Do not drink in public. Drinking alcohol in public is prohibited by law in all of Canada. （　　）

（4）Politics is generally considered a mostly private matter in Canada. You can talk about the political preferences with a Canadian. （　　）

（5）For men, light colored suit, such as pink suit is not suitable for business occasions. （　　）

同步测试：汉语版 –M7T4 判断正误

 Case Study

• **Case 1**

Xiaoli, a Chinese employee from Xiaohe Logistics International, went to Canadian DASS Export Trading Company to attend the conference. It was their first meeting. Xiaoli gave his Canadian business partners Mr. Girard, sales manager, a luxury wallet; he gave Mr. Davis, salesman, an exquisite ornament with the logo of his company, but only to embarrass them.

微课：加拿大商务馈赠

Discussion: Why were they embarrassed?

• **Case 2**

A Brazilian company went to the United States to purchase equipment. The Brazilian party wasted time in shopping and arrived 45 minutes late. Extremely dissatisfied, the U.S. representative spent a long time accusing the Brazilian party of their late arrival, which made the Brazilian party feel guilty and constantly make apologies. During the negotiation, the U.S. still blamed the other party, which embarrassed the Brazilian and made them at a loss. Having no intention of bargaining, the Brazilian party failed to consider many important details and hastily signed the contract. It was too late when the Brazilian representative realized that they had suffered a great loss.

Discussion: What negotiation strategies did the U.S. party use to achieve their goals?

Skills Training Tasks

Gift-giving Guidelines in the U.S.A.

Xiaosun, a Chinese employee from Jiuzhou Import and Export Company, went to American Johnson International Trading Company, to attend the conference. It was their first meeting. Xiaosun gave his American business partners Mr. Jones, sales manager, a designer scarf; he gave Ms. Miller, secretary, a bottle of perfume but only to embarrass them.

Scan the following QR codes to complete the tasks.

微课：美国商务
馈赠

7.4 任务工作单　　7.4 任务实施单　　7.4 任务检查单　　7.4 任务评价单

Curriculum Ideology and Politics

Making Every Effort for Peace and Development and Shouldering the Responsibility for Solidarity and Progress

How should we respond to the call of our times and ride on the trend of history to build a community with a shared future for mankind? China's answer is firm and clear:

We must uphold peace and oppose war and turbulence. We should remain committed to addressing differences through peaceful means and resolving disputes through dialogue and consultation.

We must pursue development and eliminate poverty. We should place development at the center of the international agenda, build international consensus and see that everyone in every country benefits more from the fruits of development in a more equitable way.

We must remain open and oppose exclusion. We should stay true to openness and inclusiveness and uphold the multilateral trading system with the WTO at its core and endeavor to build an open world economy.

We must stay engaged in cooperation and oppose confrontation. We should engage in dialogue, consultation and win-win cooperation, and reject conflict, coercion and zero-sum game. We should jointly oppose group politics and bloc confrontation.

We must strengthen solidarity and oppose division. We should stand against drawing lines on ideological grounds, and we should work together to expand common ground and convergence of interests to promote world peace and development.

We must uphold equity and oppose bullying. We should promote and practice true multilateralism, promote equality of all countries in terms of rights, rules and opportunities, and build a new type of international relations featuring mutual respect, equity and justice, and win-win cooperation.

Discussion: What is your understanding of " building a community with a shared future for mankind"?

Chinese Etiquette

In China, gifts are usually given to show respect, gratitude, friendship, love or hospitality. It is actually a common courtesy in the world. With a history of thousands of years, Chinese etiquette has formed and been passed down from generation to generation. For Chinese people, courtesy demands reciprocity, which means people who are well-mannered to others will receive kindness and favors. If they receive a gift, an invitation or hospitality treatment from someone, they will offer back to the one when it is suitable. The custom of reciprocity is also considered a traditional way to build and maintain friendship. For birthdays, weddings or parties, giving suitable gifts in China is just as any other countries else do. It does not matter whether your gift is expensive and big or not.

Task 5

Business Etiquette in Major Oceanian Countries

◎ Learning Objectives

■ Moral Objectives
- To cultivate students' values of equality, justice, civility, harmony.
- To have a sense of China as a responsible great power, neither humble nor arrogant, and maintain China's national image.

■ Knowledge Objectives
- To get familiar with the profile, customs and etiquette of major Oceanian countries.
- To grasp the business etiquette rules and taboos of major Oceanian countries.

■ Ability Objectives
- To be able to conduct business exchanges and communications effectively by understanding the importance of cultural differences and respecting others.
- To be able to avoid cultural conflicts, respect exotic cultures, and conduct business activities successfully under cross-cultural communication.

Lead-in: Case Study

Situation: A Chinese foreign trade salesman was invited to visit and dine at a customer's home during a business trip in Australia. The following is the conversation at dinner.

Chinese: Thank you very much for your invitation. This is a gift from me. It's a fine bottle of wine.

Australian: Thank you very much. But our country are good at producing high quality wine, so we don't usually drink wine produced by other countries.

Chinese: (frowning) Oh, sorry, I never thought about that.

Australian: Did you enjoy your dinner tonight?

Chinese: Very delicious! I'm stuffed.

Australian: Sorry, I don't know what you mean. Does that mean you're full? It is a very strange expression in Australia.

The Chinese, feeling very unhappy, thought that the Australian always spoke poorly of others in public. After finishing the dinner, he left the Australian's home in a hurry.

Discussion:

（1）Why was the Chinese annoyed by the Australian?

（2）Why was the Australian confused about what the Chinese businessman said?

Basic Knowledge

7.5.1　Australia

1. Profile

Australia is located between the South Pacific and the Indian Ocean and surrounded by seas. The northern part of Australia has a tropical climate, while the southern part has a temperate climate.

微课：澳大利亚
国家概况

Australia is a highly developed capitalist country. It has developed agriculture and animal husbandry and is rich in natural resources. Australia is rich in fishery resources and its tourism and service industries have developed rapidly.

Australia is a multicultural immigration country with a population of approximately 25.44 million. About 63.9% of residents believe in Christianity.

Australia has a superior natural environment and developed tourism. Famous tourist attractions includes the Great Barrier Reef and Sydney Opera House, etc.

2. Business dress code

Australians tend to dress conservatively in business situations. Men should wear dark, conservative business suits, such as black or dark blue, with white shirts.Women should wear beautiful skirts or business suits.

微课：澳大利亚
商务着装规范

Australians will indicate the dress code when sending you a formal dinner invitation letter. "Casual wear" is the most common one. However, casual wear does not refer to jeans, shorts and slippers. Men should wear trousers with collared tops, and women should wear skirts or pants with tops. Ladies should not wear excessive jewelry or heavy makeup.

3. Business negotiation

Australians do not value hierarchy much. Australians are very straightforward when doing business. People often like to get straight to the point in negotiations. They don't like pressure from the other side, and they also dislike pressure coming from high expectations. They appreciate humbleness and truthful information.

微课：澳大利亚商务谈判

Australian businessmen like to debate, and the best response is to use humor to respond to other people's queries. They also like to obey the rules of time and act on the agenda. Rules are higher than personal emotions.

In Australia, the business negotiation process is often short, but the decision-making process is relatively long. It's better to be patient while waiting for the other person to make a decision.

4. Business dining

Always arrive on time or a few minutes early for a dinner. The person who makes the invitation generally pays the bill in restaurants. However, it isn't unusual for friends to split the bill.

Australians follow continental-style dining etiquette (fork held in the left hand; knife in right). Barbecues — very informal "cook outs" — are popular in Australia. Sometimes guests bring their own meat or other items. The guest of honor is generally seated to the right of host.

Do not say "I'm stuffed" after a meal. This means you are pregnant.

5. Business gift giving

It is not customary to exchange business gifts during initial meetings. When invited to an Australian's home, bring a small gift (flowers, chocolates, or books about your home country or region) for your hosts. Australia produces excellent wine. Taking wine would be like taking sand to the desert.

6. Business taboos

Australia's culture is deeply influenced by both Britain and the United States. Australians are hospitable, sincere and straightforward. In the process of interacting with them, we need to pay attention to some taboos.

微课：澳大利亚商务禁忌

1) Body language taboos

In business situations, try to avoid yawning and stretching.

Even a very friendly wink is considered extremely impolite.

When talking with Australians, keep a certain distance. They value private space much.

In addition to shaking hands, try to avoid other physical contact.

2）Conversation taboo

Try to avoid discussing the history of Australia, especially the colonies.

Don't compare Australia with the UK in public.

Pay attention to the volume during business meetings, and don't overstate or exaggerate.

3）Other taboos

Australians believe in Christianity, so they are very disgusted with Friday and the number 13.

Australians also believe that rabbits are unlucky animals that will bring bad luck.

7.5.2 New Zealand

1. Profile

New Zealand is located in the southwestern Pacific Ocean and has a temperate maritime climate.

New Zealand economy is dominated by agriculture and animal husbandry, and exports of agricultural and livestock products account for about 50% of total exports. The export volume of mutton and dairy products ranks first in the world, and the export volume of wool ranks third in the world.

微课：新西兰
国家概况

New Zealand officially stipulates three official languages, namely English, Maori and New Zealand Sign Language.

About 15% of New Zealand's 4 million people are of Maori descent or belong to a tribe. The Maori have a rich and lively culture that retains their long-term connection to the spiritual and natural world.

2. Business negotiation

New Zealand businesses value equality. In business activities, we must respect and value everyone. New Zealanders value time management and insist on doing things according to plan.

微课：新西兰
商务谈判

Before starting business negotiations with New Zealanders, a few minutes of small talk can be used to break the ice. New Zealanders often use their humor to create a good atmosphere for discussion.

New Zealanders generally don't trust those who brag, and they are more direct and expect the other to be honest with each other. In business transactions, New Zealanders appreciate honest and frank people. There is no bargaining habit in New Zealand culture.

3. Business taboos

New Zealand is a multi-ethnic country, with European descent predominant, and it is deeply influenced by Europe, America and Australia. Its lifestyle and habits are basically westernized. But at the same time, the local Maori culture still plays an important role in the lives of many residents.

微课：新西兰
商务禁忌

1）Body language taboos

It is important to dress appropriately and try to avoid overexposure and too many accessories.

When yawning, cover your mouth. Chewing gum or using toothpicks in public is also considered uncivilized behavior.

In business situations, try to keep voice low.

When interacting with a woman, a man need to wait for the woman to reach out before shaking hands.

In Maori culture, the head is considered sacred and cannot be touched.

2）Conversation taboos

New Zealanders have a strong sense of time.

Appointments must be agreed in advance and be on time. Guests can arrive a few minutes early to show respect to the host.

Conversations focus on topics such as climate, sports, domestic and foreign politics, tourism, etc., and avoid personal matters, religion, race, and other issues.

When taking pictures of people, especially for Maori, it is better to ask for permission first.

If you work with business partner who has a Maori cultural background, the business card should be translated into the local Maori language.

3）Other taboos

Many New Zealanders believe in Christianity and Catholicism. They think the number 13 as a taboo and don't like to do important things on Friday.

Events for male and female are usually separated in New Zealand.

New Zealand has strict restrictions on alcohol, and restaurants licensed to sell alcohol can only sell wine.

📖 Extended Reading

Scan the QR code, read the passage about "How to do Business with New Zealand's Maori Culture" and finish the following tasks.

After-reading tasks

When you finish reading the text above, finish the following tasks.

Task 1　Read the statements and decide whether they are true or not. Mark "T" for true and "F" for false.

拓展阅读：如何
与新西兰毛利人
做生意

（1）Even though the Maori account for a small proportion of New Zealand's population, they have a important role to play in both the business and living culture of New Zealand. （　　）

（2）The concept of "papatuanuku" is the foundation of Maori business, which can be translated to "reason for being."

（3）It is more likely to make a successful business with Maori if you can provide environment-friendly options. (　　)

（4）Family and nature are highly valued in Maori's culture. (　　)

（5）Maoris regards concents such as unity and loyalty with much less importance than profit. (　　)

Task 2　Critical thinking

Supposing your company is going to set up a factory in New Zealand and send you there to negotiate with the local government and Maori, what should you pay attention to during the negotiation?

 ## Basic Knowledge Test

Read the statements and decide whether they are true or not. Mark "T" for true and "F" for false.

（1）Australians prefer carefree lifestyle, so they tend to dress casually in business situations. (　　)

（2）Australia's business culture values mutual cooperation more than the hierarchical order between people. (　　)

（3）Australians do not like to be compared with Britons in public. (　　)

（4）New Zealanders have a good sense of humor just like Australians. (　　)

（5）People can buy and drink alcohol freely in New Zealand. (　　)

同步测试：汉语
版 –M7T5 判断
正误

 ## Case Study

Lulu and Lili who are from an international company were on a business trip to the company's headquarter in Australia. They visited the headquarter and had a three-day meeting with the colleagues in Australia. On the evening of the third day, the Australian colleagues sends Lulu and Lili a formal invitation for dinner, with a "casual dress code" written on the invitation. They were very happy to see that because they had been wearing business clothes for a few days and finally had a chance to be dressed in a simple way. So Lulu chose to wear jeans and a T-shirt that night, while Lili wore a pair of shorts and sandals. They also spent a lot of time in heavy makeup, with their fluffed eyebrows and bright red lips showing off. However, when they arrived at the party, they realized that their clothes did not match those of the other partygoers, who were all peering at them in weird looks.

Discussion: What's wrong with Lulu and Lili's clothes and makeup? Can you give them some suggestions?

Skills Training Tasks

A Chinese company is planning to set up a food processing plant in New Zealand to produce high-end food from locally produced milk, fruit and other specialty products. The company sent its business representative Andy Wang to visit the factory site and negotiate with the local administration about the construction of the factory. After arriving in New Zealand, Andy Wang learned that the factory was located in the Maori inhabited area which was under the Maori's autonomy. The local chief who greeted him was also Maori, who was dressed in traditional garment and wearing a distinctive facial tattoo. Feeling very exotic, he picked up his phone to take a picture, but the official immediately raised his hand asking him to put down the phone. During the negotiation, the Maori asked Mr. Wang what benefit the plant would bring to them in the future. Mr. Wang repeatedly emphasized that it would boost local agricultural production and generate tax revenue for the local government. The Maori, however, seemed not to be interested. The Maori then offered what they thought was the right price for the land, which Andy Wang said was too high and unacceptable. He tried to make a bargain but was rejected. Finally, the negotiations ended in failure.

Tasks:

（1）List the mistakes Andy has made in talking with the Maori.

（2）Give some suggestions for the next negotiation with the Maori in New Zealand.

Scan the following QR codes to complete the tasks.

7.5 任务工作单　　　7.5 任务实施单　　　7.5 任务检查单　　　7.5 任务评价单

 Curriculum Ideology and Politics

Demand for Locally Made Mooncakes Soars in Australia

Mid-Autumn Festival is celebrated in Chinese culture. Mooncakes - pastries traditionally featuring lotus seed paste, red bean or nut fillings - are eaten and shared throughout the festival.

Mooncakes made by local food stores were a huge hit during this year's Mid-Autumn Festival in Australia. Some bakeries in Sydney started preparing for the festival days ahead of time to meet demand.

Steve Hou, managing director of Sweet Lu bakery in Sydney's Chinatown, said his mooncakes have been "flying out the bakery door" since June.

"(It is) unbelievable! It is so busy. We are just making mooncakes all the time. Some of my mooncakes are already sold out," he said. "Our factory has three shifts, from the morning to 3 am. The staff can rest but the factory never rests. The oven is always warm - it's on all the time".

Omar Hsu, owner of the Ommi's Food and Catering, a mooncake seller in Sydney's inner west said his business had more than doubled compared with last year.

As the Asian and Chinese populations in Australia continue to grow, Hsu said preferences for mooncakes were also changing, particularly among the younger generation.

"We always consider mixing traditional and modern. We don't want to lose that traditional flavor from our memory. We want to take something people already love and make it better," he said.

Discussion: Can you name some other traditional Chinese food popular in western countries?

 Chinese Etiquette

The Diplomatic Idea of "Harmony but Difference"

Since ancient times, the Chinese have advocated "harmony and difference". During the Spring and Autumn Period and the Warring States Period, vassals and lords were at odds with each other. With much differences between countries, creating a harmonious relationship was one of the most important diplomatic issues. As Mencius said, "The disparity of things is also a matter of affection". "Harmonious diplomacy is about admitting differences without seeking total agreement. *The Analects of Confucius* says: "A man of virtue pursues harmony but not uniformity; a petty man seeks uniformity but not harmony. " This is also true in diplomatic relations, as all countries are different and may have differences and contradictions. It should be recognised that it is because of these differences that the world is so rich and colourful, just as the poem goes "One flower alone is not spring, but a hundred flowers in full bloom bring spring to the garden".

Task 6

Business Etiquette in Major African Countries

 Learning Objectives

■ Moral Objectives

• To cultivate students' values of equality, justice, civility, harmony.

• To have a sense of China as a responsible great power, neither humble nor arrogant, and maintain China's national image.

- Knowledge Objectives
  - • To get familiar with the profile, customs and etiquette of major African countries.
  - • To grasp the business etiquette rules and taboos of major African countries.

- Ability Objectives
  - • To be able to conduct business exchanges and communications effectively by understanding the importance of cultural differences and respecting others.
  - • To be able to avoid cultural conflicts, respect exotic cultures, and conduct business activities successfully under cross-cultural communication.

Lead-in: Case Study

Situation: Wang, a Chinese girl, is talking with Cooper, a friend from South Africa about the gift-giving etiquette in China and South Africa.

Wang: Giving gifts in China is a common etiquette used to express appreciation or gratitude for friendship or hospitality.

Cooper: In south Africa, gift giving is not the norm in business. If you are invited to a South African home, you should bring a small gift for the hostess. A bottle of wine, flowers or chocolates work well as a gift .

Wang: In China, we receive gifts with both hands to show our respect to the gift-giver. And the recipient won't open the gift until the guest leaves.

Cooper: We use either both hands or the right hand when giving and presenting gifts. And gifts will be opened upon receipt. But do not present gifts with the left hand.

Wang: In addition, there are some taboos in Chinese giving gifts. For example, it is inappropriate to present an umbrella as a gift to a couple because the word "umbrella" has the same pronunciation with another word "scattered" in Chinese.

Cooper: Interesting!

Discussion: What differences of gift-giving etiquette in China and South Africa can we learn from the dialogue?

Basic Knowledge

7.6.1　South Africa

1. Profile

South Africa represents one of the most multicultural nations, earning it the nickname — the Rainbow Nation. South Africa has a population of about 60,000,000. Three-quarters of its population is black (African) and

微课：南非国家
概况

approximately 15% is white (European). There are six major ethnic groups and 11 official languages in South Africa. Three cities serve as the capital of South Africa. Pretoria is the seat of the executive branch. Cape Town is the seat of the National Parliament. Bloemfontein is the judicial capital. The majority of South Africans are Christians. South Africans love success stories and many admire Americans because they believe in what is known as the "American Dream."

2. Business attire

South Africans of urban cultures generally wear western dress. Men usually wear suits for business meeting. You are expected to dress well in public. Here are some tips：If you are male, choose a dark, conservative business suit for business meetings. Women should wear dark business suits or conservative, modest dresses. South Africans may dress casually, but you should dress up when heading to an initial meeting.

微课：南非商务
着装

3. Gift-giving etiquette

Gift giving is not the norm in business. If you are invited to a South African home, you should bring a small gift for the hostess. A bottle of South African wine, flowers or chocolates works well as a gift for hostess. Use either both hands or the right hand when giving and presenting gifts. Gifts will be opened upon receipt. Do not present gifts with the left hand.

微课：南非商务
馈赠

For meals, business meetings can be held over lunch or dinner in a good restaurant. Meals at the home of a white South African will include a barbecue by the pool — called a braaivleis or braai.

4. Business meeting

South African business culture relies heavily on personal trust between parties. Whenever possible, schedule a face-to-face meeting to discuss business rather than communicating via e-mail, letter or telephone. While South Africa has many different cultures within the country, most of these cultures have a strong sense of value for their elders. To avoid coming across as offensive, always behave respectfully around older individuals, even if they play a less

微课：南非商务
会面

important role in the business meeting than someone else. Make appointments far in advance, at least a month prior to the meeting. Call to confirm one day before your appointment. Be on time for your appointment. If the individual or company you meet with has no knowledge of you or your business prior to your initial meeting, you'd better ask a trusted third party to send a letter of recommendation. South Africans prefer a "win-win" situation. Do not rush deals. Negotiations move slowly in South Africa. South Africans are very casual in their business dealings. Add a deadline to your contract but view it as flexible.

There are some conversation taboos in South Africa. Don't praise the achievement of the white in front of the black. Don't make comments on relationship of different tribes. Don't make negative comments on customs of the black people. Don't call indigenous people Africans.

Handshake is the most common greeting. Maintain eye contact when you shake hands at your meeting, and this helps to build trust. Use titles and surnames to address people. Appointments should be made starting at 9 a.m.. There is no formal protocol for exchange of business cards in South Africa.

7.6.2   Kenya

1. Profile

The Republic of Kenya is an East African state. Its capital Nairobi is the largest city in Kenya. English and Swahili are the official languages. Around two thirds of Kenyans are Christian but there is also a significant Muslim minority (around 10%) and followers of Hinduism and Sikhism. Kenya is a multi-cultural society made up of around 70 ethnic groups. Kenyans value familial ties above everything. A love of music and dance is deep-rooted in

微课：肯尼亚
国家概况

Kenyan culture. Kenyans are also passionate about sports, especially track and field athletics. Don't disrespect religion. Almost everyone you meet is religious; religion here is always in fashion, so if someone asks you if you are religious, don't take offense because it is common for everyone to follow a religion here.

2. Dining etiquette

Understanding Kenyan dining etiquette will be helpful. The most honored position is next to the host. When seated, your toes and feet should not be pointing toward the food or other diners. Accept offered cups of tea and/or coffee, even if you only put it to your lips or just take a few sips. Your cup will always be refilled if it is less than half full. If you are the honored guest, you are not expected to make a statement or toast, but if you offer a small

微课：肯尼亚
用餐礼仪

compliment, it will be appreciated. The honored guest is served first, then the oldest male, then the rest of the men, then children, and finally women. Do not begin to eat or drink until the oldest man has been served and has started eating.

Take off your shoes before entering Kenyan homes. Wash your hands before and after meals. Eat with your right hand. If offered a spoon or fork, hold them in your right hand. Always allow more senior members of your party to enter the room ahead of you.

Here are some dont's for dining in Kenya：Do not put your left hand on bowls or serve ware. Do not drink and eat at the same time. Eat first, then drink. Do not pour your own drink. Wait to be served. Do not leave the meal area unless invited to do so. A small burp signifies satisfaction. Tips in restaurants are 10 percent. United States currency is usually appreciated. Hissing may appear rude in other cultures but it is a perfectly acceptable form of getting a stranger's attention in Kenya. It is normal to hiss at a waiter in a crowded restaurant.

3. Business meeting

Businesses are traditionally hierarchical in Kenya. Education and experience are revered in the Kenyan workplace so be mindful of your counterpart's position in an organization when meeting for the first time. Kenyans are known for having an indirect and polite communication style, so projecting a friendly and open demeanor will help you to gain trust and support.

微课：肯尼亚商务会面

Kenyans have a relatively good sense of time. They will be punctual when there is a scheduled meeting. This, however, only refers to the sophisticated urban population. People in rural areas will turn up late for meetings, sometimes even a couple of hours late, and will make no apologies for their lateness. Be patient. Hardly anything runs on time in Kenya. Everything runs late. Don't get pissed off or impatient. Learn to go with the flow. Things will happen, just not on time.

4. Business greeting

Don't call someone by their first name. Miss, Mrs, Mr., Dr. and Engineer are totally accepted.

微课：肯尼亚商务问候

It is considered good manners for visitors to mumble at least a salutation in the local language. Traditionally, greetings should last about a minute or two. However, it is advisable to make them slightly longer, especially if you plan to conduct a business negotiation with the person you are greeting. Longer greetings may help you negotiate a cheaper price. Kenyans are very outgoing and prefer that every encounter starts with warm greetings. A person entering a shop, for instance, would start by shaking the shop attendant's hand and would proceed to make small talk before going about their business. The same practice should be repeated on departure. Close physical contact is common in Kenya, especially among the Coastal communities. Visitors should anticipate holding hands with strangers, especially if they are leading you around.

A common and essential component of etiquette in Kenya is the hand rule. Kenyans reserve the left hand for unhygienic acts and the right for acts such as eating, touching and passing things to other people. Pointing at another person is considered rude and that goes for beckoning with the palms up, which is considered rude and may be interpreted as you being dismissive.

知识储备：非洲其他主要国家礼仪风俗

📖 Extended Reading

Scan the QR code, read the passage about "Know Before You Go: Business Card Etiquette in Africa" and finish the following tasks.

After-reading tasks

When you finish reading the text above, finish the following tasks.

拓展阅读：非洲国家交换名片礼仪

Task 1   Read the statements and decide whether they are true or not. Mark "T" for true and "F" for false.

（1）Although the business card content is similar everywhere in the world, there are regional differences in both the content details and — more importantly — with regard to the etiquette of their usage. （   ）

（2）In South Africa, exchanging business cards is a usual practice, and some ceremony usually surrounds the exchange. （   ）

（3）Business cards should always be in English and both-sided in Zambia. （   ）

（4）Make sure you present and receive business cards with the right hand only or with both hands in Ethiopia. （   ）

（5）Take the time to read the card, and do not immediately put it away in your business card holder in Egypt. （   ）

Task 2   Critical thinking

Supposing you are going to visit your African customer, what should you pay attention to as to the business card exchange?

 Basic Knowledge Test

Read the statements and decide whether they are true or not. Mark "T" for true and "F" for false.

（1）Nigeria represents one of the most multicultural nations, earning it the nickname — the Rainbow Nation. （   ）

（2）Greeting processes are very important in Nigeria. Take time to exchange pleasantries and ask about each other's well-being. （   ）

同步测试：汉语版 –M7T6 判断正误

（3）Angolans do not require a great deal of personal space when conversing. If you back away, you may give offense or the person may step forward to close the gap. （   ）

（4）Business is conducted differently in South Africa. Associates often interrupt meetings to discuss other matters. （   ）

（5）Moroccans' favorite colors are green and red. Their favourite numbers include 3, 5, 7 and 40. Moroccans don't like the white color and number 13. （   ）

 **Case Study**

• Case 1

Mr. Wang invited his colleague Mr. Adebayor and his wife to dinner. Mr. Adebayo, a Hausa man from the north of Nigeria, is the manager of the Mr. Wang's department. Mr. Wang ordered pork and scrambled eggs for Mr. and Mrs. Adebayor. To show how close they had become, Mr. Wang just called Joseph instead of Mr. Adebayor and stared at his guests passionately during the conversation. Mr. Wang wanted to know more about the country, so he asked his colleague a lot of questions about the political situation in Nigeria. Before leaving the restaurant, Mr. Wang left some tips on the table.

Discussion: What rules of etiquette did Mr. Wang break in this case?

• Case 2

Ximei Import and Export Company invited Moroccan Baraka Trading Company for business negotiations. Ximei Import and Export Company arranged the negotiation conference on 10 a.m., Monday. But on that day, Moroccan business partners did not show up until 10:30 a.m.. This really makes representatives from Ximei Import and Export Company feel uncomfortable, who thought their counterpart didn't mean to cooperate. During the negotiation, Moroccan counterparts often interrupt meetings to discuss other matters. What's more, Moroccan businessmen were still negotiating even after signing a deal, which really annoyed Chinese businessmen. The negotiations were deadlocked.

Discussion: What accounts for the deadlock of the negotiation?

 Skills Training Tasks

Cultural Differences in International Business Negotiation

American Carson Import and Export Company invited Angolan Lusus Trading Company for business negotiations. During the negotiation, Angolan partners stood close to each other and sometimes touched their American partner's shoulder; their American counterpart couldn't help to back away from them. What's more, American counterparts sometimes interrupt mid-sentence, openly challenge and state their disagreements, which really annoyed Angolan businessmen, who thought their American counterparts were really rude and aggressive.

Scan the following QR codes to complete the tasks.

7.6 任务工作单   7.6 任务实施单   7.6 任务检查单   7.6 任务评价单

 Curriculum Ideology and Politics

Chinese Aid to Africa

For decades China has been helping Africa by offering aid in agriculture, health, education, infrastructure and other livelihood-related areas. The Tazara Railway in Africa is the best example of China's sincerity and efforts. It was built when China was itself in economic difficulty and over 60 Chinese workers gave their lives while constructing it.

China has aided or financed the building of over 5,000 km of railway and roads, built more than 200 schools and nearly 100 hospitals, and trained more than 160,000 professional workers in Africa. China's 43 medical teams in 42 African countries have treated 280 million patients. We believe "it's better to pass on fishing skills than to hand out fish." Our aid is based on equality and mutual benefit, and serves Africa's economy and social programs.

China has taken solid steps to ease Africa's debt burden. Since 2000, nine loan waivers have been announced for heavily-indebted and least developed countries (LDCs). By 2009, 312 debts of 35 African countries have been cancelled, worth $3 billion in total. In September 2015, President Xi Jinping announced China's decision to write off outstanding intergovernmental interest-free loans due by the end of 2015 for LDCs, landlocked developing nations and small island developing countries, including African countries.

Discussion: What is your understanding of "It's better to pass on fishing skills than to hand out fish."?

 **Chinese Etiquette**

Chinese and the Color of Red

We Chinese like the color of red, and even we call ourselves as Chizi, which means a patriot. In China, red represents the power and happiness. Official robes of many dynasties were red. In the Qing Dynasty, different shades of red on the official caps showed different rankings. Headlines of official documents are often printed in red. For that reason, it's called "red-head documents". In addition, the Chinese character signifying double happiness used for weddings is red. During the Spring Festival, elder people will give Hongbao to the children as gifts and wishes for the new year.

模块 7
跨文化商务礼仪

模块导读

　　全球化加剧是过去 10 年中重要的进展之一。跨境业务大幅增长。在 21 世纪，与世界各地的贸易伙伴有效开展业务的能力依赖于跨文化知识和文化智慧。有远见的公司将国际商务礼仪和沟通技能的发展视为一种战略，这样就可以拥有商业优势，领先竞争对手。

　　文化多样性在日常实践和商业场合中体现出来，如商务问候、商务馈赠、商务禁忌、握手、餐桌礼仪（商务餐）、肢体语言、口语、书面语（电子邮件、短信）和其他面对面互动。适应并意识到文化多样性在商业互动中至关重要。企业如果没有意识到文化差异的重要性，在与商业伙伴沟通时会遭遇尴尬或违反职业道德，从而损害商业关系。跨文化交流将呈现一个人的个性，反映在他的行为中，体现出个人价值观、习惯和礼仪。

任务 1

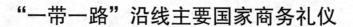

"一带一路"沿线主要国家商务礼仪

◎ 学习目标

■ **素养目标**
- 秉承平等、公正、文明、和谐等社会主义价值观。
- 具有家国情怀与大国担当，不卑不亢，维护民族形象。

■ **知识目标**
- 了解"一带一路"沿线主要国家概况、习俗礼仪。

- 掌握"一带一路"沿线主要国家商务礼仪规范和商务禁忌。

■ **能力目标**

- 能够理解文化差异的重要性，并秉持"敬人"理念进行商务交往和沟通。
- 能够规避文化冲突，尊敬异国文化，从而顺利进行跨文化交际下商务活动。

 情境导入

情境：一个马来西亚人正在和他的美国同事谈话。

马来西亚人：我可以问你一个问题吗？

美国人：（抬头）当然。

马来西亚人：现在几点了？

美国人：（看起来很困惑）现在是五点半。

马来西亚人：锅里能剩下一点汤吗？

美国人：（看起来更困惑）对不起？我听不懂你的意思。

马来西亚人：（因为同事不明白他的意思，所以他要说得更明确一些）我要去市区参加一个员工的培训项目，一直到今晚8点。到时候我会又累又饿。

美国人：（终于明白了）你想让我开车送你去餐馆吃饭吗？

马来西亚人：那太好了！

讨论：案例中的美国人为什么在开始时没有听懂马来西亚人的弦外之音？

 **知识储备**

7.1.1 马来西亚

1. 国家概况

马来西亚是一个君主立宪联邦制国家，位于东南亚的赤道地区，热带雨林气候，四季分明。

马来西亚是世界第 18 大贸易国，世界第二大棕榈油及相关产品生产国，第三大天然橡胶生产国和出口国，第三大液化天然气出口国。

根据马来西亚宪法，国家保证宗教自由，同时使伊斯兰教成为国教。大约 61.3% 的人口信奉伊斯兰教，19.8% 信奉佛教，9.2% 信奉基督教，6.3% 信奉印度教，1.3% 信奉儒教、道教和其他中国传统宗教。

2. 商务禁忌

1）饮食禁忌

马来西亚人大多数是穆斯林，在伊斯兰教文化里，不允许饮酒、吃猪肉和狗肉以及用左手进食。

宴会中不能饮酒，可以喝茶或软饮料。

2）着装禁忌

伊斯兰教文化里，商务着装不宜过于暴露。无论男女，都不要穿无袖或短袖衣服。女性应该穿着得体，遮住肩膀、上臂和膝盖。

3）体态禁忌

不要用食指指着别人。

不要用左手打招呼、握手或传递信息，因为在伊斯兰教文化中，左手被认为是肮脏的。

不要碰别人的头或背，因为他们的头和背被认为是神圣的，不能碰。

不要分开双腿坐着，或跷二郎腿。

不要在别人面前露脚底，把脚底露给别人看是一种侮辱。

4）言谈禁忌

不要谈论家庭等私人生活话题。

不要谈论忌讳的动物，即马、猪、狗和乌龟。狗被认为是肮脏的，会带来瘟疫。乌龟被认为是不吉利和色情的。

不要谈论禁忌数字，即 0、4、13。

5）商务馈赠禁忌

不要用左手拿礼物。

不要当着送礼人的面打开礼物。在马来西亚，用双手接受礼物，并一般要等送礼人离开后才打开礼物。

因为猪是禁忌，因此不要送猪皮手套、猪皮皮带等猪制品礼物。

6）商务拜访禁忌

除非马来西亚女性主动握手，否则男士不能主动握手。在商务活动中，男性之间经常握手。男性和女性很少握手，点头或鞠躬都可以。

7.1.2　俄罗斯

1. 国家概况

俄罗斯联邦有一亿四千七百万人口。首都是莫斯科。官方语言为俄语，也包括其他各地区的语言。

以下是关于俄罗斯的一些有趣的事实。俄罗斯幅员辽阔，涵盖了 9 个时区。俄罗斯是第一个将人类送入太空的国家。莫斯科为欧洲最大的城市。红色是俄罗斯文化和历史中的重要颜色。俄罗斯覆盖了半个北半球，有 12 个海域。

2. 商务问候

握手要坚定，保持直接的眼神交流。俄罗斯人非常尊重女性。"女士优先"在俄罗斯很流行。不要隔着门槛握手或送东西。到达和离开对方家时，最好先跨过门槛，然后和主人握手。

对他人不要直呼其名，除非对方允许你这么做。你可以用"Gospodin"（先生）或"Gospozha"（夫人）加上他们的姓氏。使用他们的专业或学术头衔是值得赞赏的。如果你知道那个人的全名，而且你非常了解他，那么如果你用他的名字和他的父名的组合会更受欢迎。

3. 商务谈判

耐心是俄罗斯人极为重要的美德。俄罗斯人在谈判中被称为伟大的"座席者"，这显示了他们巨大的耐心。别指望你的俄罗斯同事会准时到，这可能只是试探你的耐心。不要指望迟到的俄罗斯人会道歉，如果你的商务约会晚了一两个小时，也不要表现出任何态度。

当和别人握手时，一定要摘下手套，因为戴着手套与别人握手会被认为是不礼貌的。一定要准备足够多的名片。一面用英文，另一面用俄文。

自由地表达你的观点，不要只做一个倾听者。适合的话题包括和平、文化、历史、俄罗斯目前发生的变化等。俄罗斯人很喜欢孩子。所以，不要犹豫，向他们展示你孩子的照片。避免谈论诸如抱怨俄罗斯、与少数民族的冲突等话题，也不要将俄罗斯与其他发达国家进行比较。

4. 商务着装规范

俄罗斯商人通常穿着剪裁考究的深色西装和精致的鞋子。在谈判中，男人通常不会脱下外套。在朋友家参加晚宴时，穿休闲装和一件漂亮的衬衫，不打领带是合适的。

职场女性穿着相当保守。不要穿太花哨的衣服。妇女在参观东正教堂时应该用围巾遮住头部。应该穿裙子而不是裤子。

5. 商务宴请

在所有客人盘子里都盛上了食物，并且主人邀请你开始吃之前，先不要吃。接受别人的祝酒，也可以主动祝酒，如果拒绝别人的祝酒会有违礼节。

受到邀请出去喝一杯是非常可取的，因为这表明了对方愿意与你增进关系、表示友好。

6. 商务馈赠

如果没有当地人的帮助，在俄罗斯做生意是极其困难的。为了解决这个问题，在俄罗斯做生意时送礼物是一个好主意。

如果在家庭住宅参加晚宴，带一份礼物是合适的，如一瓶酒、甜点或一束花。确保花的数量是奇数，在俄罗斯，偶数的花通常与葬礼有关。

 **同步测试**

扫码做题。

同步测试：汉语版 –M7T1 判断正误

案例分析

案例 1

希杰国际物流邀请马来西亚吉隆坡进出口贸易公司进行业务洽谈。希杰国际物流安排了周五的谈判会议，但被告知周五不是合适的日期。然后他们决定在星期六上午 9 点。但到了周六那天，马来西亚商业伙伴直到上午 10 点才出现。这着实使希杰国际物流的代表们感到不快，他们认为对方无意合作。在谈判过程中，马来西亚商业伙伴一直在讨价还价，希杰国际物流不愿意在价格上做出任何让步。希杰国际物流设宴款待贵宾，并把中国著名白酒茅台摆在了餐桌上。他们试图说服马来西亚的商业伙伴喝酒，结果使他们大为不快。更糟糕的是，希杰国际物流忘记告诉厨师不要用猪油做饭。马来西亚商业伙伴愤怒地离开宴会，谈判陷入僵局。

讨论：谈判陷入僵局的原因是什么？

案例 2

迈克尔是贸易促进服务公司的一名英国雇员，他出席了 PT Laxam 国际公司的会议。迈克尔给印度尼西亚商业伙伴送了礼物，但他们却大为不悦。印度尼西亚华人销售经理张先生收到精美的大本钟；文秘莎丽收到可爱的玩具狗；印度尼西亚马来族人布迪收到猪皮包；印度裔印度尼西亚人辛塔收到带牛皮包装袋的派克笔。

讨论：为什么迈克尔的商业伙伴很生气？

实训项目

实训项目 1

分析马来西亚商务馈赠

1. 实训目的

通过训练，掌握马来西亚商务馈赠的习俗与禁忌。

2. 实训内容

（1）背景资料：希杰国际物流中国员工小刘赴马来西亚吉隆坡进出口贸易公司参加会议。他给马来西亚的生意伙伴送礼物，却没想到令他们感到不快。马来西亚华人销售经理张先生收到了中国名酒茅台；马来西亚人推销员 Foo 先生收到了万马奔腾装饰品；马来西亚人秘书 Min 女士收到一副猪皮手套；印度裔马来西亚甘地先生收到一条牛皮带。

（2）以小组为单位，分析此案例中小刘违反了哪些马来西亚商务馈赠禁忌；小组成员间讨论，在马来西亚还有哪些商务馈赠的禁忌；给出可供改进的商务馈赠方案。

3. 实训要求

（1）采取"组内异质，组间同质"的原则，将学生分为若干小组，每组 4~6 人。

（2）每组提交一份马来西亚商务馈赠实训报告，内容包括本案例中存在的问题及相应的改进方案。

（3）每组讲解和展示本组的工作成果。

4. **实训考核**

（1）评价方式：采取小组自评、小组互评、教师评价、企业导师评价四维评价方式，总评成绩 = 小组自评×20% + 小组互评×20% + 教师评价×30% + 企业导师评价×30%。

（2）评价指标：从素质目标、知识目标、能力目标 3 方面进行评价。

7.1.1 任务工作单　　7.1.1 任务实施单　　7.1.1 任务检查单　　7.1.1 任务评价单

实训项目 2

分析印度尼西亚商务谈判

1. **实训目的**

通过训练，掌握印度尼西亚商务谈判的规则与禁忌。

2. **实训内容**

（1）背景资料：希杰物流国际有限公司邀请了 PT. Laxam 国际公司进行国际会谈。希杰物流的谈判人员与印度尼西亚方伙伴握手后，亲切地拍了拍对方的后背，然而印度尼西亚谈判人员露出了反感的神情。谈判过程中，印度尼西亚商业伙伴一直在拐弯抹角，并不切入正题。此外，他们一直在讨价还价，希杰物流国际有限公司不愿意在价格上做出任何让步。谈判结束后，中方松了一口气，跷起二郎腿。更糟糕的是，当双方签署合同时，中方经理用左手在纸上签字。这些举动让印度尼西亚的商业伙伴难以接受，愤怒地离开了，没有签署合同。

（2）以小组为单位，分析此案例中谈判失败的原因是什么；小组成员间讨论，在印度尼西亚，人们在商务谈判时要注意哪些习俗与禁忌；给出可供改进的商务谈判方案。

3. **实训要求**

（1）采取"组内异质，组间同质"的原则，将学生分为若干小组，每组 4～6 人。

（2）每组提交一份印度尼西亚商务谈判实训报告，内容包括本案例中存在的问题及相应的改进方案。

（3）每组讲解和展示本组的工作成果。

4. **实训考核**

（1）评价方式：采取小组自评、小组互评、教师评价、企业导师评价四维评价方式，总评成绩 = 小组自评×20% + 小组互评×20% + 教师评价×30% + 企业导师评价×30%。

（2）评价指标：从素质目标、知识目标、能力目标 3 方面进行评价。

7.1.2 任务工作单　　7.1.2 任务实施单　　7.1.2 任务检查单　　7.1.2 任务评价单

思政课堂

柬埔寨 58 号公路正式通车。这条全长 174km 的公路在柬埔寨西部地区的经济和旅游发展中发挥了关键的作用。它不仅由上海的一家建筑企业承建，而且部分资金来自中国"一带一路"倡议下的优惠信贷。迄今为止，中国已经援助柬埔寨修建 3000 多公里的公路和 8 座大桥。柬埔寨的这些项目是"一带一路"倡议的一个缩影。2013 年，习近平主席在出访东南亚和中亚期间提出了"一带一路"倡议。受到古代丝绸之路的启示，"一带一路"倡议是一个全球性的基础设施发展计划，寻求共同发展和共享繁荣。截至 2000 年，中方与 138 个国家、31 个国际组织共同展开的 2000 多个项目在"一带一路"倡议下进行，包括港口、道路和桥梁的建设。在新冠疫情期间，中欧班列作为"一带一路"的标志性项目成为欧亚大陆之间的个人防护设备和其他货物运输的生命线。截至 2021 年 5 月，中欧班列共向 22 个欧洲国家运送了超过 340 万标箱的货物，为全球供应链提供了一个可靠的新方案。中国提出人类命运共同体，也是中国作为一个大国的担当。这样一种责任感，其实中国一直有。中国共产党始终认为，全人类共享同一家园，因此要通过合作而不是称霸来解决全球事务。

（资料来源：https://www.ximalaya.com/sound/459552597）

讨论：党的二十大报告中指出，要推进高水平对外开放，推动共建"一带一路"高质量发展。"一带一路"倡议具体指什么？作为世界大国，中国如何履行自己的职责？

中华礼仪

在中国文化里，"面子"一词并不单指脸。送一个人厚礼就是"给他面子"。而如果礼物是个人送的，最好别照单全收，只收一部分即可，也不要拒收。

任务 2

欧洲主要国家商务礼仪

◎ 学习目标

■ **素养目标**
- 秉承平等、公正、文明、和谐等社会主义价值观。
- 具有家国情怀与大国担当，不卑不亢，维护民族形象。

■ 知识目标
- 了解欧洲主要国家概况习俗礼仪。
- 掌握欧洲主要国家商务礼仪规范和商务禁忌。

■ 能力目标
- 能够理解文化差异重要性并秉持"敬人"理念进行商务交往和沟通。
- 能够规避文化冲突，尊敬异国文化，从而顺利进行跨文化交际下商务活动。

 情境导入

情境：一位美国商人与他的德国客户初次见面，就一批新产品的价格进行谈判。

德国人：您好，现在是 10:10，如果我没记错，我们约定的会议时间是 10:00 对吧？

美国人：（笑着说）是的。刚刚来的路上遇上了堵车，所以来晚了。

德国人：那我们开始吧，初次见面，这是我的名片（双手递出名片）。

美国人：（单手接过名片）啊，您的名字很特别，这在德国也是很少见的名字吧。

德国人：这是我公司的产品报价单，请您过目。

美国人：（看起来很没耐心）听说附近有一家很棒的餐馆。时间不早了，我们去那里吃午饭，边吃边谈怎么样？

德国人：对不起，我已经浪费一上午的时间了，我要回公司了，请另约时间吧！（生气地离开了会议室）

讨论：谈判为什么会陷入僵局？

 知识储备

7.2.1　英国

1. 国家概况

大不列颠及北爱尔兰联合王国，俗称英国，是西欧的主权国家。英国位于欧洲大陆西北海岸，包括大不列颠岛、爱尔兰岛东北部和许多较小的岛屿。英国气候温和，全年雨量充沛。

英国是议会民主政体中的君主立宪制国家，英国由英格兰、苏格兰、威尔士和北爱尔兰四个部分组成，伦敦是英国的首都和最大的城市，是一个全球城市和金融中心。

1400 多年来，在英国，基督教一直占主导地位。英国人 59.5% 是基督徒，其次是穆斯林（4.4%）、印度教徒（1.3%）、犹太教徒（0.4%）。25.7% 的人不信教。

英国的官方语言是英语。法语和德语是英格兰地区和苏格兰地区最常用的第二语言。

2. 商务宴请

如果你邀请英国人出去用餐，最好邀请一些背景相同、专业水平相近的人。下面几点可能会有用。

进餐时吸烟被视为无礼。宴会中禁止吸烟。

基督徒禁忌食用动物血做成的食物。由于英国基督徒人口众多，英国人不吃动物血制成的食物。

英国人进餐时，会一直把手放在桌子上，但是不会把肘部也放在桌子上，也不会托下巴或托腮。

3. 商务着装规范

在正式商务场合（会客、拜访、宴会等），男士一般穿三件套式西装，打领带，女士要穿晚礼服或套装以及有跟的鞋子。

英国人不喜欢条纹领带，因为条纹领带会让他们联想到旧时"军团"或老学校的制服领带。所以最好不打条纹领带。

在夏天，男士可以不穿西装，只穿短袖衬衫，但也要打领带。如果有人邀请你喝下午茶，除非有特别的规定，男士不必穿西装、打领带，可以穿休闲商务装，但是不能穿运动服或运动鞋。在正式场合，西装不能和运动鞋搭配。

4. 商务仪态

做 V 字手势时，不能手背向外。在英国、澳大利亚和新西兰，这个手势的意思是"滚开，闭嘴"，具有侮辱性。

和英国人交谈时，不要站的距离对方太近，更不要把手放在对方的肩膀上，这会让英国人感到非常不舒服。

不要跷二郎腿。

5. 商务谈判

和英国人闲聊时，可以谈论天气和运动。交谈中要多用礼貌用语及句式，如"请""谢谢""抱歉""我能荣幸地请您……"。家庭、收入、宗教、婚姻等个人私事，皇室以及政治等话题都不要谈论。

6. 商务馈赠

英国人在商务场合下通常不交换礼物。当你被邀请到英国人家里做客时，要带一份小礼物给女主人，可以送鲜花、巧克力、葡萄酒、香槟或书籍。当主人收到礼物时，会马上打开礼物。下面是赠送礼物的禁忌。

不要送给英国人白色百合和菊花，因为这些花是葬礼用的。不要送带有送礼人公司标记的纪念品。

不要选择涉及私生活的服饰、香皂之类的物品。不要用墨绿色包装纸包装礼物，因为第二次世界大战时期纳粹军服是墨绿色的，被英国人所厌恶。英国人喜欢蓝色、红色和白色。

不要送带有大象、孔雀或猫头鹰图案的礼物或这些动物的装饰品、玩偶。

7. 商务问候

下面是与英国人相互问候时的禁忌。

切忌一只脚在门里面、另一只脚在门外与人握手。切忌四人交叉握手。

在商务活动中，男性之间经常握手。

男性和女性很少握手，点头或鞠躬都可以。

7.2.2　法国

1. 国家概况

法国是西欧最大的国家。它位于欧洲大陆的西部边缘，与六个邻国接壤：北部是比利时和卢森堡，东面是德国和瑞士，东南是意大利，西南是西班牙。

法国是欧盟人口最多的国家之一。大约 84% 的法国人是罗马天主教徒。此外，8% 是穆斯林（主要是北非移民）、2% 是新教徒、1% 是犹太教徒，而 4% 不属于任何宗教。

法语是法国的母语，被视为法国文化的象征。法国人通常更喜欢说法语，也更喜欢对方说法语。此外，大量的移民人口带来了许多其他语言，增加了法国的种族多样性。

2. 商务问候

到达和离开某个商务或社交会议时，要和每个人握手。握手要快而轻。

男性可能主动与女性握手。

家人和亲密的朋友相互问候时，通常会亲吻双方的脸颊。

使用姓和适当的头衔，除非你的法国房东或同事特别邀请你使用他们的名字。名字只用于亲密的朋友和家人之间。

同级别的同事在私底下通常直呼其名，而在公开场合总是直呼其姓。

称呼别人为"先生""夫人"或"小姐"，不要加上姓氏。

Madame 是指所有 18 岁以上的成年女性，无论已婚还是单身（称呼女服务员时可以用 Mademoiselle）。

学术头衔和学位非常重要。你应该了解并正确地使用它们。

3. 商务谈判

法语使用了许多习语和比喻（如"raining cats and dogs"），如果没有额外的上下文或说话者本人的解释，非母语人士就很难理解这些习语和比喻。

法国人可能不愿意与他们不太了解的人或非法国人自由分享信息。你如果问他们私人问题，会让他们感觉不舒服，还会感到被冒犯，所以最好等你们建立了一定的信任之后，再问他们工作、生活或家庭方面的私人问题。

4. 商务宴请

法国人不喜欢在吃饭时谈论生意。晚餐更多的是一个社交场合，是享受美食、美酒和讨论的时间。当你和法国客户一起吃饭时，以下几点可能会有用。

晚餐前不要点马提尼或苏格兰威士忌——它们会让你的味觉麻木。

晚餐前，可以提供茴香酒、基尔酒、香槟、苦艾酒。酒总是随餐而上。晚餐后，供应利口酒。

高级经理只愿意与地位相当的人交往。

商务午餐不包括配偶，但商务晚宴可能包括配偶。

女贵宾坐在男主人的右边。男贵宾坐在女主人的左边。

在主人和女主人开始吃饭之前，不要先吃。等有人向你祝酒后再喝酒。

几乎所有的食物都是用刀叉切的。

第二天发一封感谢信或打电话向女主人表示感谢。

5. 商务馈赠

在法国，当商务人士第一次见面时，他们通常不会互赠礼物。表达感激之情的最好方式是举办一个特别的活动或晚宴，而不是送礼物。

被邀请到别人家里做客时，一定要给女主人带一份小礼物。如果可能的话，在聚会当天早上送花（这在巴黎很流行）。否则，可以在到达时给女主人送一份礼物。不要将礼物寄到法国人的家里。送给女主人的礼物，她可能不会当面立即打开（除非没有其他客人在场或预期没有其他人会来）。

礼物应该是高质量和包装精美的。送糖果、饼干、蛋糕和鲜花。不要送印有公司标志的礼物（法国人认为这很花哨）。不要送价值6或12英镑的礼物（这是送给恋人的）。不要送奇数的礼物（尤其是13），菊花、红玫瑰或葡萄酒（除非酒的质量特别好）也不合适。

7.2.3　西班牙

1. 国家概况

西班牙地处大西洋和地中海、欧洲和非洲的十字路口，是西欧和欧盟的第二大国家。

西班牙是一个多民族国家，由20多个民族组成。西班牙约4800万人，96%的人口信奉天主教。官方语言为西班牙语，另外，还有三种地区级官方语言：加泰罗尼亚语、巴斯克语和加里西亚语。

西班牙人以对娱乐的热情而闻名。体育在西班牙人的生活中扮演着重要角色。西班牙人喜欢踢足球和看足球，几乎每个城镇都有一些足球比赛场地。在西班牙，斗牛相当受欢迎。它被认为是国家的奇观，是一种勇气、智慧、优雅和意志的象征。

西班牙因其友好的居民、轻松的生活方式、诱人的美食、充满活力的夜生活以及世界闻名的民间传说而被视为欧洲最具魅力的国家之一。

2. 商务着装规范

外表对西班牙人来说极为重要。即使是在休闲场合，他们也会穿着优雅。下面是一些注意事项：

穿着保守。避免明亮或浮华的颜色。

鞋子是服装中最重要的元素。破旧的鞋子会毁了一套漂亮的衣服。

商务场合，即使天气温暖，男士也应该穿夹克打领带。如果高层在会议中脱下他／她的外套，你也可以这样做。

女士应该穿连衣裙、衬衫和裙子。

3. 商务谈判

对西班牙人来说，人际关系是商务谈判中的关注点。西班牙人更喜欢在开始商业关系之前了解对方。任何会议通常都会从讨论一般性话题开始，并在个人层面上相互联系，以建立稳固的工作关系。在很多情况下，社会关系可以起到担保作用，甚至可以取代书面合同。

西班牙人害怕丢面子，所以他们不会在他人面前承认自己理解起来有困难。因此在谈判中最好给每人提供一份用西班牙语写的文稿，会非常有助于他们理解。

在西班牙，决策过程可能会非常缓慢，因为各个管理层的意见都要被询问，只有地位最高的人才能做出最后的决策。

4. 商务宴请

在西班牙，许多生意都是在午餐时谈成的，晚餐往往是为了娱乐或庆祝。话题可以涉及个人、家庭等。下面是一些注意事项：

试着用西班牙语祝酒。祝酒时要简短。女士祝酒是可以接受的。

在任何就餐场合都要付小费。

西班牙人不浪费食物。宁可拒绝某样食物，也不要把食物剩在盘子里。

5. 商务馈赠

对西班牙人来说，礼物是一种表示尊重的方式，而不是贿赂。被邀请到别人家里做客时，一定要给女主人带一份包装好的小礼物。你可以选择自己国家或地区的礼物，如葡萄酒、领带和围巾。

如果你收到包装好的礼物，你应该立即打开它并表示感谢。之后你也可以写一封感谢信。

商务会议中通常不交换礼物，但在谈判成功结束时，送点小礼物是合适的。

 同步测试

扫码做题。

同步测试：汉语版 –M7T2 判断正误

 **案例分析**

青岛贝来国际贸易有限公司派销售经理小李参加广交会，在展会上他将与来自德国、法国、意大利、西班牙、葡萄牙等欧洲国家的客户进行业务洽谈。小李已经做了充分的准备，并列好了以下注意事项。

与德国人的会面，我会列出会面的详细程序，并提前发给客户。我想我们可以用英语交流。

与法国人沟通，我会尽量让他们在会议期间与我们达成协议，我认为英语也会很有用。

与意大利人沟通，我会直接给他们报价，希望他们能马上接受并达成口头协议。

与西班牙人沟通，我将以一些随意的话题开始，这样我们可以更好地了解对方。

与葡萄牙人沟通，我将表现出真诚的合作，保证我们产品的质量。

讨论：上述每一条是否合理？请给出改进建议完善计划。

技能演练

分析欧洲国家商务宴请礼仪

1. 实训目的

通过训练，掌握不同欧洲国家的商务宴请礼仪。

2. 实训内容

（1）背景资料：青岛贝来国际贸易有限公司接待一些来中国谈判的欧洲客户。谈判结束后，公司为他们精心准备了一场晚宴。由于他们来自英国、德国、法国、意大利、西班牙和葡萄牙等不同欧洲国家，经理需要总结宴会的要点，以便让厨师做好准备。

① 宴会上将提供优质啤酒和香肠。

② 法国人非常注重食物的品质和味道，所以需要选择最好的食材来烹饪。

③ 葡萄酒是必不可少的，中国白酒是一个不错的选择。我们可以在敬酒时就经济、政治等话题进行交谈，这样我们就可以和欧洲客户建立良好的关系。

④ 安排一些娱乐活动，以便他们能更好地享受宴会。

⑤ 准备足够数量的餐具，特别是勺子和筷子。

（2）以小组为单位，分析此案例中的方案违反了欧洲国家商务礼仪的哪些方面；小组成员间讨论，如果改进方案使之更合适，还可以补充哪些合理的要点，使晚宴更加成功。

3. 实训要求

（1）采取"组内异质，组间同质"的原则，将学生分为若干小组，每组4~6人。

（2）每组提交一份欧洲国家商务宴请礼仪的实训报告，内容包括本案例中存在的问题及相应的改进方案和建议。

（3）每组选派一名代表讲解和展示本组的工作成果。

4. 实训考核

（1）评价方式：采取小组自评、小组互评、教师评价、企业导师评价四维评价方式，总评成绩＝小组自评×20%＋小组互评×20%＋教师评价×30%＋企业导师评价×30%。

（2）评价指标：从素质目标、知识目标、能力目标3方面进行评价。

7.2 任务工作单　　7.2 任务实施单　　7.2 任务检查单　　7.2 任务评价单

 **思政课堂**

中国国际贸易促进委员会2022年8月29日发布的一项调研显示，欧洲跨国公司持续看好中国市场，中国经济发展的韧性以及国内大市场对欧洲跨国公司保持强大的吸引力。例如，6月，空中客车中国研发中心落户江苏苏州，专注于氢动力飞机的研究。7月，德国化工集团巴斯夫公司决定在广东湛江建设一体化基地项目。

对外经济贸易大学国际经济研究院院长桑百川表示，中国具有完整的工业体系，市场巨大、社会稳定，具有长期向好的经济基础，以及中欧班列的顺利运行，这些优势为欧洲跨国公司在华发展奠定了坚实的基础。

讨论： 党的二十大报告指出"坚持社会主义市场经济改革方向，坚持高水平对外开放，加快构建以国内大循环为主体、国内国际双循环相互促进的新发展格局"。为什么中国市场对于欧盟国家来说如此具有吸引力？欧盟市场对于中国的经济发展意味着什么？

中华礼仪

如果你不知道该给亲朋好友送什么春节礼物,送红包是最保险的。红包就是一个用红纸制成的包,红纸包中装有现金,给朋友或亲人的孩子送红包是一种表达祝福的方式。在中国习俗中,春节时长辈给小孩包红包也是他们表达爱意的方式。

任务 3

亚洲主要国家商务礼仪

学习目标

■ **素养目标**
- 秉承平等、公正、文明、和谐等社会主义价值观。
- 具有家国情怀与大国担当,不卑不亢,维护民族形象。

■ **知识目标**
- 了解亚洲主要国家概况习俗礼仪。
- 掌握亚洲主要国家商务礼仪规范和商务禁忌。

■ **能力目标**
- 能够理解文化差异的重要性,并秉持"敬人"理念进行商务交往和沟通。
- 能够规避文化冲突,尊敬异国文化,从而顺利进行跨文化交际下的商务活动。

情境导入

情境:1972 年 9 月,日本首相田中角荣访问中国,迎接他的是周恩来、叶剑英等中方领导人。当他的专机抵达北京时,田中角荣身穿一身灰色西装,快步走下飞机舷梯,主动伸出手来和周总理握手,并说了一番颇值得考究的话:"我叫田中角荣,今年 54 岁,当了日本首相,请多关照"。在此后的行程中,田中角荣受到了中方的周到接见。

讨论:
(1)田中角荣如此介绍自己有何用意?
(2)田中角荣的行为和语言体现了哪些日本的商务礼仪?

7.3.1　日本

1. 国家概况

日本是东亚的主权岛国，位于太平洋，亚洲大陆东海岸，北起鄂霍茨克海，西南至东海。

日语是日本的官方语言。日语中多数句子能用至少 8 种不同程度的敬语形式表达。日本人交流通常注重大量的细节。

日本没有国教。神道教是日本的本土宗教。此外，日本人还信仰佛教、基督教等。

2. 商务问候

日本人熟悉西方习俗。他们通常轻轻握手表示问候。鞠躬是日本人传统的问候方式。鞠躬时，你的鞠躬程度应与对方相同，表明你们之间地位平等。鞠躬时，眼睛须向下看。直视他人是不礼貌的行为。手心朝上，双手平放在大腿上。

不要因为日本人问到许多隐私问题而感到恼怒。日本人需要了解工作、职位等许多信息，才能决定与外国人谈话时用何种称谓。不要把对方的名片放在口袋里，尤其是裤子后面的口袋。

3. 商务谈判

谈判首先在主管层进行，而后在中层工作人员之间展开。由于年龄和职位同等重要，你应尊重日本团队中最年长的成员。

日本人对于工作态度严肃。切勿试图"活跃气氛"。但是不要因为担心不被人喜欢而一味地逢迎。

在日本，你须将"很抱歉"挂在嘴边。切勿直接指责或拒绝，要委婉而间接地表达此意。

与日语翻译用英语交谈时一定要保持耐心。说话速度要缓慢，中间时长停顿，避免口语性用法。翻译所用的时间可能比你说话的时间要长，因为他要用冗长的敬语来表达。

4. 商务宴请

如果应邀到日本人家中做客，你须牢记这是无比的荣幸，并且应该表示感谢。允许主人替你点餐。进餐时你应该兴致高昂，餐后对主人表示感谢。

在家中，一家人围坐在一张低矮的桌子旁。你可以盘腿而坐，或者侧腿而坐。不用筷子时，须将筷子放在筷托上。切勿用筷子指人。续杯时，不可以单手拿杯。

5. 商务馈赠

在日本，馈赠礼物很普遍。对于日本人而言，礼物的馈赠仪式要比礼物本身意义重大。

馈赠佳品包括进口苏格兰威士忌酒，法国白兰地或赠给孩子的电子玩具。避免赠送数目为偶数的物品。"4"是不吉利的数字。不要用黑色或白色的包装纸。不要赠送白色的花，因为白色易让人联想到死亡。

7.3.2 韩国

1. 国家概况

韩国，即大韩民国，位于朝鲜半岛的南部，是东亚的主权国家。韩语是韩国的官方语言。韩国的学校教育普及英语，因此韩国商人通常能够熟练使用英语。

尽管在韩国多种宗教并存，但儒教对整个社会的影响力最强，是控制所有社会关系的伦理道德体系。

2. 商务问候

韩国人见面时，微微鞠躬以示问候，有时会目视对方并握手。但是，西方男性不应与韩国女性握手，西方女性应主动与韩国男性握手。

聚会上遇到你想结识的人，应邀请第三方引荐，切勿自我介绍。在韩国，称呼他人用职称或姓氏即可。已婚女性保留娘家姓。长者受到人们的高度尊重，因此出于礼貌，你应该主动问候他们。

3. 商务谈判

在韩国，成功构建业务关系的基础是建立人与人之间相互尊敬的和谐关系。因此，多准备一些名片。名片非常重要，因为它显示着你的地位，是你在韩国文化中赢得应有尊重的关键。

保留颜面，也就是维护他人的尊严，是重要且微妙的事情。因此，切勿令人在公共场合难堪。

与北美和欧洲国家相比，韩国公司的办事节奏要慢很多。达成协议之前，你应该保持耐心，切勿谈论你的最后期限。

4. 商务宴请

一天中最丰盛的餐宴在晚上举行，韩国人大多在餐厅或咖啡屋款待客人。因此如果应邀到韩国人家中做客，这是你莫大的荣幸。不要拒绝此类邀请，并尽量在离开韩国前回请对方。

韩国人认为把筷子平行放置会带来噩运。并且筷子上沾有米粒是一种粗鲁行为。从餐盘中夹起的食物不能直接入口，应该把它先放到自己的盘子里。

5. 商务馈赠

商务场合通常赠送礼物。可以送印有公司商标的物品（切勿赠送日本或韩国生产的礼品）。赠送者在场时，不能当面拆看礼物。

根据习俗，往往需要回赠对方等值的礼物。因此，选择礼物时应考虑接受者的经济能力。如果收到一份过于昂贵的礼物，可以在表示感谢后再拒绝。

 **同步测试**

扫码做题。

同步测试：汉语版–M7T3 判断正误

案例分析

　　青岛贝来国际贸易有限公司接待了从印度来中国洽谈生意的一行客户。在谈判会议上，双方就产品价格等方面进行磋商。会议开始前，中方公司沏好了茶，准备了甜点供印方客户享用。会议一开始，中方代表小王先与印方闲谈了一会儿，主要向他们介绍了青岛的风土人情，并询问了对方来中国后的生活是否适应。之后才慢慢地引出正题。在谈到供货价格时，印方提出了20%的折扣，小王没有马上拒绝，而是说可以考虑一下。印方又提出将物流时间由一个月缩短为半个月，小王也没有一口否决，还是点点头说："我们会尽力为您缩短物流时间。"了解到客户的宗教背景后，贝来公司在会后邀请印度客户来到一家地道的清真餐厅用餐。最终，印度客户在离开中国前与青岛贝来公司签了一笔数量可观的订单。

　　讨论：为什么谈判最终取得了成功？

 实训项目

分析韩国商务礼仪

1. 实训目的

通过训练，掌握韩国的商务礼仪习俗及禁忌。

2. 实训内容

（1）背景资料：来自美国某国际贸易公司的业务员杰克应邀到韩国客户家拜访并用餐。他去之前在韩国当地的百货大楼购买了一套高档化妆品准备作为礼物送给女主人。当杰克到达客户家时，他主动热情地伸出手与客户及女主人握手，并立刻把礼物拿了出来。然而女主人表现得尴尬及不悦。在餐桌上，客户热情地款待了杰克。杰克吃罢，就将筷子平行放置在桌子上，他所用过的餐具上还有明显可见的饭渣。回国后，杰克的客户并没有购买其公司的产品。

（2）以小组为单位，分析此案例中的杰克触犯了哪些韩国商务礼仪禁忌；分享身边案例，讨论还有哪些韩国商务礼仪。

3. 实训要求

（1）采取"组内异质，组间同质"的原则，将学生分为若干小组，每组4～6人。

（2）每组提交一份韩国商务礼仪的实训报告，内容包括本案例中存在的问题及相应的改进方案。

（3）每组讲解和展示本组的工作成果。

4. 实训考核

（1）评价方式：采取小组自评、小组互评、教师评价、企业导师评价四维评价方式，总评成绩＝小组自评×20%＋小组互评×20%＋教师评价×30%＋企业导师评价×30%。

（2）评价指标：从素质目标、知识目标、能力目标3方面进行评价。

| 7.3 任务工作单 | 7.3 任务实施单 | 7.3 任务检查单 | 7.3 任务评价单 |

 **思政课堂**

中日韩合作未来十年展望（节选）

我们忆及 20 年前，中日韩领导人高瞻远瞩，在亚洲金融危机寒流中开创了中日韩合作。20 年来，三国不断增进互信、深化合作、共同发展。

我们一致认为，未来十年将是国际形势深刻演变、世界经济新旧动能转换、科技革命与产业变革迅速发展的十年。各国利益和命运前所未有地紧密相连、深度交融。作为对亚洲和平与稳定负有重要责任的国家，中日韩应加强合作，与其他国家一道，为地区和国际社会面对的广泛问题作出积极和应有的贡献。加强中日韩合作符合三国和三国人民的共同利益，对地区和世界的和平与发展具有重要意义。

（资料来源：http://www.xinhuanet.com/world/2019-12/24/c_1125383968.htm）

讨论：党的二十大报告指出："中国坚持在和平共处五项原则基础上同各国发展友好合作，推动构建新型国际关系，深化拓展平等、开放、合作的全球伙伴关系，致力于扩大同各国利益的汇合点。"中日韩三国合作对于中国经济发展有何重要意义？

🤝 中华礼仪

筷子是中餐最主要的餐具，中国人的每一顿饭都离不开它。它取材简单，只要两根小细棍；大多用竹或木头制成，却巧妙地运用了杠杆原理，可以轻松应对各种食物。和西方的刀叉一样，使用筷子同样讲究餐桌礼仪。中国人使用筷子至少有 3000 年的历史，它还传播到日本、韩国等亚洲国家。筷子取材于自然，追求简约，它体现着中国人的一种生活智慧。

任务 4

美洲主要国家商务礼仪

◎ 学习目标

■ **素养目标**
- 秉承平等、公正、文明、和谐等社会主义价值观。
- 具有家国情怀与大国担当，不卑不亢，维护民族形象。

■ **知识目标**
- 了解美洲主要国家概况习俗礼仪。
- 掌握美洲主要国家商务礼仪规范和商务禁忌。

能力目标

- 能够理解文化差异的重要性，并秉持"敬人"理念进行商务交往和沟通。
- 能够规避文化冲突，尊敬异国文化，从而顺利进行跨文化交际下的商务活动。

 情境导入

情境：美国某贸易公司邀请中国某进出口公司进行业务洽谈。谈判会议安排在星期二上午9点。但当天中国商人遭遇交通拥堵，没有及时通知他们的美国商务伙伴，迟到了30分钟。这让美国代表非常恼火。此外，中方认为美国人是开放和热情的，与美方站得很近，坐得也很近，这让美国商人感到不自在。更糟糕的是，在谈判过程中，美国同行有时会打断中方，公开质疑，表达他们的异议，中国商人也被惹恼，他们认为美国同行真的很粗鲁、咄咄逼人。谈判陷入僵局。

讨论：谈判为什么陷入僵局？

 **知识储备**

7.4.1　美国

1. 国家概况

美国，正式名称为美利坚合众国，缩写为 U.S. 或 U.S.A.，别名"America"，北美洲国家，是由50个州组成的联邦制共和国。

美元是国际交易中最常用的货币，也是世界上最重要的储备货币。美国是世界上最大、最具影响力的金融市场之一。纽约证券交易所是迄今为止世界上市值最大的证券交易所。

基督教是迄今美国人最普遍信奉的宗教：新教徒占52%，罗马天主教徒占24%，摩门教徒占2%。其他还有犹太教徒（1.9%）、穆斯林（0.9%）、佛教徒（0.7%）、印度教徒（0.7%）。

2. 商务禁忌

1）饮食禁忌

当你被邀请参加商务晚宴时，回答"是"或"否"是非常重要的。拒绝是可以的，但不要说会出席，到时却不出现。

在所有人的菜上齐和主人开始吃饭之前，不要开始吃饭。

在餐桌上打嗝、发出啧啧的声音、张嘴吃饭、大声咀嚼或擤鼻涕被认为是不礼貌的。

美国人不吃家养动物，如猫或狗。用动物器官肉做菜在美国并不常见，但在个别地方菜里可以见到。美国人非常忌讳吃马肉。

2）着装禁忌

在商务会谈时建议着装保守。

男士不适合在商务场合着浅色西装（如粉色）。黑色、海军蓝、灰色或棕色等深色西装是最常见的，通常被认为是完美的商务着装。

不建议女士在商务场合穿花哨的鞋子或露趾鞋。配饰也不要过多。避免穿过分暴露的服装。

3）体态禁忌

用手指指着东西是可以接受的，但用手指指着人是不礼貌的。

举起中指做手势是很不礼貌的，因为这代表不尊重。

4）言谈禁忌

保持谈话轻松，避免任何个人话题，如财务、政治或宗教观点。

种族问题在美国是一个敏感的话题。为了避免冒犯任何人，可以把不同族裔的美国人称为：非洲裔美国人、意大利裔美国人、亚洲裔美国人等。

5）商务馈赠禁忌

在初次商务会议上带礼物是不常见的，尽管会受到欢迎。

不要送太贵重的礼物，因为可能被视为贿赂。

6）商务问候禁忌

握手是男女在社交场合或商务场合的问候习俗。除了问候亲密的家人或朋友，美国人通常会避免拥抱和亲密的身体接触。

大多数谈话都是以问候语开始的，例如"你好吗？"或"你今天过得怎么样？"不要按字面意思直接回答这个问题。应回答"不错"或"好"。

7.4.2　加拿大

1. 国家概况

加拿大位于北美洲北部，是议会民主制国家，是威斯敏斯特传统的君主立宪制国家，由君主担任国家元首，由总理担任内阁主席和政府首脑。

加拿大的经济增长非常稳健，是世界上以 GDP 计算的第十大经济体。与许多发达国家一样，加拿大经济由服务业主导，服务业雇用了国家 3/4 的劳动力。

2011 年加拿大人口普查显示，67.3% 的加拿大人宣称自己是基督教徒，其中天主教徒人数最多，占总人口的 38.7%。约 23.9% 的加拿大人没有宗教信仰。其余为非基督教宗教教徒，其中最大的是穆斯林（3.2%），其次是印度教徒（1.5%）、锡克教徒（1.4%）、佛教徒（1.1%）和犹太教徒（1.0%）。

2. 商务禁忌

1）饮食禁忌

不要在公共场合饮酒。加拿大法律禁止在公共场所饮酒。

在不列颠哥伦比亚省禁止吸烟。禁止在所有公共交通工具、公共建筑（包括餐馆、酒吧）和工作场所吸烟。

主人开动之前不要吃东西。

不要把胳膊肘放在桌子上。

不要用手吃饭。除非食物用手拿着吃更容易，可参照主人的做法。

在许多讲法语地区，走路时吃东西被认为是不礼貌的。

2）商务着装禁忌

恰当的商务着装通常取决于地区和行业。商务场合的着装要求通常是正式的，要穿西装打领带。

无论男士或女士，配饰都应最少。女性避免穿过于暴露的衣服。

不要喷过多的香水，对于患有哮喘或过敏的人可能是一种危害，而这些人在加拿大很常见。

3）商务体态禁忌

竖中指是对别人表达愤怒／沮丧的一种极其下流的手势。

如果打哈欠没有用手捂住嘴巴，会被认为是粗鲁的。

不要指着或盯着陌生人看，这被视为没有礼貌。

避免使用"V"手势，这是一种严重的冒犯。最好换一种方式表达胜利的喜悦！

4）商务谈话禁忌

在加拿大，政治观点通常被认为是个人隐私。投票是秘密进行的，加拿大人有合法权利隐藏他们的政治偏好。因此，"你投谁的票？"会是一个令人不舒服的问题。

人们不喜欢被评价，因此宗教观点很少公开讨论。此外，试图在任何一种不请自来的环境中解释或宣扬自己的宗教信仰，总是被视为说教、烦人和自以为是。

非常重要的是，谈话的主题不要涉及加拿大讲法语和英语的人之间的关系。

提到美国或美国人常常会引起激烈的争论或讨论。不要比较和强调加拿大与美国的不足或相似之处。

5）商务馈赠禁忌

在加拿大向陌生人赠送礼物的情况很少见，除非别人帮了忙或被认为"欠"别人而做出的感谢。

"非特殊场合"馈赠礼物会让人心生欢喜，但也很有可能让接收者十分尴尬，尤其是昂贵的礼物。

不要送白百合花，因为它们是葬礼上用的。

不要以现金或金钱作为礼物，一般只在家庭内赠送。

6）商务拜访禁忌

别人伸出手却不跟他握手，被认为是极不礼貌和具冒犯性的。

外国男士不能亲吻法裔加拿大女士的手。

交谈中的眼神交流被视为一种尊重的表现，但不要盯着别人看，尤其是在大城市，这是不礼貌的。

 同步测试

扫码做题。

同步测试：汉语版–M7T4 判断正误

案例分析

• 案例 1

肖河物流国际公司中国员工小李到加拿大达斯出口贸易公司参加会议。这是他们第一次见面。小李送给加拿大业务伙伴、销售经理吉拉德先生一个名牌钱包；送给销售员戴维斯先生一个印有公司标志的精美装饰品，但却让他们感到尴尬。

讨论： 为什么他们会感到尴尬？

• 案例 2

巴西一家公司到美国去采购成套设备。巴西谈判小组成员因为上街购物耽误了时间。当他们到达谈判地点时，比预定时间晚了 45 分钟。美方代表对此极为不满，花了很长时间指责巴西代表不遵守时间，不守信用，如果老这样下去，以后很多工作很难合作，浪费时间就是浪费资源、浪费金钱。巴西代表感到理亏，不停地向美方代表道歉。谈判开始后美方似乎还对巴西代表来迟一事耿耿于怀，一时间弄得巴西代表手足无措，说话处处被动。无心与美方代表讨价还价，对美方提出的许多要求也没有静下心来认真考虑，匆匆忙忙就签订了合同。等到巴西代表平静下来后，才发现自己吃了大亏，上了美方的当，但为时已晚。

讨论： 美方运用了何种谈判策略来达成目标？

实训项目

掌握美国商务馈赠原则

1. 实训目的

通过训练，掌握美国商务馈赠的原则。

2. 实训内容

（1）背景资料：九州进出口公司中方员工小孙到美国强生国际贸易公司参加会议。这是他们第一次见面。小孙给他的美国商业伙伴销售经理琼斯先生送了一条名牌围巾，给秘书米勒女士送了一瓶香水。

（2）以小组为单位，分析此案例中商务馈赠的禁忌；小组成员间讨论，在美国还有哪些商务馈赠的禁忌；给出可供改进的商务馈赠方案。

3. 实训要求

（1）采取"组内异质，组间同质"的原则，将学生分为若干小组，每组 3～4 人。

（2）每组提交一份商务馈赠礼仪实训报告，内容包括本案例涉及的商务馈赠禁忌及相应的改进方案。

（3）每组讲解和展示本组的工作成果。

4. 实训考核

（1）评价方式：采取小组自评、小组互评、教师评价、企业导师评价四维评价方式，总评成绩 = 小组自评×20% + 小组互评×20% + 教师评价×30% + 企业导师评价×30%。

（2）评价指标：从素质目标、知识目标、能力目标 3 方面进行评价。

7.4 任务工作单　　　　　7.4 任务实施单

7.4 任务检查单　　　　　7.4 任务评价单

**思政课堂**

为和平发展尽力　为团结进步担当

如何回应时代的要求，把握历史的潮流，共同构建人类命运共同体，中国的主张坚定而明确：

要和平，不要战乱。坚持以和平方式处理分歧，以对话协商解决争端。

要发展，不要贫困。坚持把发展置于国际议程中心，凝聚国际共识，让发展成果更多更公平惠及每一个国家、每一个人。

要开放，不要封闭。倡导开放包容，维护以世界贸易组织为核心的多边贸易体制，推动构建开放型世界经济。

要合作，不要对抗。以对话代替冲突，以协商代替胁迫，以共赢代替零和，共同抵制集团政治，共同反对阵营对抗。

要团结，不要分裂。摒弃意识形态划线，团结起来为促进世界和平与发展事业凝聚最大公约数，画出最大同心圆。

要公平，不要霸凌。倡导和践行真正的多边主义，推动各国权利平等、规则平等、机会平等，构建相互尊重、公平正义、合作共赢的新型国际关系。

（资料来源：https://www.gov.cn/guowuyuan/2022-09/25/content_5711761.htm）

讨论：党的二十大报告指出"中国始终坚持维护世界和平、促进共同发展的外交政策宗旨，致力于推动构建人类命运共同体"。你如何理解"构建人类命运共同体"？

中华礼仪

在中国，赠送礼物常常是为了表示尊重、感激、友谊、爱慕或热情好客。赠送礼物是世界各地一种普遍的礼节。中国礼仪已有几千年的历史，代代相传。中国人讲究礼尚往来，这意味着对人彬彬有礼的人将获得对方的友善和帮助。如果中国人收到礼物、邀请或款待，他们会在适当的时机回赠给对方。礼尚往来也被认为是建立和维持友谊的传统方式。与其他国家一样，在中国，人们会在生日、婚礼或聚会时赠送合适的礼物。礼物是否贵重、礼物大小都不重要。

任务 5

大洋洲主要国家商务礼仪

学习目标

■ **素养目标**

- 秉承平等、公正、文明、和谐等社会主义价值观。
- 具有家国情怀与大国担当，不卑不亢，维护民族形象。

■ **知识目标**

- 了解大洋洲主要国家概况习俗礼仪。
- 掌握大洋洲主要国家商务礼仪规范和商务禁忌。

■ **能力目标**

- 能够理解文化差异的重要性，并秉持"敬人"理念进行商务交往和沟通。
- 能够规避文化冲突，尊敬异国文化，从而顺利进行跨文化交际下的商务活动。

情境导入

　　情境：一位中国外贸业务员在澳大利亚出差期间受邀到客户家中拜访并就餐。下面是他们就餐时的对话。

　　中国人：非常感谢您的邀请，这是我带来的礼物，是一瓶上好的葡萄酒，请收下。

　　澳大利亚人：非常感谢。但是我们澳洲就盛产葡萄酒，所以我们一般不喝其他国家产的葡萄酒。

　　中国人：（脸上有些不悦）哦，抱歉，我没有考虑到这一点。

　　澳大利亚人：今晚的晚餐您还喜欢吧？

　　中国人：非常美味！我的肚子都填满了。

　　澳大利亚人：对不起，我实在不明白您是什么意思？意思是吃饱了吗？在我们国家很少这样表达。

　　中国人认为澳大利亚人总是当众揭短，感到非常不愉快，吃完后便匆匆离开了澳大利亚人的家。

　　讨论：

　　（1）为什么在此情境中的中国人会对感到不悦？

　　（2）为什么澳大利亚人对中国人所说的话感到困惑？

知识储备

7.5.1 澳大利亚

1. 国家概况

澳大利亚位于太平洋和印度洋之间，北部属于热带气候，南部属于温带气候。

澳大利亚是一个高度发达的资本主义国家，农牧业发达，自然资源丰富，渔业资源丰富，旅游业和服务业迅速发展。

澳大利亚是一个多元文化的移民国家，人口约2544万，约63.9%的居民信仰基督教。

澳大利亚自然环境优越，旅游业发达。比较著名的旅游景点有大堡礁和悉尼歌剧院等。

2. 商务着装规范

澳大利亚人在商务场合中往往穿得比较保守。男士应该穿深色的、传统的商务套装，如黑色或深蓝色等，搭配白色的衬衫。女性应该穿漂亮的裙子或商务套装。

澳大利亚人在向你发出正式晚宴邀请函时，会注明着装要求。"休闲装"是最常见的。但是，休闲装并不是指牛仔裤、短裤和拖鞋。男性应该穿裤装并搭配有领上衣，女士穿裙装或裤装并搭配上衣。女士不宜佩戴过多首饰或化浓妆。

3. 商务谈判

澳大利亚人在商务场合中不太强调长幼尊卑。澳大利亚人在做生意的时候非常直截了当。人们在谈判中往往喜欢开门见山。他们不喜欢对方给自己施加压力，也讨厌由高期望带来的压力。他们欣赏谦逊和真实的信息。

澳大利亚商人喜欢辩论，最好的应对措施是用幽默来回应对方的质疑。他们同时喜欢遵守时间规则，按议程行事。规则高于个人情感。

在澳大利亚，商务谈判过程往往很短，但决策过程比较长。在等待对方做决定时，一定要保持耐心。

4. 商务宴请

参加晚宴一定要准时或提前几分钟到达。在饭店里，通常由发出邀请的人买单。然而，朋友之间分摊账单并不罕见。

澳大利亚人遵循大陆式的用餐礼仪（左手拿叉，右手拿刀）。烧烤作为一种非正式的"外出烹饪"方式在澳大利亚很受欢迎。有时客人自带肉类或其他食物。主宾通常坐在主人的右边。

不要在饭后说"我肚子填满了"。这句话有你怀孕了的意思。

5. 商务馈赠

在初次见面的会议中交换礼物并不多见。当被邀请到澳大利亚人家里做客时，要给主人带一份小礼物（鲜花、巧克力或关于你祖国或地区的书籍）。澳大利亚出产极好的葡萄酒。因此带酒无异于带沙子去沙漠。

6. 商务禁忌

澳大利亚的文化介于英美之间。澳大利亚人热情好客，真诚直率。在与他们交往的过程中，需要注意一些禁忌。

1）仪态禁忌

在商务场合，尽量避免打呵欠、伸懒腰等行为。

即使是很友好的眨眼，也会被认为是极不礼貌的。

在和澳大利亚人交谈时，要保持一定的距离，他们重视私人空间。

除握手外，尽量避免其他身体接触。

2）交谈禁忌

尽量避免讨论澳大利亚的历史，尤其是殖民地部分。

不要在公众场合把澳大利亚和英国作比较。

商务会谈时，要注意音量，不要指手画脚，动作夸张。

3）其他禁忌

澳大利亚人信奉基督教，所以对星期五和数字 13 非常反感。

澳大利亚人还认为兔子是不吉利的动物，会带来厄运。

7.5.2 新西兰

1. 国家概况

新西兰位于太平洋西南部，属温带海洋性气候。

新西兰以农牧业为主，农牧产品约占出口总量的 50%，羊肉和奶制品出口量居世界第一，羊毛出口量居世界第三。

新西兰官方规定了三种官方语言，分别是英语、毛利语、新西兰手语。

新西兰 400 万人口中约 15% 是毛利人后裔，或属于某个部落。毛利人有着丰富活泼的文化，保留了他们长久以来与精神和自然世界的联结。

2. 商务谈判

新西兰的企业重视平等。在商务活动中，一定要尊敬和重视每个人。新西兰人重视时间安排，坚持按照计划做事。

在与新西兰人开始商务谈判之前，可以用几分钟的闲聊来打破僵局。新西兰人经常用幽默来营造良好的讨论气氛。

新西兰人一般不相信那些吹嘘的人，他们比较直接，也期望对方会坦诚相待。商业交易中，新西兰人很欣赏诚实和坦率的人。新西兰的文化中没有讨价还价的习惯。

3. 商务禁忌

新西兰是一个多民族的国家，欧洲后裔占主导地位，受欧美和澳大利亚的影响很深，生活方式和习惯基本西化。但同时本土的毛利文化在许多居民的生活中依旧扮演着重要的角色。

1）仪态禁忌

穿着得体很重要，避免穿着过于暴露和佩戴过多配饰。

打哈欠的时候要捂住嘴，当众嚼口香糖或用牙签被认为是不文明的行为。

商务场合，避免声音过大。

在与女士交往中，女方先伸出手，男方才能相握。

在毛利文化中，头部被认为是神圣的，不能被碰触。

2）交谈禁忌

新西兰人时间观念较强。

约会须事先商定，准时赴约。客人可以提前几分钟到达，以示对主人的尊敬。

交谈以气候、体育运动、国内外政治、旅游等为话题，避免谈及个人私事、宗教、种族等问题。

给人拍照，特别是毛利人，一定要先征求对方同意。

如果合作对象是有毛利文化背景的人，名片最好翻译成当地毛利语。

3）其他禁忌

很多新西兰人信仰基督教和天主教，他们忌讳数字 13，也不喜欢在周五做重要的事情。

新西兰人忌讳男女同场活动。

新西兰对酒类限制很严，经特许售酒的餐馆，也只能售葡萄酒。

 同步测试

扫码做题。

同步测试：汉语版 –M7T5 判断正误

 案例分析

来自某外企的露露和丽丽出差到澳大利亚，到公司总部拜访，并与澳大利亚的同事进行了为期三天的会议。在第三天的晚上，澳大利亚同事向露露和丽丽发出正式的晚宴邀请函，请帖上注明的着装要求为"休闲装"。两人见到后非常开心，因为这几天她们一直穿着商务装，终于有机会穿得简便一些了。于是当晚露露穿着牛仔裤和 T 恤衫，丽丽穿了一条短裤，脚穿一双凉鞋。两人还花费了好长时间化了浓妆，浓浓的眉毛，鲜红的嘴唇非常显眼。然而到达会场后，她们发现自己的穿着与其他参加宴会的人相比显得格格不入，大家纷纷向她们投来异样的目光。

讨论：露露和丽丽的衣着和妆容有什么问题？你能给她们一些建议吗？

 实训项目

分析如何与毛利人打交道

1. 实训目的

通过训练，找出商务交流中的不恰当之处，提升跨文化交际意识。

2. 实训内容

（1）背景资料：中国某公司计划在新西兰建立一家食品加工厂，利用当地生产的牛奶、水果等特产生产高端食品。公司派商务代表王安迪到工厂所在地考察，顺便与当地的行政部门谈判建厂事宜。来到新西兰后，王安迪才得知工厂所在地位于毛利人聚居区，由毛利人自治。接待他的当地首领也是毛利人，他身着传统服饰，面部文着独特的花纹。王安迪感觉很新奇，拿起手机想拍照，但是对方立刻举起手示意他放下手机。在谈判时，毛利人询问王安迪该厂今后会给他们带来哪些利益，王安迪一再强调会带动当地的农业生产，并会给当地政府创收。然而毛利人似乎不为所动。毛利人之后给出了他们认为合适的卖地价格，王安迪认为价格过高，表示无法接受，于是再三砍价，但是对方一口否决。最终谈判以失败告终。

（2）以小组为单位，分析此案例中商务交流中的不恰当之处，讨论如何改进。

3. 实训要求

（1）采取"组内异质，组间同质"的原则，将学生分为若干小组，每组 4～6 人。

（2）每组提交一份如何与毛利人打交道的实训报告，内容包括本案例中出现的交流不恰当之处以及如何改进。

（3）每组选派一名代表讲解和展示本组的工作成果。

4. 实训考核

（1）评价方式：采取小组自评、小组互评、教师评价、企业导师评价四维评价方式，总评成绩 = 小组自评×20% + 小组互评×20% + 教师评价×30% + 企业导师评价×30%。

（2）评价指标：从素质目标、知识目标、能力目标 3 方面进行评价。

7.5 任务工作单　　　　7.5 任务实施单　　　　7.5 任务检查单　　　　7.5 任务评价单

澳大利亚对国产月饼的需求猛增

中秋节是中国的传统节日，传统上以莲蓉、红豆或坚果为馅料的糕点——月饼，在整个节日期间都是人们享用和赠送的佳品。

今年中秋节期间，澳大利亚当地食品店制作的月饼大受欢迎。为了满足需求，悉尼的一些面包店提前几天开始为节日做准备。

悉尼唐人街小鹿制甜面包店总经理史蒂夫·侯说，自 6 月以来，他的月饼已经"飞出了面包店的大门"。

"真是难以置信，这里太忙了。我们一直在做月饼。我的一些月饼已经卖完了。""我们工厂三班倒，从早上到凌晨 3 点。员工可以休息，但工厂从不休息。烤箱总是热的，它一直开着。"

奥马尔·徐是悉尼西部一家叫作奥米尼食品店的老板，他说他的生意比去年增长了一倍多。

徐说，随着澳大利亚亚裔和华人人口持续增长，人们对月饼的偏好也在发生变化，尤其是在年轻一代中。

"我们一直考虑将传统与现代结合起来。我们不想失去记忆中的传统味道。我们想把人们已经喜欢的东西做得更好。"徐说。

讨论：党的二十大报告指出"中华优秀传统文化源远流长、博大精深，是中华文明的智慧结晶"。传承中华优秀传统文化是每个中国人义不容辞的责任。在本案例中，中秋节在澳大利亚盛行，月饼销量大增，中华传统文化得到了弘扬。你还了解哪些在海外很受欢迎的中国传统文化或饮食？

中华礼仪

"和而不同"的外交思想

中国人自古就主张"和而不同"。春秋战国时期，诸侯并立，国家纷争。面对各国的差异，营造和谐相处的关系是重要的外交问题之一。正如孟子所说的"物之不齐，物之情也"。"和合"外交就是要承认彼此差异、不求完全一致。《论语》中讲："君子和而不同，小人同而不和。"国与国之间、不同文明之间应当平等交流、相互借鉴、共同进步。在外交关系中也是如此，各个国家都不尽相同，也会存在分歧矛盾，但是应当认识到，正是因为不同，世界才会如此丰富多彩，"一花独放不是春，百花齐放春满园"。

任务 6

非洲主要国家商务礼仪

◎ 学习目标

■ **素养目标**
- 秉承平等、公正、文明、和谐等社会主义价值观。
- 具有家国情怀与大国担当，不卑不亢，维护民族形象。

■ **知识目标**
- 了解非洲主要国家概况习俗礼仪。
- 掌握非洲主要国家商务礼仪规范和商务禁忌。

■ **能力目标**
- 能够理解文化差异的重要性，并秉持"敬人"理念进行商务交往和沟通。

• 能够规避文化冲突，尊敬异国文化，从而顺利进行跨文化交际下的商务活动。

 情境导入

> **情境**：中国女孩小王正在和来自南非的朋友库珀谈论中国和南非的送礼礼仪。
>
> **小王**：送礼在中国是一种常见礼仪，人们借此表达对友谊、款待的感激或感谢。
>
> **库珀**：在南非，生意场上礼物馈赠不是常态。如果受邀去南非人家里做客，应该给女主人带点小礼物。一瓶红酒、鲜花或巧克力都是很好的礼物。
>
> **小王**：在中国，我们一般用双手接受礼物表示对送礼者的尊敬。通常收到礼物的人在客人走后才打开礼物。
>
> **库珀**：我们接受或赠送礼物时要用双手或右手。收到礼物时会当场打开，但注意不要用左手打开礼物。
>
> **小王**：此外，中国人送礼也有一些禁忌。例如，把伞作为礼物送给一对夫妇是不合适的，因为"伞"一词与汉语中的另一个词"散"发音相同。
>
> **库珀**：太有趣了！
>
> **讨论**：从对话中可以看出中国和南非的送礼礼仪有哪些不同之处？

 知识储备

7.6.1 南非

1. 国家概况

南非是世界上最具多元文化的国家之一，因此被称为"彩虹之国"。南非有大约6000万人口，3/4是黑人，约15%是白人。南非有6个主要民族，11种官方语言。南非拥有三个首都：比勒陀利亚是行政首都，立法首都（议会所在地）为开普敦，布隆方丹是司法首都。大多数南非人信仰基督教。南非人喜欢成功的故事，他们中的许多人钦佩美国人，因为他们相信所谓的"美国梦"。

2. 商务着装

具有城市文化的南非人一般都穿西服。男士通常穿西装参加商务会议。在公共场合要穿着得体。这里有一些建议：如果你是男性，在开商务会议的时候，可以选择深色保守的商务西装。女性应该穿深色西装或保守朴素的连衣裙。南非人可能会穿得很随便，但你初次参加会议时应该穿得很正式。

3. 商务馈赠礼仪

生意场上礼物馈赠不是常态。如果受邀去南非人家里做客，应该给女主人带点小礼物。一瓶南非生产的红酒、鲜花或巧克力都是送女主人很好的礼物。接受或赠送礼物时要用双手或右手。收到礼物时会当场打开。不要用左手打开礼物。

关于就餐，商务会议可以在午餐或晚餐时在一家高级餐厅举行。去南非白人家里吃饭如果是在泳池边的露天烧烤，南非人称为"braaivleis"或"braai"（烤肉）。

4. 商务会面

南非的商业文化在很大程度上依赖于各方之间的信任。如有可能，尽量安排面对面的会晤来洽谈生意，而不是仅通过邮件、信函或电话沟通。尽管南非国内有很多不同的文化，但是大多数文化都特别尊重老年人。为了避免给人留下冒失的印象，坐年纪较大的人身边时一定要表现出尊重的态度，即使他们在商务会议中的作用不如其他人重要。会议至少要提前一个月预约，预约日的前一天要打电话确认，准时赴约。初次见面时，如果会面的人或公司不了解你的业务，可以让受信任的第三方写一封推荐信。南非人喜欢"双赢"。不要急于成交。南非谈判进度极为缓慢。南非人做生意非常随意。可以给你的合同加上截止日期，但是要灵活对待。

南非的谈话禁忌：不要在黑人面前对白人歌功颂德。不要评论不同部族之间的关系。不要批评黑人习俗。不要称土著人为非洲人。

握手是最常见的问候方式。握手时保持眼神的交流会有助于建立信任。用头衔加姓氏称呼对方。预约应该定在早上9点之后。在南非，交换名片没有特别正式的礼仪要求。

7.6.2 肯尼亚

1. 国家概况

肯尼亚共和国位于非洲东部。首都内罗毕是肯尼亚最大的城市。官方语言是英语和斯瓦希里语。肯尼亚约2/3的人信仰基督教，约10%的人信奉伊斯兰教，其他人信奉印度教和锡克教。肯尼亚是一个多文化的社会，有70多个民族。肯尼亚人认为家庭高于一切。肯尼亚人深爱音乐和舞蹈。肯尼亚人也热爱体育，尤其是田径类运动。他们尊重宗教，几乎你遇到的每一个人都是信教的。宗教在这里一直都很盛行，所以如果有人问你信不信教，千万别介意。因为这里人人信教，这是很寻常的。

2. 用餐礼仪

了解肯尼亚的就餐礼仪非常有用，主人旁边的位置是最尊贵的座位。就座后，脚和脚趾不要朝向食物或其他宾客。接过递给你的茶和/或咖啡，哪怕只放在嘴边或只是轻轻抿一口。杯子不满一半的时候就会被斟满。如果你是贵宾，不一定非要祝酒，但是如果能稍稍恭维一下主人，主人会很高兴。先给贵宾上菜，其次是最年长的男性，然后是其他男性客人，再给孩子，最后是女性。等最年长的客人开始就餐之后，大家才可以开吃或开喝。

进入肯尼亚人家里的时候要脱掉鞋子。饭前、饭后要洗手。用右手吃饭。用右手递勺子或叉子。进门时，让年长者或级别高者在前。

在肯尼亚就餐时不能做的事情：不要将左手放在碗或餐具上。不要边吃边喝。应该先吃再喝。不要给自己倒酒，应等待别人给你倒。除非被邀请，否则不要离开就餐区。可以打个小小的饱嗝表示你很满意。餐厅习惯留10%的小费。美元比较受欢迎。在别的文化里，发出嘶嘶声是很粗鲁的行为，但是在肯尼亚却是一种吸引陌生人注意力的常见方式。在嘈杂的餐厅中，人们常用嘶嘶声召唤服务员。

3. 商务会面

肯尼亚公司里等级森严。肯尼亚职场推崇教育背景和经验。第一次会面的时候，一定要留意对方在公司的位置。肯尼亚人以说话委婉、彬彬有礼著称。友好、开放的举止会助你赢得信任和支持。肯尼亚人较有时间观念。如果有预约好的会议，他们会准时到达，但仅限于城市居民。农村地区的人们会面时往往迟到，有时会晚几小时，也不会为迟到道歉，因此要有耐心。一切都可能晚，不要生气或不耐烦，要学会顺其自然。事情总归是要办的，只不过会迟一点罢了。

4. 商务问候

不要直呼其名。小姐、女士、先生、医生、工程师都是可以接受的称呼。如果不知道对方姓名，可以称其为女士或先生。只有当对方要求时，你才可以直呼其名。

来访者如果能用当地语言打招呼，会被视作是非常有礼貌的。通常，问候会持续一两分钟。建议问候时间可以再长一点，尤其是你计划要与问候的人进行商业谈判时。稍长的问候有助于你砍价。肯尼亚人性格外向，每次见面都喜欢以热情的问候开始。例如，一个人进入一家商店，会先和店员握手，然后闲聊，之后才会开始谈正事。离开的时候会重复同样的事情。在肯尼亚，人们之间密切的身体接触很普遍，尤其是沿海地区。陌生人有时会握住游客的手，哪怕他们只是在领游客参观。

肯尼亚礼仪中一个重要的组成部分是手势。肯尼亚人左手用于不卫生的动作，右手用来吃饭、接触和传递物品。用手指指着人是非常不礼貌的行为。召唤人时，手掌朝上示意也是非常粗鲁的，会让人认为你很不屑。

同步测试

扫码做题。

同步测试：汉语版–M7T6 判断正误

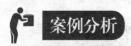

案例分析

• 案例 1

王先生邀请他的同事阿德巴约先生和他的妻子共进晚餐。阿德巴约先生是尼日利亚北部豪萨人，是王先生所在部门的经理。王先生为阿德巴约夫妇点了猪肉和炒蛋。为了显示他们已经很亲密了，王先生没有称阿德巴约先生，而是直呼约瑟夫。谈话过程中，他热情地盯着客人。王先生想更多地了解这个国家，所以他问了他的同事很多关于尼日利亚政局的问题。离开餐馆时，王先生在桌上留了一些小费。

讨论：案例中王先生违反了哪些礼节？

• 案例 2

希枚进出口公司邀请摩洛哥巴拉科贸易公司进行业务洽谈。希枚进出口公司安排了星期一上午 10 点的会议。但当天，摩洛哥商务伙伴直到上午 10 点 30 分才出现。这着实让希枚进出口公司的代表们不舒服，认为对方无意合作。在谈判时，摩洛哥商务伙伴频繁打断会议，讨论别的问题。更糟糕的是，摩洛哥商务伙伴在签署协议后仍然讨价还价，这着实惹恼了中国商人。谈判陷入僵局。

讨论：谈判陷入僵局的原因是什么？

 **实训项目**

掌握国际商务谈判中的文化差异

1. 实训目的

通过训练，掌握国际商务谈判中的文化差异。

2. 实训内容

（1）背景资料：美国卡森进出口公司邀请安哥拉卢苏斯贸易公司进行业务洽谈。在谈判过程中，安哥拉伙伴总是站得很近，有时还会触碰对方的肩膀，让美国商人不由自主地向后退。更糟糕的是，在谈判过程中美国同行有时会中途打断对方，公开质疑，表达他们的异议，这着实惹恼了安哥拉商人，他们认为美国同行真的很粗鲁、咄咄逼人。

（2）以小组为单位，分析此案例中商务谈判的文化差异；小组成员间讨论，给出可供改进的商务谈判方案。

3. 实训要求

（1）采取"组内异质，组间同质"的原则，将学生分为若干小组，每组4～6人。

（2）每组提交一份商务谈判文化差异实训报告，内容包括本案例涉及的商务谈判文化差异、改进方案以及国际商务谈判的注意事项和禁忌。

（3）每组讲解和展示本组的工作成果。

4. 实训考核

（1）评价方式：采取小组自评、小组互评、教师评价、企业导师评价四维评价方式，总评成绩＝小组自评×20%＋小组互评×20%＋教师评价×30%＋企业导师评价×30%。

（2）评价指标：从素质目标、知识目标、能力目标3方面进行评价。

7.6 任务工作单	7.6 任务实施单	7.6 任务检查单	7.6 任务评价单

 **思政课堂**

中国对非洲国家的援助

长期以来，中国秉承真实亲诚理念，在农业、卫生、教育、基础设施等民生领域对非洲国家提供了大量力所能及的无私援助。当年，中国在经济十分困难的情况下，仍慷慨援建坦赞铁路，60多位中国援建人员为之献出宝贵生命。

中国对非援助和融资修建的铁路、公路均已超过5000千米；援建学校200多所，医院近百个，为非洲培训人才超过16万人；在非洲42个国家派驻了43支医疗队，累计诊治 2.8 亿非洲病患。"授人以鱼，不如授人以渔。"这些援助遵循平等互利精神，主要服务于当地经济和社会发展。

2000 年以来，中国先后 9 次宣布免除重债穷国和最不发达国家对华到期无息贷款债务，切实减轻了有关国家债务负担。2000—2009 年一共免除 35 个非洲国家 312 笔债务，共计 189.6 亿元人民币（约 30 亿美元）。2015 年 9 月，习近平主席正式宣布中国免除对有关最不发达国家、内陆发展中国家、小岛屿国家截至 2015 年年底到期未还的政府间无息贷款债务，其中包括许多非洲国家。

（资料来源：The Daily Telegraph）

讨论： 党的二十大报告指出"中国愿加大对全球发展合作的资源投入，致力于缩小南北差距，坚定支持和帮助广大发展中国家加快发展"。本案例中中国对非洲国家的援助有哪些？

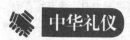

中国人和红色

中国人很喜欢红色，甚至称自己为"赤子"。红色在中国象征着权力和喜庆。很多朝代的官服是红色的；在清代，官帽上深浅不同的红色代表了不同的官位。公文的标题通常也用红色，这就是它们被称为"红头文件"的原因。另外，用于婚礼的双喜字也是红色的。春节期间，人们也会给小孩发红包，当作新年的礼物和祝福。

参考文献
References

[1] 张真，刘玲玉. 国际商务礼仪（双语版）[M]. 北京：清华大学出版社，2016.

[2] 杨丽. 商务礼仪 [M]. 3 版. 北京：清华大学出版社，2021.

[3] 特里·莫里森，韦恩·A. 康纳维，乔治·A. 伯顿. 国际商务礼仪指导手册 [M]. 魏春宇，赵雪，译. 北京：电子工业出版社，2020.

[4] 孙金明，刘繁荣，王春凤. 商务礼仪实务 [M]. 2 版. 北京：人民邮电出版社，2018.

[5] 吕彦云. 国际商务礼仪 [M]. 2 版. 北京：清华大学出版社，2020.

[6] 周加李. 涉外礼仪 [M]. 北京：机械工业出版社，2018.

[7] 王艳，王彦群. 国际商务礼仪 [M]. 北京：电子工业出版社，2017.

[8] 杜明汉，刘巧兰. 商务礼仪：理论、实务、案例、实训 [M]. 3 版. 北京：高等教育出版社，2010.

[9] 李冬梅，余凤英. 商务谈判 [M]. 北京：外语教学与研究出版社，2014.

[10] 李博，王晓娟. 商务礼仪 [M]. 北京：清华大学出版社，2019.

[11] 薛凤敏. 跨文化商务礼仪研究 [M]. 天津：天津大学出版社，2019.

[12] 王琦，舒卷，朱凤梅. "一带一路"沿线国家商务礼俗一本通 [M]. 成都：西南交通大学出版社，2017.

[13] 庄恩平. 跨文化商务沟通教程阅读与案例 [M]. 上海：上海外语教育出版社，2014.

[14] 刘白玉，韩小宁，刘夏青. 国际商务礼仪（英文版）[M]. 北京：清华大学出版社，2018.

[15] 褚倍. 商务礼仪 [M]. 北京：清华大学出版社，2020.

[16] 康开洁，柳娜，孙艺敏. 商务礼仪实务 [M]. 2 版. 北京：清华大学出版社，2020.

[17] 李兰英，肖云林. 商务礼仪 [M]. 上海：上海财经大学出版社，2021.

[18] 史锋. 商务礼仪 [M]. 5 版. 北京：高等教育出版社，2021.

[19] 王常红，孟文燕，秦承敏. 商务礼仪与职场处世 [M]. 大连：东北财经大学出版社，2021.